Making Christ Real

Princeton Theological Monograph Series
K. C. Hanson, Charles M. Collier, D. Christopher Spinks,
and Robin A. Parry, Series Editors

Recent volumes in the series:

Robert A. Hand
Theological Epistemology in Immanuel Kant's Transcendental Idealism and Karl Barth's Theology

Scott P. Rice
Trinity and History: The God-World Relation in the Theology of Dorner, Barth, Pannenberg, and Jenson

Hakbong Kim
Person, Personhood, and the Humanity of Christ: Christocentric Anthropology and Ethics in Thomas F. Torrance

Lisanne Winslow
A Trinitarian Theology of Nature

Matthew T. Prior
Confronting Technology: The Theology of Jacques Ellul

Edmund Fong
Obedience from First to Last: The Obedience of Jesus Christ in Karl Barth's Doctrine of Reconciliation

Chad Michael Rimmer
Greening the Children of God: Thomas Traherne and Nature's Role in the Ecological Formation of Children

Steven Schafer
Marriage, Sex, and Procreation: Contemporary Revisions to Augustine's Theology of Marriage

Making Christ Real
The Peril and Promise of Kenosis

Samuel J. Youngs

☙PICKWICK *Publications* • Eugene, Oregon

MAKING CHRIST REAL
The Peril and Promise of Kenosis

Princeton Theological Monograph Series 248

Copyright © 2022 Samuel J. Youngs. All rights reserved. Except for brief quotations in critical publications or reviews, no part of this book may be reproduced in any manner without prior written permission from the publisher. Write: Permissions, Wipf and Stock Publishers, 199 W. 8th Ave., Suite 3, Eugene, OR 97401.

Pickwick Publications
An Imprint of Wipf and Stock Publishers
199 W. 8th Ave., Suite 3
Eugene, OR 97401

www.wipfandstock.com

PAPERBACK ISBN: 978-1-7252-9505-6
HARDCOVER ISBN: 978-1-7252-9506-3
EBOOK ISBN: 978-1-7252-9507-0

Cataloguing-in-Publication data:

Names: Youngs, Samuel J., author.

Title: Making Christ real : the peril and promise of kenosis / by Samuel J. Youngs.

Description: Eugene, OR: Pickwick Publications, 2022 | Princeton Theological Monograph Series 248 | Includes bibliographical references and index.

Identifiers: ISBN 978-1-7252-9505-6 (paperback) | ISBN 978-1-7252-9506-3 (hardcover) | ISBN 978-1-7252-9507-0 (ebook)

Subjects: LCSH: Incarnation. | Jesus Christ—Person and offices.

Classification: LCC BT220 Y68 2022 (print) | LCC BT220 (ebook)

10/25/22

Contents

Introduction | vii

1. Understanding Kenosis (I): Modernity's Christological Challenges | 1
2. Understanding Kenosis (II): The First Two Waves of Kenotic Christology | 23
3. Understanding Kenosis (III): The Third Wave and Its Commitments | 35
4. Critiquing Kenosis: Insights from Transformation Theology | 46
5. Refocusing Kenosis (I): Framing Christological Attentiveness | 65
6. Refocusing Kenosis (II): Christ in Transformed Key | 78
7. Renovating Kenosis: The Kenotic Christology of Jürgen Moltmann | 97
8. Transforming Kenosis (I): What Does the Kenotic Christ Accomplish? | 108
9. Transforming Kenosis (II): Where is the Kenotic Christ? | 129
10. Transforming Kenosis (III): What Does the Kenotic Christ Make Possible? | 143

Bibliography | 163

Index | 177

Introduction

Christ and Reality

THIS IS A BOOK about christology, but it is also a book about theological method and ultimately a book about the Christian church. It is only in the atomizing shadows still thrown by the Enlightenment that such an initial sentence would need to be written. For before then to talk about Christ (christology) was to say something automatically about theology's very ground (method) and thereby to necessarily indicate something about Christian living in the world (the church). For if Christ is *really alive and present*, a true dynamic in the world of human life and activity, then to speak of him ought to pivot us *toward* the world of his acting. Theology, in this case, would shoulder a method marked by resolute attentiveness to the world, and the church of Christ would more readily embrace its vocational praxis in the world.

One of the greatest risks to meaningful praxis, worldly attentiveness, and, indeed, to thinking about and following Jesus, is *abstraction*. Abstraction separates ideational content from lived concreteness. It is to make a conceptual *idea* out of the real *world*. But it is in the world of empirical space and time that God has acted, and it is in the world that we are acted upon, and it is in the world that we live and move and have our being—and scripture sees this truth in no competition with the pervasiveness of divine reality.[1] So, to make of Christ an abstraction, an idea under our cognitive dominion, produces a twofold risk. First, it can cause us to remove ourselves from his summons, to seclude ourselves in a conceptual fortress in which the real-world work of God is made into a series of dictums or syllogisms, to be debated and cogitated but not obeyed and pursued. Second, abstraction in theology can make Christ fundamentally *unreal*, a piece of a doctrinal puzzle, detached from the

---

1. Acts 17:28; 1 Cor 8:6.

INTRODUCTION

world, transmuted from a person into an idea—and thereby so much less than the living Lord of the church's confession.

Christians' talk of Christ, their theological attention, and their ecclesial action must be aligned with one another. To note the sundering of these vital connections, and to plot a path toward their mending, is the concern of this book. The pursuit of such a concern, however, would be irreparably hypocritical if it was about praxis apart from method, or about method apart from Christ. So, it is a book on christology, and thereby on theology itself, and thereby on the life of the church in the world.[2]

I focus on *kenotic christology* in particular because I detect in this stream of Christian reflection one of the most marked realizations of the dangers of abstraction. As we will see, such danger has not been embraced willfully, but in reaction to the sweeping intellectual climes of the modern era. This brings up another needful point for theological method. Christology is always done *from somewhere*. Human context, far from a distortionary film to be cleared away so that empyrean truth may peek through, is the way—*the very medium*—through which God has chosen to speak and move. The incarnation is grounded simultaneously in the reality of historically specific human life and the saving work of God. It is grounded *in* human life *as* the saving work of God. It is this sort of radical attentiveness to the world of God's acting, the world from and in which we speak, that pushed Dietrich Bonhoeffer to ask: "Who is Christ actually for us today?"[3]

Kenotic christologies have posed answers to this question, and have done so on the basis of alleged commitments to the true humanity of Christ and its implications for the church. My analysis will argue, however, that their participation in a program of abstraction defunds these commitments and has rendered many kenotic approaches impotent, unable to meaningfully connect christological reflection to worldly attention and ecclesial praxis. In this sense, many kenotic approaches have made Christ *unreal*. They are certainly not the only theological programs to do so, but they are taken as the central test case and seedbed of this present study.

The point of the book should not be misconstrued. It is not to debunk or invalidate kenotic christology. Rather, it aims to rehabilitate it, renovate it by naming and overcoming its *problems* so that its vibrant *possibilities*

---

2. This emphasis is, in different registers, indebted to both Barth and Bonhoeffer. For summary commentary and explication with pertinent focus to the outlook of this book, see, on Barth, Bender, *Barth's Christological Ecclesiology*; on Bonhoeffer, see Hooton, *Bonhoeffer's Religionless Christianity*.

3. Bonhoeffer, *Letters and Papers*, 362.

might be more clearly seen and brought into meaningful connection with the life of the church.

My critical stance is drawn largely from the recent movement known as "transformation theology." While the writings of its principal architects are complex and wide-ranging,[4] transformation theology can be distilled essentially as a *radical reorientation of theological attention*, steeped in Bonhoeffer's later thought as well as a neo-Kantian sensibility for the proper limits of reason. Paul Janz, one of the founding voices of transformation theology, sums its outlook in the following way:

> In plain language, [transformation theology teaches] that it is only as I draw closer to the real world of my own creaturehood, or to the real world of sensible-rational human embodiment in space and time, that I may draw closer to God. And with every retreat from this world into conceptual abstraction, God also must inevitably become more distant.... [Transformation] theology is concerned to identify especially an array of powerful idealistic, analytical, phenomenological, foundationally textual, and cultural-linguistic developments over the past two centuries under the influence of which theology has in many of its most predominant and influential trends today effectively ceased to be a discipline which is genuinely *dependent* on the reality which grounds it.[5]

These emphases in transformation theology will not be new to anyone familiar with the likes of Rowan Williams or Donald MacKinnon. But it is the uniquely and stridently christological fixation which pervades the writing of transformation theology that makes it a highly fitting interlocutor for our present study.

The first movement of the book, what can be called its *curating* movement, describes the emergence of "properly kenotic" christological thought, beginning with Gottfriend Thomasius and then tracking through varied historical manifestations. The stage is set in chapter 1, describing prominent developments in Enlightenment-era christology, focusing especially on Schleiermacher, Hegel, and their heirs and critics. Chapter 2 describes the initial flowering of kenotic christology as a reaction to the trends of "liberal" christology. Chapter 3 discusses the recent resurgence of kenotic christology among American and UK theologians, noting that

---

4. Davies et al., *Transformation Theology*; Davies, *Theology of Transformation*; Janz, *Command of Grace*; Janz, "What is Tranformation Theology?"

5. Janz, "What is Transformation Theology?", 11–12, emphasis original.

it too has gestated as a kind of apologetic strategy against less-traditional christological approaches.

The second movement of the book, the *critical* movement, critiques kenotic christology from within the reoriented attentiveness provided by transformation theology. Chapter 4 critiques kenotic christology on the basis of its own stated commitments, demonstrating how its abstract conceptual strategies undermine its ecclesial usefulness. Chapters 5 and 6 establish the foundation of a different christological trajectory, drawn from transformation theology, that redirects attention to empirical realities and guards against excess abstraction. This movement concludes with the establishement of three "transformational questions" that a properly attentive christology must be able to answer: (1) What did Jesus Christ accomplish in the world?, (2) Where is Jesus Christ?, and (3) What does Jesus Christ make possible?

The third movement of the book, its *constructive* movement, posits the christology of Jürgen Moltmann as an example of a reflection on Christ that is both *deeply kenotic* and also *deeply transformational*. Chapter 7 encapsulates and summarizes Moltmann's unique expression of kenotic christology, which I have detailed more fully elsewhere. Chapters 8–10 then apply the transformational questions established in chapter 6 to Moltmann's christology, producing a co-reading of Moltmann and transformation theology that has concrete bearing on the living praxis of the church and produces a rehabilitative discourse for kenotic forms of christology.

It is worth noting at the outset that this present book forms a conceptual sequel to my earlier book on Jürgen Moltmann's christology, in which I sought to establish his christology's inherently kenotic character and expound on it.[6] This present book presumes and builds upon that work, especially in chapters 7–10, utilizing my outlook on Moltmann's kenotic christology and attempting to demonstrate its significance for the crucial issues that are highlighted by transformation theology.

---

6. Youngs, *Way of the Kenotic Christ*.

Understanding Kenosis (I)
Modernity's Christological Challenges

IT IS A KEY development of late modern discourse that we increasingly recognize the provisional and dialogical nature of the theological enterprise.[1] Each *kairos* has summoned forth its own voices and challenges, invariably coloring our theological inheritance. Martin Kähler put it forcefully and quite poetically: "As the blood and sweat of past generations water the cultural field on which our modern life blossoms or decays, so the mistakes of seeking and striving spirits are the steps on which we move ahead."[2] To properly discern the hue of a contemporary theological concern, we must trace the colors to their source.

And so, this first chapter attempts the following *descriptive* task: to detect and describe the pressing issues in eighteenth and nineteenth century thought about Jesus Christ, setting the stage for the emergence of kenotic Christology as a response. Kenotic forms of Christology did not arise in a vacuum. They were responses to a roiling ocean of historical and theological critiques that had battered the church for decades.

Christology and Its "Modern" Problems

Classical christology presupposed a particular metaphysic. The notion of a "hypostatic union" between divine and human "natures," vital as it may have been for the centuries surrounding the Council of Chalcedon (451 CE), had lost a great deal of its interpretive force as the Enlightenment emerged on the stage of history.[3] It is no secret that the Age of Reason challenged

---

1. See McCormack and Bender, *Theology as Conversation*. Moltmann uses the metaphor of dialogue and conversation for his relationship to theological tradition and contemporary issues, e.g., *Trinity and the Kingdom*, xiv.

2. Quoted in Thielicke, *Modern Faith*, vi.

3. See McCormack, "Person of Christ," 149–51.

traditional theology across many fronts. Claude Welch remarks, following Peter Gay, that the Enlightenment's *rationalistic* calling card was not due to its (oft-alleged) conception of the "omnipotence of reason" but rather "the omnicompetence of criticism."[4] No set of ideas, no matter how traditional or culturally ensconced, was immune from question, trial, and subsequent revision or eradication. The *agon* between scientific inquiry and authoritarian tradition—most famous in Galileo but of course adumbrated by the Reformation itself[5]—as well as the rightful place of human reasoning in our understanding of the world,[6] served to foster a heretofore unmatched critical inquiry into the received truths of theology. The immediate ramifications of such developments for Christology are what concern us here.

Humanity and *history* were the two categories that came to reshape christological reflection most radically during this period. The Enlightenment had little use for the doctrine of original sin.[7] The (supposed) autonomous, responsible, and moral constitution of human beings relegated such a doctrine to infeasible and unpopular status. This, in turn, raised questions in the face of christological tradition—what role plays the Virgin Birth with no avoidance of the transmission of sin, and what guarantees the practiced sinlessness of Jesus in the absence of an essential impeccability? (More obviously, a key plank of differentiation between Jesus and other human beings was removed if he was born in the same manner and under the same conditions as all who came before him and all who followed.) The need of humanity for a savior, in any traditional sense, diminished further as the Enlightenment's estimation of human

---

4. Welch, *Protestant Thought in the Nineteenth Century*, 32.

5. Accessible highlights can be found in Olson, *Journey of Modern Theology*, 31–41. Jerome Langford's *Galileo, Science, and the Church* offers more details, though without tracing the theological implications as clearly. On Luther and the Reformation's highly "modern" consequences, see Erdozain, *Soul of Doubt*, chs. 1–2, as well as Gregory, *Unintended Reformation*.

6. Descartes being most often credited with "dethroning" God and "enthroning" human reason through both his *Meditations on First Philosophy* and *Discourse on Method*—see, e.g., Olson, *Journey of Modern Theology*, 47–52; Moltmann, *Trinity and the Kingdom*, 14–15. However, as significant as Descartes is, Ernst Cassirer rightly notes that it was the observational and analytical reasoning of Newton that came to hold more sway in practice, see *Philosophy of the Enlightenment*, 6–8.

7. McGrath, *Making of Modern German Christology*, 24–25; Welch, *Protestant Thought in the Nineteenth Century*, 34, 39–40, 48. On the characteristic modernist redefinition of the doctrine in social terms by A. Ritschl, see Olson, *Journey of Modern Theology*, 153–54.

nature and innate morality expanded.⁸ The personal and moralistic emphases of movements like Pietism often worked to push Jesus into an *exemplary*, rather than *salvific*, role.⁹

As the perceived stock of man's natural reason increased, paralleling the growing distrust for institutional religion, "natural religion" became the highly touted subject of interest, and the writings of John Toland and Matthew Tindal argued for a traceable confluence between the core truths of Christianity and a rational, deistic faith.¹⁰ But this confluence could not be maintained for long; eventually the (especially English) deists came to posit a great chasm between Christianity and the "religion of nature." This conflict reached a climax through the deist-influenced writing of Hermann Reimarus, "the great iconoclast."¹¹

Reimarus's watershed attack on not only traditional Christianity but also on the veracity of the New Testament brought the conflict between faith and history to the doorstep of all subsequent Christian thinking, a consequence that is well-summed by McGrath:

> [Reimarus's] explicit distinction between the legitimate historical Jesus and the fictitious Christ of faith proved to be of enormous significance. The resulting "question of the historical Jesus" arose as a direct result of the growing rationalist suspicion that the New Testament "portrayal of Christ (*Christusbild*)" was a dogmatic invention.¹²

---

8. See Jacobs, *Original Sin*, 148–51 and references; also Welch, *Protestant Thought in the Nineteenth Century*, 34.

9. With consequences for Immanuel Kant and the many who fell under his considerable influence; see Head, "Scripture and Moral Examples in Pietism and Kant's *Religion*," 217–34.

10. Toland's *Christianity Not Mysterious* (1696) and Tindal's *Christianity as Old as Creation, or the Gospel as a Republication of the Religion of Nature* (1730) are perhaps the most significant of such treatises that attempted to see "natural religion" and "revealed religion" as essentially the same, as demonstrated by reason to share a common ethical core. Note Tindal: "As long as men believe the good of society is the supreme law, they will think it their duty to be governed by that law; and believing God requires nothing of them but what is the good of mankind will place the whole of their religion in benevolent actions" (*Christianity as Old as Creation*, 151).

11. Especially in the so-called *Wolfenbüttel Fragments*, as published by Lessing, with those published in 1778 causing the greatest stir. On Reimarus and the questions inaugurated by him, see Welch, *Protestant Thought in the Nineteenth Century*, 34–39; McGrath, *Making of Modern German Christology*, 27–35; Wright, *Jesus and the Victory of God*, 16–19.

12. McGrath, *Making of Modern German Christology*, 35.

G. E. Lessing, who had disseminated Reimarus's work, encapsulated the range of modernist distrust which beset Christology. For Lessing, famously, there existed a *garstiger breiter Graben* ("broad, ugly ditch") between the events of New Testament and the present day, which could not be traversed.[13] McGrath helpfully distills Lessing's ditch into three sub-ditches (as it were) and these will be conceptually helpful for us as we move forward:

1. the *chronological* ditch (reports of past, miraculous events cannot bind us to faith in the present);
2. the *metaphysical* ditch (facts of history are contingent and context-based, but the rationally-discovered truth is universal; thus, autonomous reason takes precedence over any alleged "revelation");
3. the *existential* ditch (even if the previous two ditches were to be ignored, the archaic gospel saga cannot relate to the daily concerns of the contemporary person).

In short, Lessing's influential work argued that the Gospels and their portrayal of Christ were an untrustworthy basis for personal faith, irrational as a basis for truth claims, and absurd as a basis for meaningful living in the modern day.

Christ Quite Close—The Response of Liberal Christologies

In response to such rationalistic critiques, emerging Christology would take distinctive forms in the hands of Friedrich Schleiermacher and G. W. F. Hegel. Though their christological reflections—not too mention greater theological systems—took different shapes, there were core concerns which they shared and which we can summarize here:

1. **Historicity of miracles left ambiguous**: In this way, the liberal christologies responded to Lessing's "chronological ditch," not to mention the wider and deeper rationalist and materialist critiques of miracles,[14] and it led to the devaluation of the distinctly miraculous accounts in the Gospels.

---

13. "On the Proof of the Spirit and of Power," 53–55.

14. Given its decisive shape, which has remained virtually unchanged to the present day, by David Hume's "Of Miracles," in his *Enquiry Concerning Human Understanding* (1772). For a contemporary popular use of Hume's argument see Hitchens, *God is Not*

2. **Absolute embodied in the concrete**: Lessing's "metaphysical ditch" caused the prodigious christologies of both Schleiermacher and Hegel to view Jesus Christ as the supreme embodiment of an experiential or rational "absolute" which is available to all people in some measure. This not only served to hurdle the given ditch, but to do so in-step with the optimistic anthropology of the Enlightenment. In short, Jesus was seen to be greater in *degree* from all other people (this is, axiologically) but not in *kind* (that is, ontologically).

3. **Continuing relevance in terms of effective example**: The existential ditch found an answer in both Schleiermacher's and Hegel's christological systems by the way Christ was seen to exemplify (in an effectuating manner) the heart of divine reality.

Though Schleiermacher and Hegel do not belong to the same "school" in many respects,[15] the clear congruence in their christological themes will be evident as our next sections unfold, under the light of the three points above.[16] We will jointly refer to their visions of Christ as *anthropo-inspirational Christology*.

The label of *anthropo-inspirational* for both of these christologies highlights mainly their shared envisioning of Christ ontologically as a *human being*, lacking a divine origin or "nature" in any classical sense, who was nonetheless connected to the "divine" in a significant way and whose life was effectual enough to *inspire* a community of followers, giving rise to a new awareness of heretofore vaguely-grasped realities and thus inaugurating the Christian faith. For both Hegel and Schleiermacher, what we call "God" is accessible (to some degree) to all people in all manner of religious expression,[17] but the clearest and most unique point of this expression

---

Great, 141–42. For a constructive rebuttal of Hume's argument, see Earman, *Hume's Abject Failure*.

15. On the divergences (and marked professional tension) between Schleiermacher and Hegel, see Crouter, *Friedrich Schleiermacher*, ch. 3.

16. McCormack ("Person of Christ") explicitly links Schleiermacher and Hegel together as the two "makers" of modern Christology. They were also teaching and writing concurrently, in the era between 1799 (publication of Schleiermacher's *On Religion*) and 1831 (Hegel's death; Schleiermacher died three years later).

17. In *On Religion*, Fifth Speech, Schleiermacher presents his view that religion must be plural (here speaking to the "cultured despiser"): "To be satisfied with a mere general idea of religion would not be worthy of you. Would you then understand it as it really exists and displays itself, would you comprehend it as an endlessly progressive work of the Spirit that reveals Himself in all human history, you must abandon the vain and

comes through Jesus Christ. These christologies are certainly worth studying in their own right, but we can only give them a straightforward summary here. We consider each in turn.

Schleiermacher—Potent God-Consciousness

Unmitigated rationalism is a cold companion on the highways of theology, and dissatisfaction with it brewed even from within the Enlightenment itself, with romanticism being a prominent example of this in late-eighteenth century Germany. Resisting firm definition, it is enough for us to circumscribe romanticism via its acute focus on inward sensation, near-mystical self-appraisal, and the priority given to feelings, experience, awe, and aesthetics.[18] Friedrich Schleiermacher's eclectic friendships and Pietist background inclined him toward the emerging romanticist movement, and this had a considerable effect on the shape of his theology.[19] The definition of religion famously associated with Schleiermacher is the "feeling" (*Gefühl*) of "absolute dependence," denoting a deep intuition or awareness of "[the] infinite and eternal factor in all that lives and moves, all growth and change, in all action and passion . . . ."[20] This immediate feeling, sometimes called "piety" but most distinctively referred to as *Gottesbewusstsein* (God-consciousness), is a feeling of absolute dependence on that which is not to be identified with the world but to which the world owes its creation and continuance. For Schleiermacher, all things in the world mutually condition each other, and thus all things "relatively" depend on each other in interrelated ways. But the divine does not depend in any way on the world, and hence, all created things are "absolutely" dependent upon it.[21]

---

foolish wish that there should only be one religion; you must lay aside all repugnance to its multiplicity," (213–14). Hegel in his *Lectures on the Philosophy of Religion* (1824), makes it clear that all higher human thinking relates to the Absolute in various ways.

18. See Welch, *Protestant Thought in the Nineteenth Century*, 52–55; Tarnas, *Passion of the Western Mind*, 366–87.

19. See Vial, *Schleiermacher*, chs. 1 and 2.

20. Schleiermacher, *On Religion*, 77.

21. McCormack notes that Schleiermacher, even as the "father of liberal theology," bears many marks of a classical theist. His theism aligns substantially with the immutability, impassibility, timelessness, unconditionedness, and absolute causality that would be expected of most patristic and medieval thought (see Schleiermacher's discussion in *Christian Faith*, 194–232). The discussion of this aspect of *Christian Faith*, however, requires some nuance. John Cooper, for instance, sees Schleiermacher as very close to panentheism (see *Panentheism*, 82–88) while noting that process philosophers prefer to

All human beings have consciousness of this reality "whether they reflect on it or not."[22] The history of religions, then, can simply be understood as different expressions of such God-consciousness.

In Schleiermacher's view, theology or the construction of doctrine is a second-order activity, in which religious affections or intuitions are given formalized or symbolic expression: "Christian doctrines are accounts of the Christian religious affections set forth in speech."[23] We can note, along with McGrath, the Kantian strain here, in which a first-order content (Kant = sensory perception; Schleiermacher = *das Gefühl*) is ordered and expressed via a "grid"—human reason for Kant, doctrine for Schleiermacher.[24] It is this "space" between the immediate perception of consciousness and theological articulation which allows later liberal theologies to discuss the historically-conditioned nature of religious experiences, mediated through theological construction.[25] This is what makes Schleiermacher, famously, the "father" of liberal theology. As Thandeka articulates: "[The] gap between theological reflection and a foundational neuro-biological human experience is the space of liberal theology, the place where every theological claim becomes a culturally determined description rather than an invariable God-ordained definition."[26]

Thus, the religions of the world, including Christianity, are "relativized" to a significant degree by Schleiermacher, insofar as they are all seen as granting expression to the same baseline human feeling of absolute

---

see Schleiermacher as a pantheist (87). The difficulty of pinning down Schleiermacher's view of God relates both to his apparent conflation of God and the world in some significant respects (see Cooper, *Panentheism*, 84–85) and to his overriding divine determinism, identifying God as "absolute causality" and "absolute vitality" (see Schleiermacher, *Christian Faith*, para. 51). But such a blurring between the omni-God of classical theism and a pantheistic (or panentheistic) concept of God is hardly the sole remit of Schleiermacher, as work on Baruch Spinoza and Jonathan Edwards has highlighted. On Spinoza, see Griffin, *God, Power, and Evil*, ch. 8, esp. 96–98; on Edwards, see Crisp, *Jonathan Edwards on God and Creation*, ch. 7.

22. Olson, *Journey of Modern Theology*, 136; see further 135–37.

23. Schleiermacher, *Christian Faith*, 76.

24. See McGrath, *Making of Modern German Christology*, 42 and references. Many commentators on Schleiermacher articulate this process in one or another, e.g., Mariña, "Christology and Anthropology in Friedrich Schleiermacher," 151–52; Thandeka, "Schleiermacher's *Affekt* Theology," 202–3; Olson, *Journey of Modern Theology*, 138.

25. It is worth noting that Schleiermacher's "Kantianism" is the basis for much of his methodological friction with and contrast from Hegel; see Crouter, *Friedrich Schleiermacher*, 92–93.

26. Thandeka, "Schleiermacher's *Affekt* Theology," 207.

dependence. The Enlightenment fomented a castigation of metaphysics (e.g., in Kant) as well as intense historical criticism, as we've seen. So, Schleiermacher turned to human experience to try and reconstruct theology.[27] What sort of Christology arises?

In brief, Schleiermacher's Christ represents a "vital receptivity"[28] to God's activity. Jesus is thus the foremost instantiation of God-consciousness. Two-natures Christology, and really any classical notion of preexistence or incarnation, is excluded.[29] But Christ is far from just a hyper-religious or hyper-intuitive individual; Christ is the unique and fundamentally unrepeatable occurrence of a full God-consciousness that is not only exemplary, but also effectual.[30] It both *demonstrates* the ideal openness to God (Christ is thus *Urbildlichkeit*) and *initiates* that openness in others (Christ is thus also *Vorbildlichkeit*)—it is a redeeming life, the life of the Redeemer.[31] It could then be said that Christ's God-consciousness is "potent" in the dual sense of the term in English ("concentrated" and "powerfully effective"). The life of Christ and his work are "a life in which every impulse was motivated by the divine will, a life in which his relationship with God took up, processed, and directed every physical input and every thought in action. In making his inner life visible, he evoked our receptivity to being taken up into that same relationship with God."[32] Schleiermacher claimed to want to begin with our current experiences (as those who are redeemed, as those who belong to the church, etc.) and from thence reason backwards to the Jesus Christ presented in the Gospels. Because theology can be variously articulated from age to age, and since God-consciousness is recognized in different times and places and in myriad ways, Schleiermacher is able to critique and/or avoid many traditional and orthodox affirmations about both the person of Christ (he regarded the two-natures conception as highly problematic) and

---

27. This point, often articulated, resonates quite forcefully from Olson, *Journey of Modern Theology*, 135 (he makes it on the heels of citing the famous lines from Alexander Pope, "Know then thyself: presume not God to scan. The proper study of mankind is man").

28. Schleiermacher, *Christian Faith*, 387.

29. Schleiermacher, *Christian Faith*, 393; McCormack, "Person of Christ," 158; Olson, *Journey of Modern Theology*, 144.

30. Thielicke is particularly clear on this score: *Modern Faith*, 225–27.

31. For a critical take on this christological composition, see McGrath, *Making of Modern German Christology*, 43–45; for a take that counters oft-recurring distortions of Schleiermacher's Christology, see McCormack, "Person of Christ," 158–59.

32. Kelsey, *Thinking About Christ with Schleiermacher*, 70.

the work of Christ (most traditional ways of speaking about the atonement he found to be "magical" in character).[33]

So, what was gained in Schleiermacher's reconstruction of Christology? McGrath highlights that Schleiermacher's Christology (1) avoids ontological entanglements by rejecting or completely revisioning the two-natures model; (2) excels over the vague "degree christologies" that emerged during the Enlightenment, since Schleiermacher's Christ is possessed of a God-consciousness that is unique and irreducible; and (3) bridges the gap between historical skepticism and knowledge gained by reason, arguing that Christ simply exemplifies and perfects that which is presently available to all human reflection.[34] Moreover, it is not said as often as it should (especially in more conservative theological circles) that Schleiermacher deeply understood the technique and implications of theological inquiry. His work resonates with numerous methodological points and critical questions that have proven worthwhile to theologians—both liberal and conservative—ever since.[35] He holds the situation of humanity and the constitution of Christ tightly together, reflecting with technical precision the axiom that the Redeemer must be equal to the task of redemption. But in what way ought Christ be constituted in order to redeem humanity? Schleiermacher's answer famously threads between the Scylla of docetism and the Charybdis of Ebionitism—Christ must be sufficiently similar to humanity in order to impart redemption to them, but not so much like them that he is unable to effect redemption (or that he might stand in need of redemption himself).[36]

But what were the costs of Schleiermacher's renovation project? Christologically (leaving aside here the issues relating to Schleiermacher's view of God and revelation), not only are the two natures and enhypostasis denied,[37] but the Virgin Birth, miracles, resurrection, and ascension are all discounted

---

33. McGrath, *Making of Modern German Christology*, 45.

34. McGrath, *Making of Modern German Christology*, 45; Thielicke, *Modern Faith*, is also appreciative of Schleiermacher's ability to preserve much of the concerns of Christian faith in a "modern" way (227).

35. So effective is Schleiermacher at demonstrating how one ought to "think theologically" that Catherine Kelsey's recent work on his Christology (*Thinking About Christ with Schleiermacher*) treats his exposition of this doctrine as a kind of guiding-light test case for students of theology.

36. Schleiermacher, *Christian Faith*, 380–98.

37. Two-natures, Schleiermacher, *Christian Faith*, 393; enhypostasis, 402–3.

to varying degrees.³⁸ Much of the historic affirmation of the church's thinking about Christ is thereby lost. In addition, on Schleiermacher's own outlook, if he has misdiagnosed the problem for humanity (insufficient God-consciousness),³⁹ then this christological edifice crumbles.

However, what emerges most strikingly from the Christology of Schleiermacher is its near-complete lack of a trinitarian dimension. Famously, Schleiermacher relegates the Trinity to a kind of appendix,⁴⁰ and the traditional understanding of the doctrine finds no overt place within his theological system.⁴¹ With a highly diminished view on the resurrection or ascension, and without a distinctively *Christian* doctrine of God (that is, without *trinitarianism*), Schleiermacher's theology may have been bold and robustly developed, but it was destined to be assailed by the dual hammers of those who believed he had gone too far and those who dared to go farther.

Hegel—The "Idea" of Incarnation

Unlike Schleiermacher, Hegel's mature Christology underwent various and obvious stages before culminating in a climatic (though still debated) form in his later *Lectures on the Philosophy of Religion* (1827).⁴² His early Christology was intensely critical of church tradition and largely emphasized the

---

38. Virgin Birth, Schleiermacher, *Christian Faith*, 403ff.; on the miracles, see section 47, as well as Dembski, "Schleiermacher's Metaphysical Critique of Miracles," 443–65; on the resurrection and ascension, see Kelsey, *Thinking About Christ*, 90–94 and references.

39. Schleiermacher, *Christian Faith*, 271.

40. Schleiermacher, *Christian Faith*, 738–51. Moltmann is heavily critical of Schleiermacher's treatment of the Trinity—e.g., *Trinity and the Kingdom*, 2–3, 62.

41. On balance, we should note the recent study: DeHart, "Ter mundus accipit infinitum," 17–39. DeHart eloquently argues for a correspondence between much of the *Glaubenslehre* and the short conclusion on the Trinity, setting forth a bolstered view of Schleiermacher's trinitarianism. Though DeHart is able to articulate the pneumatological shape of Schleiermacher's ecclesiology in more coherent strokes than it usually receives (29–31), it does not change the fact that Schleiermacher's trinitarian thinking is solidly Sabellian (32–36) and that his Christology explicitly resists any form of actual "incarnation" (27–28). Note Hart's summary of Schleiermacher's handling of John 1:14: "'Word' is the activity of God expressed in the form of consciousness, and 'flesh' is a general expression for the organic" (DeHart, "Ter mundus accipit infinitum," 28).

42. I draw principally on the one-volume edition edited by Peter Hodgson (1988). I abbreviate in the notes as *LPR*. It is worth noting also that these lectures went through several different editions, and the debate on Hegel's views here often centers on differences between these editions.

moral teachings of Jesus; in this way, the earlier Hegel had a view of Christ that was typically Kantian. Over time, however, his explorations of Christian theology and other religions deepened, resulting in a christological expression of remarkable theoretical force.[43]

To begin, it is essential to realize the basis of Hegel's religious philosophy. It is complex, animating hundreds of pages of Hegel's own writing and a regular rotation of secondary scholarship. But we can sum up effectively enough for our purposes. In essence, all of human history—inclusive of religion, philosophy, and all other forms of human thought and culture—is a gradual movement in which God (the "Absolute Idea" or "world spirit") reveals and develops Godself via the finite world. All of worldly history is, in fact, the self-realization of God. This realization is *dialectical* (a word one can never escape in theology and philosophy, largely owing to Hegel); in essence, this means that history proceeds in a detectable, cascading pattern, in which various "truths" of history emerge as a "thesis," only to be counteracted or opposed by a differing series of "truths" (as an "antithesis"), and both of which are finally resolved in the creation of a "synthesis," which in turn becomes the new thesis and the cycle repeats. This dialectical view allows Hegel a degree of remarkable confidence in examining the development of human civilization and seeing it all as repeatedly synthesizing upward toward the full realization of the Absolute in history (his own day and philosophy of course being something like the pinnacle). This Hegelian system is sometimes identified as dialectical *idealism*, insofar as "the world process is a process of thought. All processes [in Hegel] are materialized thought processes of the world spirit. In simplified form, one might say that all that is and happens consists of thoughts of God that have taken form as reality."[44]

The finite world is a fitting vehicle for this infinite unfolding because it shares its essential identity; the world and God are not opposed, but intertwined and in fact mutually constitutional. The absolute, infinite divine constitutes the world as its self-expressive revelation and the world constitutes the divine as its own realized thoughts and advancing self-disclosure within and to itself.[45] While this is true of all material reality, it is most perceivable

---

43. Though the overriding focus on the moral instruction of Jesus remained prominent, see Hegel, *LPR*, 458–62; also De Nys, *Hegel and Theology*, 125–26.

44. Thielicke, *Modern Faith*, 369.

45. As O'Regan phrases it: "the divine infinite necessarily expresses itself in the finite" (*Heterodox Hegel*, 201).

and pivotal in humanity, for "Hegel sees in the finite human spirit a transitional point in the self-development of the world spirit."[46] Indeed, the human spirit and God are essentially identical.[47]

However, for much of history human beings have labored under a state of "alienation," not comprehending their essential oneness (or "reconciliation") with the Absolute. For Hegel, this situation is what animates all religion. Religious thought implicitly reflects, albeit in varied and fragmentary ways, the fundamental truth of divine-human unity. In this sense, Hegel finds all religions to have an "incarnational" impulse, claiming that "the thought [*Gedanke*] of the Incarnation ... permeates all religions."[48] It is characteristic of religion to convey its witness to this truth under the symbolism of diverse *Vorstellungen*, an important term in Hegel that encapsulates the "thought forms" of myth, doctrine, and cultic activity.[49] Relatedly, great figures in history, in their exemplification of certain remarkable qualities or virtues, also bear implicit witness to the Absolute; Hegel famously discusses ancient and even mythic figures in this extension (e.g., Hercules, Socrates) while also highlighting more typical conquerors and rulers, such as Alexander the Great and Napoleon Bonaparte.[50]

Such people and such *Vorstellungen* represent and convey various dimensions of the *Begriff*, the concept-in-truth, of Absolute reality, i.e., God. But as these *Vorstellungen* are but partial and symbolic, history demands a more crystalline manifestation of the divine-human unity. Indeed, the onward roll of human civilization must, according to Hegel, "finally proceed to grasp in thought that which has at first been exhibited to Spirit in feeling and representation."[51] What is needed, then, for the human situation is not any kind of "salvific" reconciliaton with God, but rather a revealing of the reconciliation, the oneness, which already exists. Again, Thielicke:

> There is no need of a reconciliation which demands the intervention of a third party or at least a deliberate Nevertheless which reconciles

---

46. Thielicke, *Modern Faith*, 369. Indeed, in this revelatory schema humanity in some sense "makes God possible," (377) a dimension of his thought that most occasioned the eventual and blistering censure of Kierkegaard.

47. Thielicke, *Modern Faith*, 367.

48. Hegel, *LPR*, 1:77, cited in Yerkes, *Christology of Hegel*, 201.

49. Yerkes, *Christology of Hegel*, 117.

50. See Thielicke, *Modern Faith*, 363 (Napoleon), 373–74 (Alexander).

51. Hegel, *Vorlesungen uber die Philosophie der Weltgeschichte*, 1:45. See also Livingston, *Modern Christian Thought*, 121.

the two parties in the antithesis. What brings reconciliation is simply a process of knowledge. . . . What is historical takes place only on the plane of the self-unfolding of this [divine] identity.[52]

As we noted, Hegel sees all of history, especially human history, participating in an implicit recognition of the Absolute's own self-disclosure. However, he claims, that it is only in the *Christian* revelation, specifically in the historical person of Jesus, that this *implicit and universal* truth was made *explicit and effectual* in history: "The recognition of the identity of the Subject and God was introduced into the world when the fulness of Time was come: the consciousness of this identity is the recognition of God in his true essence."[53]

For Hegel, Jesus brings a "new consciousness" into the world, a "new religion" that testifies to this unity.[54] This newness is powerfully conveyed by the important *Vorstellung* of "the kingdom of God," which Hegel expressly renders as an internal state ("it is God who rules in the heart"[55]). In Livingston's interpretation of Hegel, the kingdom is said to represent "the universal reconciliation of the divine and human that was implicit from the beginning."[56]

Hegel is very clear that this "work" of Christ is not concerned with the ancient preoccupation of battling dark spiritual powers, nor with the more medieval categories of formal atonement, nor with any "mediation" as such, but rather with a direct "elevation" of human consciousness into its true identity with the divine, which Hegel describes as an "immediate self-transposition into the truth, into the kingdom of God."[57] This requires a certain detachment from thinking of oneself as different or separate from Godself. Indeed, the effect of Christ's advent and teaching is to "draw those who are to achieve the consciousness of reconciliation away from present actuality, requiring of them an abstraction from it."[58]

---

52. Thielicke, *Modern Faith*, 380–81.

53. Hegel, *Lectures on the Philosophy of History*, 323. See also Livingston: "The *implicit* unity of God and humanity is made *explicit* in Christianity. . . . In Jesus Christ the God-man unity is realized in a concrete temporal event" (*Modern Christian Thought*, 123).

54. See Hegel, *LPR*, 458–60.

55. Hegel, *LPR*, 460.

56. Livingston, *Modern Christian Thought*, 125; see also Yerkes, *Christology of Hegel*, 116.

57. Hegel, *LPR*, 460.

58. Hegel, *LPR*, 460.

Such is the work of Christ in Hegel's thought. Jesus transcends the previous, occluded representations of the *Begriff*, of the Absolute Idea, of God, and displays this radical disclosure in his very self. The resonances with the schema of Schleiermacher are obvious. But they become even more obvious when we inquire about how, precisely, Hegel discusses the "unity" between the man Jesus and "God." The following passage makes clear not only Hegel's overriding discomfort with the classical notion of two natures but also his impassioned attempt to secure an intractable unity of the divine and human in Jesus, over and beyond the vision of Jesus as a simple spiritual "teacher" so common to the modern era:

> Christ speaks not merely as a teacher, who expounds on the basis of his own subjective insight and who is aware of what he is saying and doing, but rather as a prophet. He is the one who, because his demand is immediate, expresses it immediately from God, and God speaks it through him. His having this life of the Spirit in the truth, so that it is simply there without mediation, expresses itself prophetically in such a way that it is God who says it . . . .[The] confirmation of this expression is envisaged as God's doing . . . .not as something suprahuman that appears in the shape of an external revelation, but rather as God's working in a human being, so that the divine presence is essentially identical with this human being.[59]

One can see what Hegel is after here, and may even commend it, but his normally acute philosophical precision founders at this point as he fails to provide clear reasoning or description regarding the nature of Jesus's unity with God.[60] Cyril O'Regan, after surveying other passages in Hegel to similar effect, remarks as follows: "Whatever the cogency of Hegel's argument here, it is perfectly clear that he is as anxious as orthodox Christian theologians before and after him to distinguish the Christian espousal of incarnation from the non-Christian."[61] This observation is pivotal, as it points up Hegel's difficult position in the history of Christology. He attempts, like Schleiermacher, to bravely answer the challenges of Lessing and his ilk, recalibrating theological method and doctrinal language to do so. But embracing such manuevers constantly risks imperiling the doctrinal uniqueness and devotional challenge necessary for orthodox Christology. Yerkes is clear in his

---

59. Hegel, *LPR*, 462.

60. Nor is it clear why God could only thusly be revealed in a *single* person rather than multiple individuals. De Nys does not even attempt to give an answer to this question, so lacking is such an explanation in Hegel: *Hegel and Theology*, 124.

61. O'Regan, *Heterodox Hegel*, 203.

book-length treatment of Hegel's Christology that the notion of "incarnation" has to be a *shared* property in Hegel's understanding; it is an idea that Christianity must have in common with all other religions. Yerkes elucidates further, writing, "If this were not so, then Christianity could not be understood as the *completion* of man's [sic] religious consciousness. It would appear as advocating a 'strange truth' unrelated to all of man's [sic] preceding (and succeeding) religious history."[62] Owing to the Enlightenment's widespread consideration of reason as "universal," mediating voices like Schleiermacher and Hegel could not see Christ as somehow "discontinuous" with other spiritual traditions or philosophical truths. To do so would deepen each of Lessing's ditches.[63] Moreover, it would beg into question all the more the wisdom of a God who limits eternal and salvific truth to a single, particular individual in first-century Palestine.[64]

However, as with Schleiermacher's "absolutely potent" God-consciousness, Hegel attempted to distinguish Jesus by *degree* if he could not do so in *kind*. As Thielicke has it, "Here [in Jesus] the finite spirit has become a *clear* mirror for the absolute spirit."[65] Relatedly, Hegel is adamant about the historicity of Jesus, and that it is just this historicity that makes the Christian *Vorstellung* the "'absolutely adequate' expression or instantiation of the ontological incarnational truth of the divine Idea in-and-for-itself."[66] Indeed, Hegel is critical of gnostic and docetic tendencies in Christology expressly along these lines. He is convinced that Christ's sensible existence, his embodied materiality as an actual fact of history, is key to the world-transforming power of Christianity: "In order that it should become a certainty for humanity, it had to be a sensible certainty, which, however, at the same time, passes over into spiritual consciousness, and likewise is

---

62. Yerkes, *Christology of Hegel*, 114; see further 117–18. It is worth noting (as Yerkes does) an important commonality with Tillich on this score; see his *Systematic Theology*, 2:135.

63. Note Thielicke's keen observations on how Hegel's Christology hurdles Lessing by, in essence, combining "reason" and "history" into a single category (*Modern Faith*, 380–83), an ingenious maneuver within all metaphysical idealisms.

64. This was a representative critique in the later modern era; Thomas Paine exhibits it well throughout Part I of *Age of Reason*. As is well-known, "neo-orthodoxy," especially in Barth, thoroughly rejected any such notion of continuity in its ironclad "no" to natural theology. See Barth, *Church Dogmatics*, II/1.

65. Thielecke, *Modern Faith*, 378, 381; emphasis mine. See also Livingston, *Modern Christian Thought*, 124.

66. Yerkes, *Christology of Hegel*, 127.

converted into the immediately sensible—in such a way that the movement and history of God is seen in it, the life that God himself is."[67]

The Dissolving of Jesus by the Young Hegelians

The legacy of Hegel is mixed indeed. His speculative philosophical system contained nearly limitless propensity for theological application, and much subsequent consideration of the God-world relationship has labored in his shadow. From the sparks of Hegel's thought erupted both the Right Hegelians and the Young Hegelians—the first group was expressly conservative and often theological, seeking to further meld the creativity of the Hegelian system with orthodox Christianity; the second group (also known as Left Hegelians) was expressly iconoclastic and eventually atheistic, but caught up in the whirlwind power of Hegel's view of dialectical historical progress.[68] The rise of kenotic Christology cannot be understood without this latter group, especially two of its luminaries: D. F. Strauss and Ludwig Feuerbach. Under their scouring critiques, Christology again staggered, and Schleiermacher's and Hegel's attempted *modus vivendi* between the Gospels and modernity was devastated.

Strauss—Myths Against Faith

If Reimarus was the great iconoclast of the era, then Strauss certainly resides directly below him on the totem pole of subversion. In many ways, Strauss's *Das Leben Jesu* (1835), especially in its fourth edition, is a book with which conservative Christian faith must *still* contend.[69] Strauss had been influenced by both Schleiermacher and Hegel,[70] more so by the latter, but came gradually to subject all elements of his personal religious outlook to rationalistic philosophy and critical-historical inquiry. He became highly

---

67. Hegel, *LPR*, 469–70.

68. "The Hegelian heritage proved to be profoundly ambiguous" (McGrath, *Making of Modern German Christology*, 55, see further 55–58). See also Dalimayr, "Discourse of Modernity," 683.

69. Livingston, *Modern Christian Thought*, 216.

70. McGrath, *Making of Modern German Christology*, 58; Livingston, *Modern Christian Thought*, 215, notes that Strauss "lost sympathy" for Schleiermacher's theology rather quickly. However, he always valued Schleiermacher's attempted path between "rationalism" and "supranaturalism" [supernaturalism]—see Strauss, *Life of Jesus Critically Examined*, 768–69.

dissatisfied, as did most Left Hegelians, by what he saw as false unities in some of the great, modern theological statements of his day; in turn, his focus migrated toward attacking and dismantling these structures.[71] The investigations that resulted in the 1835 *Life of Jesus* caused a tremendous stir and launched Strauss into a controversial limelight (a height he would not attain again; the denouement of his career reached an ignoble end when he was excoriated by Nietzsche in 1873).[72]

Strauss's *Leben* was, in essence, a historical investigation of the Gospel accounts which stridently pointed to apparent inconsistencies or absurdities, along the way countering any attempted "rationalistic" reinterpretation of the miraculous or the supernatural. Enamored as he was with his own philosophical background, Strauss proclaimed himself uniquely suited for such an undertaking:

> The majority of the most learned and acute theologians of the present day fail in the main requirement for such a work [as this], a requirement without which no amount of learning will suffice to achieve anything in the domain of criticism, namely, the internal liberation of the feelings and intellect from certain religious and dogmatical presuppositions; and this the author [Strauss himself] early attained by means of philosophical studies. If theologians regard this absence of presupposition from [my] work as unchristian, [I regard] the believing presuppositions of theirs as unscientific.[73]

The ghost of Hegel can be clearly detected in another section of the same preface, in which Strauss notes that even if the birth, miracles, and resurrection of Jesus are all questionable "as historical facts" they nonetheless represent "eternal truths."[74] Hegel, as we have seen, forged a key distinction between *Vorstellung* and *Begriff* in his philosophy of religion, and, though he attempted to precariously balance the significance of both these elements, subsequent Left Hegelianism found in these categories justification for unraveling the historical ground of Christianity.[75] For Strauss, the

71. Thielicke, *Modern Faith*, 428.

72. Livingston, *Modern Christian Thought*, 216. On the relation between Nietzsche and Strauss (as well as the context of Nietzsche's reaction to Strauss's last work, *Der alte und der neue Glaube*), see Cooper, "Reading Beyond Community," 456–70.

73. "Preface to the First Edition," in Strauss, *Life of Jesus*, x.

74. "Preface to the First Edition," in Strauss, *Life of Jesus*, x.

75. Thielicke gives a trenchant analysis of the relationship between Strauss and Hegel on this score: *Modern Faith*, 430–35.

category of note is *myth*. The traditional church, and arguably the later writings of the New Testament itself, saw the fundamental salvific power and transformative orientation of the entire Christian proclamation as originating in concrete, actual historical happenings.[76] Miracles, however, cannot take place; for Strauss, miracles are simply "holes" in the net of real history (after all, miraculous accounts fly in the face of empirical science and experiential rationality); hence miracles are myths, and as such they are attempted articulations of ideal truth (the realm of philosophy) in religious language, as Livingston articulates:

> Myth, for Strauss, is the natural mode of perception in the pre-scientific, prehistorical mind. Unmindful of this, or refusing to accept such a view, the supernaturalists are forced to exempt the events of biblical history from the laws of general experience, whereas the rationalists are forced to admit that the witnesses misinterpreted what they saw or that the writers were misinformed. In any case, unconscious or conscious deception is at work. For Strauss no such tortured arguments are required. Myth is the natural language of religion.[77]

Such a "mythic" reading of the Gospel narratives "could only amaze and shock theologians and historians standing outside the Idealist camp."[78]

Strauss's treatment of Schleiermacher is not altogether negative,[79] but he avers that in seeking to vindicate both Christian piety and the historical ("scientific") concerns of the modern age, Schleiermacher only succeeded in running afoul of both:

> [Schleiermacher's] Christology is undeniably a beautiful effort of thought, and . . . does the utmost towards rendering the union of the divine and the human in Christ conceivable; but if its author

---

76. E.g., "For I [the apostle Paul] handed on to you as of first importance what I in turn had received: that Christ died for our sins in accordance with the scriptures, and that he was buried, and that he was raised on the third day in accordance with the scriptures, and that he appeared to Cephas, then to the twelve. Then he appeared to more than five hundred brothers and sisters at one time. . . . Then he appeared to James, then to all the apostles. Last of all, as to one untimely born, he appeared also to me. . . . [If] Christ has not been raised, then our proclamation has been in vain and your faith has been in vain. . . . If Christ has not been raised, your faith is futile and you are still in your sins. Then those also who have died in Christ have perished. If for this life only we have hoped in Christ, we are of all people most to be pitied" (1 Cor 15:3–19, NRSV).

77. Livingston, *Modern Christian Thought*, 217; cf. Strauss, *Life of Jesus*, 77–80.

78. Livingston, *Modern Christian Thought*, 216.

79. See Strauss, *Life of Jesus*, 768–73.

supposed that he kept the faith unmutilated and science unoffended, we are compelled to pronounce that he was in both points deceived. Science opens its attack on the proposition that the ideal man was historically manifested in the person of Christ.... [the Christology's] disagreement with [traditional] faith is the most conspicuous in the position that the facts of the resurrection and ascension do not form essential parts.[80]

Thus, for Strauss, Schleiermacher's efforts to hurdle the Enlightenment's ditches (chronological, metaphysical, existential) were internally inconsistent or insufficiently realized.

When later in his career Strauss published *Die christliche Glaubenslehre* (1840–1841), it became clear that any historical, miraculous, or "supernatural" moorings of Christianity which had fallen under his attack in the *Leben* had been dispensed with, replaced by a purely secular ideology of Absolute Spirit and a humanistic ethic, with no need for a redeemer or savior. *Humanity* and *history*, as they had been throughout the Enlightenment, once again barred the way to relevant and biblically satisfactory Christology, and all the ditches of Lessing yawned deep once again.

Feuerbach—Humans All the Way Down

Hegel and Schleiermacher both fell under a second axe, this one wielded with peerless gusto by Ludwig Feuerbach. A student of Hegel who became the anti-Hegel (perhaps, both rhetorically and literally, we could say he was Hegel's *antithesis*), Feuerbach represents the utmost range of the Young Hegelians' polemic. Often famously distilled by the adage "Theology is anthropology," Feuerbach's thinking used Hegelian frameworks to argue that human beings, in the construction of theology, are in the end only talking about themselves. McGrath elaborates:

> [In Hegel, the] process by which the conscious subject identifies the object of that consciousness is defined as 'objectification' (*Vergegenständlichung*) or 'externalization' (*Entäusserung*). It is this process of 'objectification' which is taken up by Feuerbach, and developed in an anti-theological direction.... Whereas Hegel understood the subject of the dialectic of self-differentiation to be the Absolute Idea (in order to rationalize the manner of its unfolding), Feuerbach took it to be humans as a species. With this

---

80. Strauss, *Life of Jesus*, 770, 772.

> dramatic shift in the point of reference, a universal pantheism [in Hegel] became little more than an atheism [in Feuerbach].[81]

Feuerbach saw God as the "alter-ego" of humanity, the projected idealization of human nature and "the historical sign of humanity's unconscious self-estrangement."[82] Failure to recognize this marks all theology and is in fact constitutive of religious consciousness. Feuerbach thus classified theology, the project of thinking about God and having faith in God, as humanity thinking its own thoughts about itself—doing so quite loudly, and with much pomp and circumstance, but nothing more.[83] Feuerbach put it bluntly: "Consciousness of God is human self-consciousness; knowledge of God is human self-knowledge . . . . What was earlier religion is taken to be idolatry: humans are seen to have adored their own nature . . . the antithesis of divine and human is altogether illusory."[84]

Sometimes dramatically referred to as *Hegel's fate*, Feuerbach may more accurately be regarded as the fate of all theological reflections whose major point of departure is anthropocentric. For if Schleiermacher had sought to counter the anthropocentric critique of theology by doing theology via anthropology,[85] then Feuerbach had undermined the legitimacy of theology done in precisely this way.[86] But it was not solely the anthropo-inspirational theology and Christology of Schleiermacher that fell within the path of the Feuerbachian scythe, but that of his erstwhile master, Hegel, as well:

> The much lauded speculative identity of spirit and material, infinite and finite, divine and human, is nothing more than the accursed

---

81. McGrath, *Making of Modern German Christology*, 68–69. See also Livingston, *Modern Christian Thought*, 223–27; Welch, *Protestant Thought in the Nineteenth Century*, 171–75.

82. Livingston, *Modern Christian Thought*, 224.

83. Here we are echoing Barth's verdict that Schleiermacher had sought to speak of God by speaking of humanity in a loud voice—e.g., Barth, *Word of God and the Word of Man*, 196.

84. Feuerbach, *Essence of Christianity*, 12–13.

85. Olson, *Journey of Modern Theology*, 135; McGrath, *Making of Modern German Christology*, 75.

86. "Feuerbach's critique of religion called into question the propriety of inferring the existence of nature of 'God' from religious feeling, in that this feeling cold only be interpreted anthropologically, and not theologically . . . [The] relation between the 'archetypal Christ' and the Jesus of history might be purely illusory, resulting from the erroneous objectification and externalization of human aspirations" (McGrath, *Making of Modern German Christology*, 75).

paradox of the modern age: the identity of belief and unbelief, theology and philosophy, religion and atheism, Christianity and paganism, at the very summit, the summit of metaphysics. Hegel conceals this contradiction by making of atheism, the negation, an objective component of God—God as process, and atheism as one component of this process.[87]

In short, Feuerbach took the anthropocentric orientation of Schleiermacher and Hegel to its utmost conclusion, unveiling crippling implications and generating a critique of religion that has held global significance down to the present day, especially via Feuerbach's significant influence on Karl Marx.[88] Schleiermacher and Hegel had vigorously attempted to stitch-up the rendings of Reimarus and others, but the results were uneven at best, and the questions of *humanity* and *history* remained unspooled on the floor of theology's workshop.

Conclusion: The Road to Kenosis

This (admittedly brief and selective) survey of Enlightenment-era Christology has set the stage. Though "kenosis" had been afoot in christological discussions since the beginning of Christianity,[89] and though the language had gained a degree of specificity within Lutheranism,[90] it took the convulsions of the modern era to produce *properly kenotic Christology*, in which Christ's humanity is preserved via a divestment, limitation, or modification of certain divine attributes. While this certainly challenged various classical commitments—divine immutability chief among them—it also demonstrated the creative force of the kenotic impulse. We will explore this

---

87. Feuerbach, "Zur Kritik der Hegelschen Philosophie," 277, quoted in Livingston, *Modern Christian Thought*, 222.

88. This influence was both negative and positive. Negatively, Marx was critical of Feuerbach, seeing him as not going far enough to draw practical and political consequences from his materialist philosophy (see his "Theses on Feuerbach"). Positively, Feuerbach's notion of religion as the projective work of the human consciousness was a vital underpinning to Marx's own evaluation of religion, exemplified, for instance, in Marx, *Critique of Hegel's 'Philosophy of Right,'* 30, 131–32. See also Pals, *Theories of Religion*, ch. 4.

89. Dawe, *Form of a Servant*, chs. 2 and 3.

90. Luther in many ways "seeded" various themes and tendencies in theology that provided impetus for the later emergence of kenotic Christology, as adumbrated in the Tübingen vs. Giessen debates in the early seventeenth century. On these dynamics, see Law, "Luther's Legacy and the Origins of Kenotic Christology," 41–68.

impulse thoroughly in our upcoming chapters, providing a survey of what I have termed the *first, second,* and *third waves* of kenotic Christology. In the course of understanding the form of these christologies, as well as their concerns and commitments, we will be positioned to see both the problems of kenotic Christology as well as its vibrant promise.

Understanding Kenosis (II)

The First Two Waves of Kenotic Christology

STRAUSS HAD ATTACKED "FROM below," with history, strip-mining the scriptural texts and doctrinal traditions. Feuerbach had attacked "from above," arraying epistemology, anthropology, and psychology against post-Enlightenment theological constructions. For orthodox Christology, however, this two-pronged assault was a mixed blessing. *Strauss had raised most of the true problems for orthodox christologians to contend with, and Feuerbach's trenchant critiques had crippled (though not destroyed) the anthropo-inspirational models of Schleiermacher and Hegel.* From this point, liberal theology adapted in its own way, and the ethics-focused anthropo-inspirational models of Ritchl, and later Harnack, grew to prominence in their own spheres.[1] But the door now remained ajar for more-traditional Christology to rise and meet afresh the challenges of both *history* and *humanity*, as presented by the modernizing trends of the Enlightenment. Donald Dawe notes that this was the predominant motivation for the pontification of kenotic Christology:

> By the nineteenth century, through the work of men like D.F. Strauss and F.C. Baur, the challenge to church dogma had grown to the point of a strident denial of the validity of the orthodox picture of Christ. The battle was soon joined between the proponents of historical criticism and the defenders of orthodoxy. In this struggle the kenosis motif was to play a vital role.[2]

David Brown, correcting the sometimes-assumed notion that kenosis originally marked a perilous liberalization in Christology, notes its role as

---

1. See McGrath, *Making of Modern German Christology*, 76–98; Olson, *Journey of Modern Theology*, 147–63, though Olson gives little space to the necessary restructuring in liberal theology in light of the Young Hegelian critiques.

2. Dawe, *Form of a Servant*, 89, see also 92.

essentially *rational* and *apologetic* in character, attempting to defend traditional doctrine from the challenges of the day: "[K]enosis is advocated not as some new 'liberal' idea to be valued for its own sake but rather as the best means for 'orthodoxy' to deal with the new challenges that were now being presented to faith from philosophy and historical studies alike."[3]

This chapter agrees with this assessment of the motivations of kenotic Christology and will seek to articulate it more fully in what follows, eventually arguing that though kenotic Christology accomplished many advances in christological discourse, it is beset by certain oversights. Whereas many twentieth-century criticisms of kenotic Christology have raised issues of a mainly doctrinal nature, this present work assumes a doctrinal cogency and even needfulness for kenotic thought while seeking to recalibrate the *hermeneutical outlook and shape* of kenotic Christology. In short, it will be argued that the fundamental orientation of early kenotic Christology was *conceptual* and *apologetic* in character, and as such it predominantly engaged in discussions about ideas, abstractions, and conceptual systems, rather than discussions about sensible, embodied reality, or, as we've mentioned in the Introduction, *reality in a Christian key*.[4] Kenotic Christology took on conceptual, apologetic, and mediating significance, committed to the historic faith, yes, but defending that faith through a problematic preoccupation with conceptual and analytic tools.

The following exposition focuses only on the christologies of Gottfried Thomasius and Charles Gore, as representatives of the first and second "waves" of kenotic Christology, respectively. As kenosis, in both Germany and England, received treatment at the hands of a wide array of able theologians, we cannot hope here to justly survey even a fraction of them. (The reader interested in such a survey will find several classic and recent publications to this effect in the footnotes and bibliography.)

Thomasius and Gore are singled out for three reasons: (1) They are both rightly considered, in their own ways, to be "fathers" of kenotic Christology (Thomasius on the Continent, Gore in England) and most subsequent kenoticists in these respective regions labored in their shadow; (2) they effectively represent the two most commonly arising "schools" or "trends"

---

3. Brown, *Divine Humanity*, 40. See also Law, *Kierkegaard's Kenotic Christology*, 37. (Brown and Law stand as two of the most pre-eminent contemporary commentators on kenotic Christology.)

4. We might also say that if kenotic Christology did ever apply itself to "reality-bearing" concerns (as could be argued in the thought of P. T. Forsyth especially), it did not do so with adequate force or consistency.

in kenotic Christology;[5] and (3) owing largely and ironically to the evident force of their theological acumen, both Thomasius and Gore readily, if unintentionally, highlight the pitfalls which attend their kenotic outlooks.

Father of the First Wave—Thomasius

Beyond doubt, the most rigorously articulated, thoroughly criticized, and demonstrably fertile treatment of kenotic Christology has been at the hands of Thomasius. Some earlier shuffles in the direction of properly kenotic Christology can be detected,[6] but it was the Lutheran divine's first presentation of such a Christology that sprinted the discussion into full gallop. In his article "Contributions to a Churchly Christology"[7] it became immediately apparent that his motivation proceeded from what he called "the destructive tendencies in present-day thought," specifically identified as the recent writings of Strauss and others.[8] Traditional christological formulations had been attacked on two fronts: as not being supported by the actual narratives of the Gospels and as being developed in the alien soil of Greco-Roman philosophy.[9] Thomasius's "Contributions" sought to counter these accusations in a mediating fashion—by agreeing where

---

5. There exist several listings and typologies for the "schools" of kenotic Christology, e.g., in Bruce, *Humiliation of Christ*, 138ff., and more recently in Law, *Kierkegaard's Kenotic Christology*, 52–59. These listings overcomplicate matters by not distilling the categories in terms of the most salient and recurrent theological issues. The following pared-down schema more efficiently focuses only on the extent of the kenosis as manifested in the person of Christ: (1) Divested Models, in which the eternal Son is not sustaining the universe while also being incarnate—he is thus "divested" of certain divine modes, attributes, properties, or roles, found, e.g., in Thomasius. (2) Divided Models, in which the Son is kenotically limited in the sphere of the incarnation but still retains traditional divine properties and sustains the universe in "another sphere," apart from the incarnation, found, e.g., in Martensen, Weston, and Gore; (3) Deep Models, in which the kenosis is so deeply rendered that the Son "ceases" to be God, at least in a certain sense, for the span of the incarnation, found, e.g., in Gess and Godet.

6. E.g., in E. W. C. Sartorius, K. F. Gaupp, and others; see Law, *Kierkegaard's Kenotic Christology*, 38.

7. Thomasius, "Beitrag zur kirchlichen Christologie," 1–30, 65–110, 218–58.

8. Dawe, *Form of a Servant*, 91–92; Welch, *God and Incarnation*, 26, 32n2; Welch, *Protestant Thought in the Nineteenth Century*, 233, 235n2.

9. Of course Strauss's *Das Leben Jesu* raised such points, but they were given even greater critical weight by his *Die christliche Glaubenslehre*, 2 vols. (Tübingen, 1840–1841) and Baur's *Die christliche Lehre von der Dreieinigkeit und Menschwerdung in ihrer geschichtlichen Entwicklung*, 3 vols. (Tübingen, 1841–1843).

the tradition had made missteps, but on the whole seeking to defend the "intention and direction" of traditional Christology as rooted in the scriptures and expressed in light of modern developments.[10] In particular, the concerns of humanity and history caused Thomasius to argue with fervor for both the historically rendered humanity of Christ (minus any doctrinal "distortions") and the thoroughgoing unity of his divine-human person. For Thomasius, there was no way to cogently explicate both these elements of "churchly" Christology without the notion of kenosis. Following his initial statement, criticism and further reflection[11] occasioned a much fuller treatment, *Christi Person und Werk*, published in its second, definitive edition in 1863.[12] It will behoove our project to summarize this Christology along the lines of its central doctrinal movements.

True Kenosis as the Emptying of the Logos Asarkos

Kenosis had appeared in various forms throughout the history of ecclesial reflection on the person of Christ.[13] But the "properly" kenotic Christology of the nineteenth-century, beginning with Thomasius, attributed this self-emptying to the *logos asarkos* itself (rather than the *logos ensarkos*);[14] thus the kenosis was seen as a logically (if not temporally) prior step to the incarnation, rather than an aspect of the incarnation itself. The self-emptying actually affects the divine life; there is a change in the Godhead, and for this there was little precedence in tradition. For Thomasius, as for many subsequent kenotic thinkers, this innovative step meant jettisoning the classical understanding of divine immutability.[15]

---

10. Welch gives an excellent summation of the scope and aims of the *Beitrage*'s arguments, *God and Incarnation*, 26–28.

11. I. A. Dorner and others had criticized the "Contributions" for not being sufficiently trinitarian and for not adequately addressing the state of the Logos's rule over the cosmos during the incarnation (Dawe, *Form of a Servant*, 95–96).

12. Welch's text (*God and Incarnation*) reproduces the relevant material from Thomasius's *Christi Person und Werk*. We will be referencing Welch's translation intratextually in what follows as *CPW*, followed by the relevant page number(s).

13. See Dawe, *Form of a Servant*, 47–85.

14. See Law, *Kierkegaard's Kenotic Christology*, 38; McGrath, *Making of Modern German Christology*, 79–80.

15. Impassibility came under suspicion concurrently, anticipating one of the more significant developments in twentieth century theology and Christology. For an example, see Thomasius, in Welch, *God and Incarnation*, 64; for commentary on the anticipation, see McGrath, *Making of Modern German Christology*, 80.

Assumption of Humanity Requires Divine Kenosis

Chalcedonian Christology, in its desire to preserve divine immutability and related attributes, could stomach no notion of "change" (and certainly not of "limitation" or "emptying") on the part of the Logos in the course of becoming incarnate. Rather, it had long been maintained that the Logos simply added to itself an anhypostatic human nature.[16] However, when such a notion is paired with the axiom of *finitum non capax infinitum,* then it necessarily follows that whatever aspect of the Logos is hypostatically united with human nature, this cannot be the "whole" of the Logos—it will still exist in an infinite capacity apart from the actual incarnation. Thomasius saw this "duality" of the incarnate Logos to be untenable: "For scripture knows nothing at all of a duplication of [Christ's] personality, but only of one subject, of one ego, and this is the same which was in the beginning with the Father and, having come from there into the flesh, lived 'in the flesh'. . . ."[17] If such a "duplication" is to be avoided, Thomasius argues forcefully that the assumption of the human nature *requires* a kenosis of the divine nature:

> As the assumption of human nature, the incarnation is at the same time the self-limitation of God the Son; and conversely, the self-limitation of the Son of God mediates the assumption of the flesh. . . . The two moments, coincident in time and deed, are rather only the two sides of one and the same act by which the Christ of God came into being.[18]

---

16. See Law, *Kierkegaard's Kenotic*, 46–47.

17. Thomasius, *CPW*, 55. This point—divesting the Logos of a further sphere of activity and existence beyond the incarnate Son of God in Jesus—is one of the most sustained by Thomasius. Another key passage comes earlier in *CPW*: "[If the eternal Son of God] persists in his trans-worldly position, in the unlimitedness of his world-ruling and world-embracing governance, then the mutual relation of the two also remains always afflicted by a certain duplication. . . . Thus here [would be] a twofold mode of being, a double life, a double consciousness; the Logos still is or has something which is not merged into his historical appearance, which is not also the man Jesus—and all this seems to destroy the unity of the person, the identity of the ego" (46–47; note further 54, 70). Brown recounts that many critics have taken extreme exception to this, one of the most prominent contemporary examples being Pannenberg (see Brown, *Divine Humanity*, 51; Pannenberg, *Jesus—God and Man,* 311–12). Oakes in his *Infinity Dwindled to Infancy* has well-noted the similar objection from Barth; see 326–68.

18. Thomasius, *CPW*, 49, see also, 48, 53–54, 56, 58; Thompson, "Nineteenth Century Kenotic Christology," 80–81; Welch, *Protestant Thought in the Nineteenth Century*, 236.

It is tenaciously maintained within most kenotic schools of thought that this mutability in the divine nature is no defection or weakness, but rather demonstrates the range to which the persons of the Trinity can willingly self-determine to be limited through acts of sacrificial love.[19] It is in this sense that it has been argued that kenotic Christology is also pleromic Christology.

Kenosis as the Divestment of Relative Attributes

In what, precisely, does such a limitation of the divine consist? The famous answer of Thomasius required a division in the attributes of deity: those which were understood as relating God to the created order (omnipotence, omniscience, omnipresence)[20]—which Thomasius termed the "relative attributes"—and those which were understood as characterizing God's essential, immanent, trinitarian being (love, freedom, holiness)—which he termed the "immanent attributes". Thus, so long as the incarnate Christ, in accord with his kenotic divestment which facilitates the assumption of human nature, retains the immanent attributes, then "he lacks nothing which is essential for God to be God."[21] However, even the immanent attributes of the Son should be understood as operating within particular bounds consistent with human existence—thus Thomasius will state that "Christ knows himself to be the incarnate Son of God"[22] but will later go on to argue that Christ gradually realized this as he matured.[23] Even divine love and divine freedom must take on human parameters in order to be consistent with a truly human life and the Gospel narratives.[24]

    19. Thomasius, *CPW*, 60–61: "[The] essence of love is precisely that it is able to give up everything except itself, that it is able to take upon itself every limitation, even the uttermost, even to make the greatest sacrifice, in order to satisfy its holy urgency to restore its created image which has fallen into corruption" (61). On self-limitation as self-determination, see Dawe, *Form of a Servant*, 94.

    20. The simple idea being that God, without a creation, would have nothing over which to exercise power (hence, no omnipotence), nothing to know outside his triune self (hence, no omniscience), and nowhere to be pervasively present (hence, no omnipresence).

    21. Thomasius, *CPW*, 73. Clearly, divine immutability is turned on its head with such suppositions; see the helpful doctrinal-historical notes in Brown, *Divine Humanity*, 49–54.

    22. Thomasius, *CPW*, 59.

    23. Thomasius, *CPW*, 65.

    24. Thomasius, *CPW*, 67–70.

The Incarnation's Trinitarian Shape

It is especially important to note that in their emphasis on the humanity of Christ, kenotic christologians have been among the most effective interpreters of Jesus as "dependent" on both the Father and the Spirit in the course of his ministry, death, and resurrection. Thomasius set the tone for this, emphasizing, for instance, that the miracles of Christ arose from the trifold confluence of the Son, the Father, and the Spirit: "Even the miracles which he performed prove [that] these are the works which the Father gives him; he does not do them out of his own capability . . . . they belong to the works of vocation, for which humanity is anointed with the Holy Spirit."[25] Thus, on this level at least, Thomasius perceives a trinitarian layer supervening throughout the incarnate life of Christ.

Father of the "Second Wave"—Gore

Kenotic Christology in Germany collapsed primarily due to its occupation of a theological demilitarized zone; objections came against it from both the right and the left, and its relatively few proponents could not contend.[26] But with the publication of *Lux Mundi*, Anglican theology whispered the beginnings of its own kenotic endeavor. With only a brief mention of the themes of kenosis (in an essay that was primarily concerned with historical hermeneutics and scripture),[27] Charles Gore precipitated various critiques and exchanges which would foster the growth of his own kenotic Christology, until it reached its apex of expression in *Dissertations on Subjects Connected with the Incarnation*,[28] a "more strictly theological" supplement to his Bampton Lectures of 1891.

---

25. Thomasius, *CPW*, 70. Perhaps even more salient than this point about the miracles is Thomasius's repeated assertion that it is the Holy Spirit working upon the mind of Christ which, in essence, illuminates his divine knowledge for him; e.g., "For even if it happens that these divine thoughts come only gradually to consciousness for him through the mediation of the Holy Spirit, this is still only a development of what is contained in the depths of his own being; it arises for him in the form of human knowing" (70). See further: Thompson, "Nineteenth Century Kenotic Christology," 83.

26. Ably discussed in Thompson, "Nineteenth Century Kenotic Christology," 95–102; see also Welch, *Protestant Thought in the Nineteenth Century*, 239–40; Dawe, *Form of a Servant*, 102–3.

27. Gore, "Holy Spirit and Inspiration," 358–60; Dawe, *Form of a Servant*, 129.

28. Gore, *Dissertations on Subjects Connected with the Incarnation*.

But, as with Thomasius, this was not constructive theology emerging from tradition and taking account of the reality-bearing aspects of lived human existence—it was conceptual, mediating theology, engaging in doctrinal speculation and defending the faith through apologetic concerns. *Lux Mundi* is seen as one of the great mediating documents of this period in Anglican thought, and Gore's reputation, then and now, is one of an "Anglican apologist" (to use R. J. Page's term).[29] Lawson states that

> The men who developed the kenotic theory in English Christology were neither sceptics nor humanists. They did not seek to overthrow the traditional orthodox Christology of Christendom: on the contrary, *they sought to establish it, by removing it from where it was in danger of being attacked by modern critical methods.*[30]

This stream of nineteenth century kenoticism thus shared the *apologetic* tendency with kenosis in Germany.[31] But though Gore thought that the traditional doctrine stood in need of restatement, he went about the process more modestly than Thomasius—it was in fact rather standard for the English kenoticists to be less speculative and bold in their theological ruminations.[32] For Gore, it was not a thickly circumscribed discussion of the divine attributes that should animate an understanding of kenosis, but rather the sobering shape of the Gospel narratives as they delineate the "consciousness" of Christ.[33] Thus, Ramsey gives a typical assessment of Gore's kenosis: "What was vital for Gore was not the assertion of a

---

29. Page's dissertation, in its focus on Gore as an "apologist" whose theology should be viewed as a response to modernism and the "New Theology" is highly instructive on this score. See Page, *Charles Gore, Anglican Apologist*, chs. 3–5. Michael Ramsey also notes that *Lux Mundi* arose from "a common desire to grapple with the intellectual questions which Christians were having to face at the time" (*Era in Anglican Theology*, 2).

30. Lawson, *Conflict in Christology*, 121–22.

31. On the modern attacks on Christology, see Lawson, *Conflict in Christology*, 36–43; on Gore and his opposition to Modernism: Ramsey, *Era in Anglican Theology*, ch. 5; Page, *Charles Gore*, ch. 3—Page notes well Gore's progressive leanings, in so far as he sympathized with much of the New Theology's discontentment (as exhibited in R. J. Campbell, for instance), but also Gore's conservative moorings, insofar as he questioned the extremities to which the New Theology was willing to go—see 110–34.

32. See the comments in Dawe, *Form of a Servant*, 127–29; Ramsey, *Era in Anglican Theology*, 32–33. For examples of Gore's lack of speculation on knotty theological issues, see Gore, *Dissertations*, 86–87, 90, 203–4.

33. The second, and most significant, dissertation focuses entirely on this topic and its treatment in the history of theology, Gore, *Dissertations*, 71–225.

metaphysical theory so much as the assertion of the historical fact of Christ's human limitations."[34]

But phrasing like Ramsey's can also give the wrong impression. Gore did not remain apart from speculative theological topics entirely, even if he trod more reservedly on that territory than his German predecessors.[35] In fact, on the first and third of the four points of kenotic Christology that we noted above, Gore differs from Thomasius. The major thrust of that difference originates in Gore's complete opposition to the notion that the Second Person of the Trinity was not still ruling and sustaining the world at the same time that he was incarnate.[36] For Gore, the Logos retained another "sphere" of activity beyond the life of Jesus. Thus, the Logos *qua* deity is not kenotically emptied, but simply partially lives in a "sphere" of human conditions; no attributes of God are lost or modified by the Logos, they are simply concentrated differently between the two spheres of activity.[37]

Gore's model, alongside the model of Thomasius, came to be, in differing versions, one of the most long-lived versions of the kenotic model. However, it has serious drawbacks, the most obvious being the fact that, for all Gore's concern for the testimony of scripture concerning Jesus, the Gospels emphatically present the picture of a unified self-understanding in Christ. There is no scriptural testimony for a supramundane oversight of the Logos during the Gospel events. Jesus is not divided—he possesses a unitary identity, and thus any supposition of a transworldly existence alongside that historical persona is speculative and theologically questionable. It is here that the constant warnings from Thomasius against dividing the "one person" of Jesus resonate most loudly.[38] If such a conversation is going to be maintained, the view of Gore (and Martensen,

---

34. Ramsey, *Era in Anglican Theology*, 34.

35. Ramsey feels that though Gore may have been preceded historically by German kenoticists, he appears to have developed his notion of kenosis, at least initially, independently of their influence (*Era in Anglican Theology*, 33). But Dawe notes that A. B. Bruce's summary of foregoing German kenotic theories was available as early 1876 (see *Form of a Servant*, 129). Regardless, Gore never attributes the origin of his kenotic thinking to any other theologian.

36. "Thus, if we are asked the question—Can the functions of the Son in the Godhead and in the universe have been suspended by the Incarnation? we cannot but answer with the theologians of the Church from Irenaeus to Dr. Westcott, that it is to us inconceivable" (Gore, *Dissertations*, 93).

37. The most thorough discussion comes when Gore explicitly compares his model of kenosis to others: Gore, *Dissertations*, 184–201.

38. Thomasius, *CPW*, 36–38, 46, 55.

and Weston, and others) is the least viable, for it divides the person of Christ, stretches its scriptural evidence, tends toward referred docetism, and operates on such a limited trinitarian and cosmological basis that the operation of the incarnation is allowed to bring no true novelty into the divine life. If the Word "became" flesh (John 1:14), this is quite different, linguistically and otherwise, from the Word "assuming" flesh[39] or the Word "partially inhabiting" the sphere of flesh.

Sounds of Silence—Kenosis as Mere Concept

However, such discussions derived from speculative and conceptual schemas are not the point of this project. In fact, it is, in its own specific way, opposed to them. This manner of theologizing points away from the world—the world of experience and of embodied existence. However, this is precisely the world that we live in, and thus it is precisely this world to which theology needs to speak, and nowhere more so than in christological reflection. Gore's Christology leaves us stuck in the realm of concepts, not truly relating to Christ, no more aware of his meaning for our lives and reality here-and-now. Kenosis, as a resource for Christology, can certainly connect Christ with reality in significant and transformative ways, but the kenosis of Gore does not; he keeps us in our heads, conceiving of theological ideas and parsing the data of Bible and tradition, but not connecting theology with the real, physical, causal-sensible aspects of our experience and knowing.

Most tellingly, Gore compares his conception of the "double life" (one kenotic, one not) of the Son to an *intellectual* exercise:

> Sympathy, love—this is the keynote of the Incarnation. . . . And surely here—in the region of love and sympathy—we have something analogous to a double life, and a double life which affects the intellect as much as any of our powers. To sympathize is to put oneself in another's place. Redemptive sympathy is the act of the greater and better putting himself at the point of view of the lower and the worse. He must not abandon his own higher standing-ground if he is to benefit the object of his compassion; but remaining essentially what he was he must also find himself in the place of the lower[.] [40]

---

39. But see Barth's protestations in *Church Dogmatics* I/2, 159–62.
40. Gore, *Dissertations*, 218.

There are few examples more clear-cut than this. The incarnation here sounds like Christ doing his best (like a social superior) to "understand" the world of humanity, stooping in his consciousness, but not actually stooping, not *actually identifying* with them, and certainly not committing the whole of the divine self to the *via crucis* and the washing of our feet.

Thomasius, though sporting a more systematic and consistent doctrinal understanding of kenotic Christology,[41] fares little better. In examining the kenosis of Thomasius, we can note many positives. The Christology strives to balance theological tradition with the ever-present need to re-articulate that tradition in newly nuanced ways. It has a strong basis in biblical narrative[42] and succeeds in making sense of much of the perplexing Gospel materials as they relate to Jesus's person. But it is precisely this "making sense" element which falls under the critique of this project. Responding to a particular series of intellectual attacks, the shape and tone of Thomasius's Christology is apologetic and conceptual in character—it spends most of its energy seeking to abstractly analyze the "data" of the incarnation (drawn from the propositional statements of scripture and metaphysics, analytically rendered) and does little to annunciate the continuing, reality-bearing significance for any of these doctrinal discussions. In a very serious way, this method of christologizing (if we may invent the verb) also turns "away" from the world of spatio-temporal perception and embodiment and turns "inward"—to the world of conceptual schemas and speculative theology. This was the source of the assaults from Strauss and company, and in seeking to meet them on the field of engagement, kenotic Christology sacrificed its vital potential to truly connect the core expression of Christian faith (Christ) with what he came to redeem and transform (*this* world, the world of our experience).

In seeking to counter the Enlightenment-influenced critiques of Christology, Thomasius's kenotic thinking only succeeded in producing a different note in the same song; a duel of concepts formed the frame within which Christology was re-articulated. This can be clearly seen in Thomasius's chief doctrinal innovation—the distinction between the relative and immanent

---

41. This opinion is not mine alone. Brown faults Gore "for not going far enough" in his articulation of kenosis (*Divine Humanity,* 139), and Dawe, speaking of all British kenoticists, says that "they did not advance the understanding of kenosis. Rather, they settled for a limited and unsystematic application of the kenotic motif to the problem of Jesus' consciousness" (*Form of a Servant,* 130–31).

42. Thomasius is very clear that, in his view, "scripture forces us to [the conclusion of kenosis]" (55). See his full discussion of the scriptural basis, *CPW,* 50–56.

attributes of God. Whereas many have critiqued such a notion as being untenable, the grounds of such objections fall under the same critique that we are here applying to Thomasius. It is a speculative doctrine, drawn from a conceptual and metaphysical framework which defines itself based on negations of sensible reality. So long as theology draws our mind's eye away from the world and into some detached, speculative, cognitively-reified system, no matter how coherent it may be within that system, it will struggle to apply itself to this world and the transformation of it. Thomasius, like Gore, also cannot help but compare the incarnation to an intellectual exercise, rather than an act of sacrificial ministry to the world:

> The unity [of Christ] is always such that this person has intrinsically two sides, and in its actual knowing and willing constantly comprehends two movements. Even in the human limitation Christ knows himself to be the incarnate Son of God . . . . There is a similarity to the way in which our self-consciousness embraces the two sides of our life, the higher and the lower, and our will embraces two directions of our being, the upward and the downward.[43]

In short, a *transformational* critique of early kenotic Christology takes the following form: Insofar as kenosis is articulated within a speculative, abstract system of theology and treated as an analytic tool for rendering the incarnation intellectually coherent, it will fail to fully connect theology to its ultimate source and ground (the actual lived history of Jesus) and its site of intended revelation and application (the actual lived experiences of the church today).

Conclusion: The Waves Roll On

While the emergence of kenotic Christology is deeply intelligible given the critical intellectual environment of the modern era, and while it was conceived and articulated with impressive force in both Germany and England, the program was ultimately one of mere conceptuality with little ecclesial substance or concrete bearing on Christian activity. These issues, notable as they are, would be exacerbated in many regards in the later-arising third wave of kenotic Christology, which our next chapter engages in some detail.

---

43. Thomasius, *CPW*, 59.

Understanding Kenosis (III)

The Third Wave and Its Commitments

KENOTIC CHRISTOLOGY IN ITS first and second waves gave way under myriad pressures. As an innovative yet creedally committed movement in Christian dogmatics it received criticism from both conservative and liberal wings, making any long tenure on the highroads of theology unlikely.[1] Beneath the assailment of Karl Barth,[2] any of its lingering intellectual purchase effectively crumbled, and those not inclined toward Barth could find a different range of critique in Wolfhart Pannenberg.[3] Finally, history itself shifted the sands which helped to bury kenotic Christology, and once the dust of the World Wars had settled, it would be several decades before any proper resurgence could gather steam. True, there were occasional flickers of life,[4] indicating that doctrinal dormancy, rather than permanent death, had set in,[5] but by and large the first (German) and second (British) waves of kenotic Christology had spent their force.[6] The

---

1. See Welch, *Protestant Thought in the Nineteenth Century*, 239–40; Olson, *Journey of Modern Theology*, 254–55. Even the less-bold British kenotic models received little love from traditionalists; see e.g., the first statement by an American on kenosis: Hall, *Kenotic Theory*.

2. Barth maintained that the kenoticists (esp. Thomasius and Gess) had "good intentions," saying that "they wanted to clear away the difficulties of the traditional teaching and make possible a 'historical' consideration of the life of Jesus." But he firmly concluded that they "abandoned" the key fact that "the Godhead of the man Jesus remains intact and unaltered" and thus they had "reduced [orthodox Christology] to absurdity" (*Church Dogmatics*, IV/1, 176, see further 175–77).

3. Pannenburg, *Jesus—God and Man*, 311–12.

4. E.g., Dawe's survey, *Form of a Servant*, which makes significant constructive statements of its own (e.g., 188–204). Anglican theology allowed kenosis, albeit in a qualified form, e.g., Taylor, *Person of Christ in New Testament Teaching*, 260–76.

5. E.g., in the spiritually incisive work of W. H. Vanstone: *Love's Endeavour, Love's Expense*.

6. Sykes describes the various death knells that were sounded of kenoticism: "Strange

fact that kenotic Christology has indeed re-emerged with vigor in the past forty years is one of the more remarkable developments in the contemporary state of christological study.

In this chapter I will briefly situate the current and ongoing "third wave" of kenotic Christology within its broader theological context. Following on this, the core "christological commitments" (that is, the goals and focuses which direct the christological work) of contemporary kenotic Christology will be enumerated in detail and then critically examined. My analysis will indicate that many present-day iterations of kenotic Christology are inhibited from fulfilling their own christological commitments, and that this fact trammels their christological and ecclesiological significance overall.

Third-Wave Kenotic Christology

Not surprisingly, challenges to orthodox commitments are what stoked the coals of kenotic Christology back into flame. In this regard there is a fundamental similarity in the emergence of the first and second waves and the current, ongoing third wave. 1977 saw the publication of a work that resounded through the halls of christological reflection for decades to come: *The Myth of God Incarnate*. This was an academic *tour de force* in which numerous English and American scholars sought to update, redefine, and/or relativize traditional understandings of the incarnation through incisive essays on various aspects and applications of the doctrine. The essay which sparked the most enduring controversy was that of the volume's editor, John Hick. The twin specters of backwards dogma and failed logic loomed large in Hick's assessment of traditional christological formulations:

> [The Chalcedonian understanding of the incarnation] remains a form of words without assignable meaning. For to say, without explanation, that the historical Jesus of Nazareth was also God is as devoid of meaning as to say that this circle drawn with a pencil on paper is also a square.[7]

Persistence," 350, 356–57. Louis Berkhof, in the 1930s, said summarily that kenosis had "died out" and that it "finds very little support at the present time" (*Systematic Theology*, 2:329).

7. Hick, "Christology and the World Religions," 178.

Traditional Christology has for too long, according to Hick, tried to render as literal what should have remained metaphorical—Jesus's status as the "son of God." Christ was a man remarkably open to God, bringing an ethical kingdom, and a figure from whom people of all religious traditions could draw inspiration if only the "Ptolemaic" theological tendencies of conservative Christianity would desist (and thereby declare the notion of two-natures, enshrined at Nicaea and Chalcedon, to be defunct and parochial).[8] Hick claimed throughout his career that a metaphorical understanding of Jesus "incarnating" the will and love of God was both closer to the biblical evidence and more religiously viable than any literal or metaphysical rendering of the doctrine.[9] Other essays in *The Myth* offered further points along these lines, though none was perhaps more bold than Don Cupitt's description of the church's historic practice of worshiping Jesus as a "cult" and "paganization."[10]

"Furor" is a term that has been employed to describe what *The Myth of God Incarnate* brought about,[11] and in the midst of that furor several christological thinkers deemed the kenotic model a useful tool to revive and put to use in defense of the traditional faith.[12] The gauntlet had been thrown, so to speak, and the task of *rendering the incarnation intelligible* was taken up with renewed apologetic and philosophical passion.

The third wave of kenotic Christology officially commenced as Stephen T. Davis and David Brown produced resuscitations and defenses of kenotic models in the 1980s.[13] In a work also clearly meant (in its title and

---

8. Hick retained this fundamental orientation, writing nearly 25 years later that "[the] assumption that Jesus's combined deity and humanity is a literal truth . . . will satisfy many good Christian people. It will not, however, satisfy any who realize that the fully God, fully man mystery is a philosophical proposal. It is not a divine revelation but a human creation. And its mysteriousness consists in the fact that it is a form of words with no intelligible meaning," ("Literal and Metaphorical Christologies,"150).

9. See Hick, "Literal and Metaphorical Christologies," 151–52.

10. Cupitt, "Christ of Christendom," 142–43.

11. See the comments and summary in Langmead, *Word Made Flesh*, 31–32. Stephen Davis also uses the expression; see his *Logic and the Nature of God*, 119.

12. This has always been the role of kenotic Christology—seeking to defend orthodox claims by re-articulating them in the midst of critique. Thus, the complaint that kenosis is a "liberal" trajectory in Christology is ill-founded, or at least poorly stated. Brown makes this point repeatedly: *Divine Humanity*, 24–25, 40–41, 126.

13. Davis, *Logic and the Nature of God*, esp. ch. 8, which proffers a kenotic model explicitly against Hick's critiques; Brown, *Divine Trinity*, 102–58, 219–71, with explicit mentions of Hick, et al. at 222, 239.

content) to counter *The Myth of God Incarnate*, Thomas Morris produced a philosophical-apologetic Christology that, though it did not endorse kenosis as its own position, saw kenosis as the only other viable candidate for a coherent Christology.[14]

But third-wave kenotic Christology has also been set in sharp relief over the past three decades through the continued historical work on the Gospel narratives, e.g., in what have come to be known as the "Third" Quest and "New" Quest for the historical Jesus.[15] Both these trajectories have produced pictures of Jesus Christ that have resulted in much defensive maneuvering on the part of christologians. The New Quest has proven the most vituperative to orthodox commitments; a main branch of such scholarship is Robert Funk's "Jesus Seminar," which, in its emblematic publication of *The Five Gospels*, proclaimed that:

> It was once assumed that scholars had to prove that details in the synoptic gospels were *not* historical. D.F. Strauss undertook proof of this nature in his controversial work. . . . The current assumption [in scholarship] is more nearly the opposite and indicates how far [we have] come since Strauss: the gospels are now assumed to be narratives in which the memory of Jesus is embellished by mythic elements that express the church's faith in him. . . .[16]

The Jesus which emerged from the Seminar's sifting of the supposed mythic elements in the Gospel narratives was more of a wandering, iconoclastic cynic than the God-man of Chalcedon. Along the way, the historicity of many distinctive aspects of the career of Jesus were called into question. Such conclusions should hardly have been unexpected, but the Jesus Seminar's pointed attempts to disseminate their findings widely beyond academia spurred many theologians to respond. C. Stephen Evans's interdisciplinary

---

14. See the discussion in Morris, *Logic of God Incarnate*, 89-102, where he is critical of kenosis on some fundamental grounds (mostly provided *ab initio* by his commitment to an Anselmian account of deity) but treats it as a serious contender to the mantle of most coherent incarnational strategy.

15. In short, the Third Quest sees the originary backdrop of Judaism as paramount in interpreting Jesus in his historical milieu, and is often, from E. P. Sanders onward, associated with the so-called "New Perspective on Paul." The "New" Quest is distinct from the Third Quest on several fronts, primarily in its focus on the alleged interpretive constructions given to the Gospels by early Christian communities, a hermeneutical strategy aligned closely with Bultmann and the resultant developments of form criticism. For robust discussion and distinctions, as well as critical commentary on both movements, see Wright, *Jesus and the Victory of God*, 28-124.

16. Funk, *Five Gospels*, 4-5.

work *The Historical Christ and the Jesus of Faith* thus appeared a few years later, citing *The Five Gospels* and related works, claiming that, in contrast to their denuding of the Gospels of their historical force, "much of what is religiously significant about Jesus lies precisely in the historicity of his story, and much is lost when the story is emptied of that historicity[.]"[17] Notably, Evans's arguments for the historicity and rationality of traditional Christology also featured a strong kenotic understanding of Christ's person.[18]

The Third Quest also caused its own share of christological worry, primarily issuing from the work of N. T. Wright, who had, for a variety of reasons, been identified as an ally by many relatively conservative Christian theologians. But that alliance was sorely tested when Wright wrote the following: "Jesus did not, in other words, 'know that he was God' in the same way that one knows one is male or female, hungry or thirsty, or that one ate an orange an hour ago. His 'knowledge' was of a more risky, but perhaps more significant, sort: like knowing one is loved. One cannot 'prove' it except by living it."[19] C. Stephen Evans also responded to this, suggesting that Wright was operating on the basis of methodological naturalism by denying Jesus a divine source of knowledge,[20] and further adding that "a commitment to what is called 'kenotic Christology' does not lead to any such [naturalistic] methodology."[21] This exchange between Wright's statement and Evans's response calls to mind the pivotal role that was played by the self-understanding and consciousness of Jesus in the second wave of kenotic Christology, in British thought, typified in the reflections of Charles Gore.[22]

The foregoing discussion has been necessarily concise, but it has intended to highlight the fact that third-wave kenotic Christology has emerged over the past four decades and has seen itself as both a defender and renovator of traditional (two natures) Christology, over and against doctrinal, philosophical, and historical challenges (e.g., Hick, the various

---

17. Evans, *Christ of History*, vi.

18. See Evans, *Christ of History*, ch. 6, esp. 132–36. This chapter also aligns itself with response to the metaphorical Christology of Hick and others, see 120–22.

19. Wright, *Jesus and the Victory of God*, 652–53. See further Wright, "Jesus and the Identity of God," 42–56.

20. Evans, "Methodological Naturalism in Historical Biblical Scholarship," 195.

21. Evans, "Methodological Naturalism in Historical Biblical Scholarship," 198.

22. Sections from Gore's major statements on this topic are helpfully drawn together in the recent thematic anthology of his writings: Waddell, *Charles Gore, Radical Anglican*, 47–56.

"Quests", etc.). It thereby perpetuates the *mediating* character that also attended the first and second waves of kenotic Christology.[23] Mediation, as a mode of theology or a description of such a mode, has been taken to mean a variety of different things since it was first employed in nineteenth-century Germany.[24] My application of the term here follows the usage of Donald Dawe, who identifies kenoticists as "mediating" figures in the following sense:

> They felt the necessity for uniting in their theology Christian orthodoxy, usually as interpreted in the doctrinal formulas of their own confessions, with the valid insights into Christian faith and history that were coming from the philosophical and critical historical studies of their time.... [Such kenotic thinkers] were united in the desire to incorporate into the structure of Christian thought set by the ecumenical creeds... the valid insights of modern historical and philosophical scholarship.[25]

Dawe asserts that kenoticists often see denunciations of traditional dogma not only as attacks to defend against but also as occasions for retooling foregoing doctrinal formulations, thus rendering them more relevant and cogent in the midst of current intellectual and existential climes.[26] C. Stephen Evans and Stephen Davis underscore this dimensionality of third-wave kenotic Christology: "[Christians] must be able to explain in contemporary terms, both to themselves and to the unbelieving world, who Christ is. Such explanations are especially necessary in times (like ours) of Christological ferment and confusion."[27]

Reflective of this orientation is the fact that all major waves of kenotic Christology discourse—from Thomasius to Charles Gore to the present

---

23. Again, the first wave was German and characterized most prominently by Thomasius; the second wave was English (and, to some extent, Scottish) and characterized most prominently by Gore.

24. See the analysis of the terminology and its various applications by Matthias Gockel, "Mediating Theology in Germany," 301–6.

25. Dawe, *Form of a Servant*, 91. See also comments by Thompson, "Nineteenth Century Kenotic Christology," 77. Ramsey speaks of *Lux Mundi* in a similar fashion: "The writers were a group of young teachers in theology who [embraced] a common desire to grapple with the intellectual questions which Christians were having to face at the time. ... Novelty lay in the willingness of a group of High Churchmen to treat contemporary secular thought as an ally rather than as an enemy" (*Era in Anglican Theology*, 2–3).

26. Thomas Senor makes a similar point about the emergence and continuance of kenotic Christology: "Drawing on Many Traditions," 102–3.

27. Davis and Evans, "Conclusion: The Promise of Kenosis," 313.

day—have been overlaid by three fundamental theological commitments: (1) a focus on Christ's *true* history; (2) a focus on his *true humanity*; and (3) a focus on Christ's *current significance for the church*.[28] Interestingly, these three commitments map quite logically onto the three "ditches" of Lessing (chronological, metaphysical, existential) and so can be seen as protractions of the now centuries-long quest to respond to them. Moreover, these three christological commitments can be viewed in an interlocking way: the more that a proper focus on the humanity of Christ is neglected, the harder it then becomes to understand his relevance and significance for the life of the people who constitute the church in the present day. We will proceed to illustrate kenotic Christology's allegiance to these commitments, and in so doing we will be focusing our attention on a handful of principal thinkers who have formed the spearhead of third-wave kenotic Christology: C. Stephen Evans, Stephen Davis, and Ron Feenstra.[29] Alongside these, the work of David Brown, Thomas Morris, and Peter Forrest—though differing in certain important ways from that of the first three[30]—highlight further key elements of the current discourse surrounding the advocacy of kenotic forms of Christology. All of these figures have authored or contributed to multiple major publications on kenotic Christology in recent decades.

---

28. These focuses have always characterized the major voices of kenotic Christology, and demonstrate why one of Thomasius's first major works on kenotic Christology was entitled "Contributions to a Churchly Christology" ("Ein Beitrag zur kirchlichen Christologie"]) and why Gore's first foray into the topic came in the publication of *Lux Mundi*.

29. Thompson groups them likewise (though he includes David Brown, whom I separate from this trio): "Nineteenth Century Kenotic, Christology," 103.

30. The differences can be summed concisely as follows:
Brown is a part of the third wave of kenotic Christology (and could be in fact be considered one its initial proper voices—see his 1985 work *Divine Trinity*, esp. 231–34), but he is more revisionist with tradition and more open to the findings of textual-historical criticism in his handling of scripture than is the triad of Davis, Evans, and Feenstra (who are all relatively "conservative" in these regards). See e.g., Brown, *Divine Humanity*, 3–25, 172–219.

Thomas Morris is a conservative theologian himself whose skill in philosophical theology, and apologetic interest in meeting the charges of Hick and others, have made him one of the most notable expositors of the logical force of kenotic Christology (though he himself does not ultimately subscribe to the view): see his *Logic*, esp. 87–107; "The Metaphysics of God Incarnate," 217–24.

Peter Forrest is much more beholden to an aggressive form of kenotic Christian *theism* than any of these other thinkers, though his exposition of his own kenotic Christology would place him in the rough orbit of third-wave kenotic Christology as well; see his *Developmental Theism*, esp. 168–87; "Incarnation," 127–40.

Analyzing the Christological Commitments

In his summative introduction to an important collection of essays showcasing contempoary kenotic Christology, C. Stephen Evans delineates the movement's commitment to a full exposition of Christ's humanity, saying that "the [kenotic] attempt to understand the identity of Jesus is valuable" because many Christians who "ardently affirm the divinity of Jesus are not comfortable with Jesus' *full humanity*."[31] Gordon Fee's essay in the same collection relates several anecdotes from his teaching career in which his students are repeatedly scandalized by Fee's unflinching declaration of Jesus's humanity.[32] He goes on to state that his students could be described as regularly subscribing to "a kind of naive docetism."[33] Evans broadens the application of this realization, stating that a "mild docetism" runs through much "popular piety" within the Christian faith,[34] and Stephen Davis significantly preempts a flagship discussion of his own kenotic Christology position by twice denouncing docetism.[35]

Third-wave kenotic Christology has consistently ennumerated important implications which flow from their commitment to Christ's *humanity* and its concomitant emphasis on Christ's *history*. (These are mutually constituitive and often treated together; after all, Christ's humanity is hardly *true* or *full* humanity if he did not actually live a human life in history.) One such implication concerns the use of scripture. Evans and Fee focus sharp attention on the "very human" portrait of Jesus in the Gospels,[36] and kenoticists have long noted that many forms of past Christology have avoided, or even distorted, passages which portray Jesus as lacking in knowledge or beset by human frailty.[37] Over and against the

---

31. Evans, "Understanding Jesus the Christ as Human and Divine," 3, emphasis added.

32. Fee, "New Testament and Kenosis Christology," 26–27.

33. Fee, "New Testament and Kenosis Christology," 25.

34. Evans, "Introduction," 3. Among prominent historical kenoticists, the second-wave advocates A. B. Bruce, Hugh Ross Mackintosh, and Frank Weston present perhaps the most sustained anti-docetic volley against christological tradition: Bruce, *Humiliation of Christ*; Mackintosh, *Doctrine of the Person of Jesus Christ*; Weston, *One Christ*, 68–78. See also Brown, *Divine Humanity*, 89, 118, 146.

35. Davis, "Jesus Chris: Savior or Guru?," 47–49.

36. Evans, "Introduction," 3; Evans, "Kenotic Christology and the Nature of God," 195–96, 199; Fee, "New Testament and Kenosis Christology," 35–42.

37. Brown's survey does a masterful job at showing how strongly this point is sustained throughout the first and second waves of kenotic Christology: *Divine Humanity*,

notion that kenotic Christology hinges solely on the interpretation of the "kenosis hymn" found in Phil 2:6–11, third-wave advocates argue for the breadth of the biblical witness to be brought to bear on Christology in a holistic and integrated sense.[38]

A related implication radiates from the commitment to articulating Christ's *signficance for the church*. Specifically, it concerns the church's use of scripture and scripture's relationship to theological method (especially its oft-utilized philosophical constructs). Across myriad encounters with non-kenotic forms of Christology, especially those which attempt to defeat kenosis on the philosophical premises of divine immutability, eternity, aseity, or perfection, kenoticists claim that "biblical teaching ought to trump disputed *a priori* theological intuitions."[39] Evans, Davis, Feenstra, and Brown agree that philosophical systemizations are not sufficient to override what seems, to them, to be the putative "picture of Jesus that the four evangelists paint."[40]

Another implication of kenotic Christology's commitments emerges when Evans claims that kenotic Christology involves real "implications for the practical life of Christians and the Church."[41] Though he does not expound on this point in detail, he seems to imply that these practical implications will involve the sacraments of the church and Christ's current relationship to them. Contrasting kenotic Christology with versions of Christology which deny Jesus's full divinity, Evans says that the "practical consequence [of non-divine christologies] will be that practices such as the Eucharist and Baptism must be understood differently from the way they have been traditionally, if they are continued at all."[42]

A final implication has to do with Christology's effect on the life of the Christian. Evans describes this by pointing out how an undistorted view of the humanity of Christ conveys a powerful solidarity with the

---

esp. the sections on Gess, Godet, Garvie, and Gore: 62–75, 104–8, 135–38.

38. E.g., Fee, "New Testament and Kenosis," 30–42; Brown, *Divine Humanity*, 4–14.

39. Davis and Evans, "Conclusion," 317. See also Ron Feenstra, "Kenotic Christological Model of Understanding the Divine Attributes," esp. 154–64.

40. Quote from Davis and Evans, "Conclusion," 318. For Feenstra's similar affirmations, see "Kenotic Christological Model," esp. 159–63; Brown states this less stridently, being more open to historical criticism in terms of the biblical text (*Divine Humanity*, 173–83). On the questions of divine immutability and aseity in particular, see Davis, "John Hick on Incarnation and Trinity," 263–64.

41. Evans, "Introduction," 3.

42. Evans, "Introduction," 3. See also Forrest, *Developmental Theism*, 180–83.

Redeemer, reflective of his true sharing in the full depth of human travail. A Christology that is even implicitly docetic, according to Evans, "makes it difficult for Christians to think of Jesus as fully identifying with the human condition (and thus with their own situation)."[43] This is why, third-wave kenoticists claim, the issues surrounding kenotic Christology cannot be seen as "a purely theoretical affair."[44] David Brown provides further commentary to this end, writing at length on the significance of the kenosis of Christ for understanding God's willingness to stand in camaraderie with an afflicted created order and "embroil divinity in the contingencies of human existence."[45] It should be emphasized that all of these resultant implications are interlocking and cohesive, and that they are largely shared by third-wave kenoticists.

Conclusion—Commitments to What End?

To sum up and synthesize, our overview yields the following four implications which attend third-wave kenotic Christology's commitments to an exposition of Christ's *history, humanity,* and his *churchly significance*:

1. the importance of an integrated and holistic approach to scripture (that is, not being selective in attention to the biblical text);
2. the importance of not allowing *a priori* philosophical intuitions or deductions to disproportionately direct christological work;
3. the necessary role that Christ's deity and kenosis play in the sacramental thinking and acting of the church;
4. the practical value of a kenotic understanding of the depth of Christ's solidarity with the human situation.

These commitments and their resultant four implications certainly pave a distinctive path for a christological program.

But it remains to be seen how effectively the kenoticists have been able to "make good" on these commitments. Indeed, as the next chapter

---

43. Evans, "Introduction," 3.
44. Evans, "Introduction," 3.
45. Brown, *Divine Humanity*, 189. See further 188–93. In his earlier work, wherein Brown presents cases for both kenotic Christology and a more traditional model without electing one over the other, he still makes the point that a kenotic understanding of the incarnation "would enable God to experience directly the human situation in a way that is impossible in [more traditional formulatons]" (*Divine Trinity*, 271).

will elucidate in detail, these alleged commitments of kenotic Christology are often eclipsed by another, and quite overt, commitment that has long dogged this kind of christological reflection: the commitment to *render the incarnation coherent* against primarily *conceptual* critiques. This fundamental orientation has led, consistently, to a problem in the "christological attentiveness" of kenotic Christology, and this problem spawns a host of others which, *en masse*, overwhelm the ability of kenoticists to deliver on their other, ostensible commitments.

4

Critiquing Kenosis

Insights from Transformation Theology

THE STUDY NOW BEGINS to draw more actively on the methodological and critical orientation proffered by transformation theology. As the reader will recall from the book's Introduction, this movement in theology pursues a fundamentally *limiting* program in which *reality*, the world of empirical sensing and embodied life, strikes the boundaries within which doctrine must live if it is going to be meaningful for real acting in the world. Crucially, then, theology which is excessively speculative and/or overly preoccupied with strategies of abstract cogitation will not suceed in making a real difference in the present world nor in demonstrating the significance of Christian commitments for that world. I refer to this critical and delimiting stance as the "transformational critique."[1]

Kenosis as Coherence-Making Device

Importantly, in its typical apologetically oriented modes,[2] kenotic Christology has largely been concerned to employ the "idea" of kenosis in an "analytic" fashion, that is, seeking to "make sense" of traditional christological statements through the semantic entailments or certainties that can be derived via the analysis of the meanings and definitions of terms, and thereby carrying on the bulk of its discourse in purely conceptual or abstract

---

1. The whole of Janz, *Command of Grace* is illustrative of this critique, though chs. 1–3 are the most foundational. See also chs. 2 and 3 in Davies, *Theology of Transformation*.

2. I have already illustrated this at length for the ongoing third wave. For historical commentary revealing the similarly apologetic motivations of the first wave (which sought to counter the legacies of both Schleiermacher and Left-Wing Hegelianism, as we have seen), note Dawe, *Form of a Servant*, 89–93; McGrath, *Making of Modern German Christology*, 36–80.

registers.³ Kenoticists have fixated the bulk of this abstract discourse on the issues arising from the ascription of divine attributes to Jesus's personhood.⁴ On most treatments of kenotic Christology, it is Christology's presumed ontological and metaphysical difficulties which stand to be "resolved" via the proper deployment of kenosis as a conceptual, sense-making device.⁵ Basically, insofar as many critical treatments of Christology have claimed that traditional doctrine is incoherent, kenosis is seen by its third-wave advocates as the mediating idea whereby the incarnation's conceptual coherence might be convincingly defended. In fact, this is precisely how C. Stephen Evans describes what he identifies as the *primary* reason for pursuing a kenotic form of Christology, averring that it "may allow Christians to give an answer to criticisms that what the Church asks them to believe is impossible and/or unintelligible."⁶

This commitment to the conceptual coherence of doctrinal statements is the most pervasively resounded in the literature of third-wave kenotic Christology.⁷ The goal and function of the entire undertaking is readily described by its protagonists as "a theory that *explains* the Incarnation,"⁸ or

---

3. I am employing the term "analytic" (or "analytical") in the Kantian sense in which it is employed by Paul Janz, referring to modes of reasoning that "are concerned solely with what reason can come to by itself, or can establish by itself, i.e. purely by a conceptual *analysis* of a certain hypothetically 'given' or a presuppositionally specified subject matter" (*Command of Grace,* 39).

4. See Brown: "The objection [from critics] here would be that the doctrine of the Incarnation is inevitably shown to be incoherent, as soon as one tries to apply both human and divine attributes to the one person, a hopeless, irresolvable muddle being the result" (*Divine Trinity,* 252).

5. The doctrinal framework is seen to consist in the (largely analytical or definitional) philosophical issues that are "left open" by Chalcedon—they are listed thusly: "Are the two 'natures' individual entities of some sort, or is a 'nature' here to be taken as an abstract entity, a set of properties? Does having both a divine and human nature imply that Christ has both a human and divine mind? Does the duality of natures really allow for the unity of the person?" (Evans, "Introduction," 2).

6. Evans, "Introduction," 2.

7. Commenting on the christologies of Brown, Davis, and Feenstra, James Anderson correctly states that these thinkers "have sought to defend and refine earlier kenoticism in the face of subsequent criticisms [and also] have offered their treatment in the explicit context of developing *logically consistent* interpretations of the doctrine of the Incarnation" (*Paradox in Christian Theology,* 81).

8. Davis, "Is Kenosis Orthodox?", 113, emphasis added; also Davis, "Jesus: Savior or Guru?", 53.

"an attempt to *get clear* on the person of Jesus,"[9] or an articulation of the incarnation that "*accounts* for perplexing biblical claims."[10] In the words of T. R. Thompson: "It is the goal of a kenotic Christology to *make . . . understandable* how it is that the pre-existent Son can enter into a fully human condition while retaining both his divinity and unity of person."[11]

By way of illustration, it is not uncommon for third-wave thinkers to list human attributes (e.g., limited knowledge) and divine attributes (e.g., omniscience) side-by-side, describe their contradictory ramifications for the person of Christ, and then "apply" kenosis as the coherence-making technique by which the incarnation can be logically understood.[12] Of course, the thinkers display variation in the specific mode and tone of this application. Brown, characteristically, states things in extremes: "Divine attributes apply exclusively before the Incarnation, human attributes apply exclusively to the period of the Incarnation, and divine attributes again exclusively to the post-Incarnation period[.]"[13] (This statement reflects Brown's pronounced sympathy for the kenotic model of W. F. Gess, the most radical of the first-wave kenoticists, whereas most other contemporary kenoticists favor the reasoning of Thomasius as a first-wave representative.[14]) Thomas Morris, though not himself a kenoticist, has offered an alternate suggestion for how kenosis can intelligibly render the human possession of divine attributes.[15] His suggestion, which has been gratefully taken up by active kenoticists like Davis and Feenstra,[16] is worth quoting:

> It is possible to reject a kenotic analysis of any divine attribute such as omniscience and yet square the kenotic perspective with

---

9. Davis and Evans, "Conclusion," 313, emphasis added.

10. Feenstra, "Kenotic Christological Method," 139, emphasis added.

11. Thompson, "Nineteenth-Century Kenotic Christology," 77–78, emphasis added.

12. E.g., Davis, "Savior or Guru?", 50–54, and more recently in "Metaphysics of Kenosis," 119–22. See also Law, *Kierkegaard's Kenotic Christology*, 35.

13. Brown, *Divine Trinity*, 257.

14. For Brown's sympathetic treatment of Gess, see *Divine Humanity*, 62–69. Brown notes, as I do, that Evans, Davis, and Feenstra "follow Thomasius" (244–45). Brown ultimately comes to prefer Martensen's kenotic model (radicalized) over that of Gess (he briefly circumscribes a critique of Gess in 244). Thompson is another notable third-wave figure who has expressed a preference for the Gessian model: see "Nineteenth-Century Kenotic Christology," 111.

15. Morris, *God Incarnate*, esp. 96–102.

16. E.g., Davis, "John Hick on Incarnation," 262; Feenstra, "Kenotic Christological Model," 152.

strong modal claims for deity by specifying that the conditions or requisites of divinity, the properties ingredient in or constitutive of deity, are not simply the divine attributes . . . but rather are properties composed of these attributes *qualified by* kenotic limitation possibilities. . . . What would be claimed is that it is not precisely *omniscience* which is a requisite of deity. It is rather a distinct property, the property of being omniscient-unless-freely-and-temporarily-choosing-to-be-otherwise, which is a logically necessary condition of deity.[17]

Forrest and Feenstra have also developed modal renderings of the divine attributes along these lines, both relying heavily on Morris's analysis.[18] And while such conceptual argumentation is adroit, and obliges unswervingly to meet certain critics on the grounds of an abstract discussion of alleged divine and human ontologies, I suggest that, as a mode of christologically significant discourse, it is importantly deficient. This deficiency fundamentally revolves around what I have referred to as *christological attentiveness*. This phrase now requires further explanation.

Christological Attentiveness to Reality

In every arena of discourse, a given field of study is defined predominantly by its subject matter, that is, the objects or sources of concern to which the study directs its attention. Different fields clearly have different concerns; that is, they "pay attention" to different things and orient themselves to differing ranges of human inquiry. The concerns of a field of study are pursued most effectively when directed by a proper "attentiveness" to the fitting object(s) of its study. The issue, then, with many forms of kenotic Christology, could be articulated as follows: the attentiveness which should (indeed, according to kenoticists' own stated commitments) characterize the study of Christology *is historical, particular, and engaged with spatio-temporal events in the world*. But third-wave kenotic Christology instead foregrounds a primarily analytical and apologetic focus, causing it to consistently seek to "defend" its christological affirmations, and to do so primarily via *conceptual*

17. Morris, *God Incarnate*, 99.
18. Forrest, "Incarnation," 228–32; Feenstra, "Reconsidering Kenotic Christology," 140–42. Senor sees Morris's suggested strategy as rather *ad hoc* and instead suggests renovating our understanding of the attributes more integrally rather than modifying them with Morris's proposed caveat—thus he takes a path similar in some respects to Thomasius (see "Drawing on Many Traditions," 104–10).

avenues. And while such avenues have a place in christological discourse, contemporary kenotic Christology often pursues them to the near wholesale neglect of more *concrete* christological attentiveness. Thus, its christological statements tend toward abstract categorization and speculative ontological discussions which are fundamentally remote from the world of history and action, of space and time, of life and reality.

It deserves to be stated here quite clearly that I am not saying that abstract thought *per se* has no use in Christology; abstract conceptualization, logical deduction, and other such mentally discursive operations are necessary and key elements of rational inquiry and understanding. Moreover, Donald Mackinnon (an important thinker in these regards) has made a resonant and enduring case for ontological considerations in the christological enterprise.[19] The issue, rather, is that kenotic Christology's attention is fixated so paramountly on this aspect of Christology that it inhibits much of its potential contribution to its other claimed commitments.[20]

By way of illustrating and supporting this critique, I will proceed in the next several sections to analyze the discourse of contemporary kenotic thinkers, taking care to note specific ways in which the attention to *conceptual coherence* compromises their ability to deliver on their other commitments which we outlined in chapter 3.

Christ's Humanity and the Problem of A Priori Parameters

As already expressed in more general terms above, kenotic christologians consistently attend to abstract and ontological categories in order to render the incarnation "coherent." In both Davis and Morris, for instance, we find explicit defenses of the "logic" of the incarnation—aiming to counter the work of Hick and others—which name kenosis as one of the most productive means for explicating the ontological composition of Christ in a lucid and orthodox manner.[21]

19. See e.g., Mackinnon, "'Substance' in Christology," 244–53.

20. This study is focusing on kenotic Christology in this regard, but it could well apply to other schools of christological reflection that are current in philosophical debate. See Cross, "Incarnation," and Senor, "Drawing on Many Traditions," for an effective survey of examples.

21. Thomas Senor refers to his elucidation of his own kenotic Christology as an exercise in "developing a *philosophically satisfying* Christology" ("Drawing on Many Traditions," 89, emphasis added).

For Davis, the primary concern is to demonstrate the logical (conceptual) feasibility (intelligibility) of the doctrine of the incarnation. How can one personage be both God and man? Cognitive coherence is the directing goal.[22] But in order to match swords with critics of the philosophical basis for traditional Christology, Davis sees himself compelled to separate the term "God" from its biblical, historical, and ecclesiological dimensions:

> When we ask whether the incarnation is possible, i.e. whether God can become man while remaining God, we must specify in what sense we are using the term 'God'. One possibility is that the term 'God' is a proper name, i.e. a term denoting Yahweh, the being who alone (so Christians believe) is divine. Another possibility is that the term 'God' is a title or descriptive term for any divine being. . . . Unless otherwise indicated, the term 'God' in this chapter will be used in the second way. I will be asking the question: *Can any truly divine being also be truly human?*[23]

Here it is made clear that the term "God," when discussed in the context of the incarnation's logical coherence, is being discursively reduced to an analytically reified concept—quite apart from the "Yahweh" of scripture whom the church confesses. This deity-concept will bear all the typical definitional constraints necessarily derived from axiomatic (and tautological) properties of divinity—aseity, simplicity, infinity, incorporeality, the omni-attributes, etc. Kenosis, *ab initio*, thus appears as a *method for conceptualizing*, or re-conceptualizing, the *idea* of "deity," and thus to render coherent that deity's act of incarnating itself, within these philosophically and cognitively orchestrated parameters.[24]

In Morris's landmark work *The Logic of God Incarnate* we find a similar range of concerns and similar initial methodological and hermeneutical moves. Morris avers that his account of the incarnation (which is conceived with impressive force at the intersection of analytic philosophy

---

22. "I am going to try to show that the statement 'Jesus Christ is truly God and truly man' is coherent . . . . I hope to present a convincing case that 'Jesus Christ is truly God and truly man' is entailed by a coherent statement or series of statements" (Davis, *Logic*, 119).

23. Davis, *Logic*, 120. Emphasis original.

24. Many kenotic christological thinkers have taken issue with at least some divine attribute or another; Davis, for instance, takes special care to emphasize that he does not think omniscience ought to belong to the "essential" properties of God (Davis, *Logic*, 121, 126–28). Immutability, however, stands apart as the traditional attribute most roundly criticized by kenoticists; Brown's commentary is representative: *Divine Trinity*, 256–57.

and Anselmian theology) preserves doctrine and also "stands triumphant against all contemporary challenges of a philosophical nature."[25] In Morris, then, we find a clearly parallel apologetic maneuver, in-step with the third wave of kenotic Christology as a whole and exemplified specifically in what we have just seen in Davis.[26]

However, a very particular sort of challenge confronts this fundamental starting point within christological reflection. Categories arising from the rational distillation of ideas are cognitive objects; they are abstract. That is, they do not exist in the world of space and time. Yet *it is only in the world of space and time that God has revealed Godself and that the incarnate, human life of Christ has taken place* (and continues to take place). Thus, rather than a fundamental basis in abstract categories (concerning ontological properties, predicates, attributes, etc., all secured by deductive, intellectual operation) it is rather the specific *life* (in empirical history) of Jesus and the *life* of the church (in the concrete existence of past and present space-time) in the world that must direct our attention to Jesus's humanity and what that humanity means. Christology originates from, and must be continually shaped and informed by, the historically-manifested, divinely causal force of revelation, the revelation of God in Christ. Insofar as Christology turns toward a program of argumentation concerning a humanity that is subordinated to *a priori* conceptual parameters, it simultaneously turns away from the real-world events which animate the historical progression and continuing efficacy of Jesus's human life. (As things proceed in our next chapter, this spatio-temporal focus as a component of christological attentiveness will be shown to be necessary in any Christology which hopes to effectuate relevant and praxiological reflection upon and awareness of the mode of Christ's working in the world today.)

The *a priori* starting points which are seen in Davis/Morris catalyze a prominent issue which comes, in many cases, to characterize the abstract program of many kenotic Christology discussions. One such issue is what we have alluded to above as the self-referential nature of the discourse. This can be found, for example, in its preoccupation with the supra-sensible

---

25. Morris, *God Incarnate*, 14. Further: "The book as a whole should be viewed as a defense of the orthodox doctrine of the Incarnation, the two-natures view of Christ, against contemporary philosophical attacks" (16).

26. Again, it is worth noting for clarity's sake that Morris personally advocates for a "two minds" Christology, rather than a kenotic model. However, he discusses and praises the explicatory power of kenotic models often in his own work, which is very much a part of the selfsame apologetic-christological *Zeitgeist*.

divine "essence" and human "essence" and their posited attributes, properties, and/or parts. In spite of their manifest rigor and commendability on other fronts, many such discussions remain enclosed in abstract analytics or "conceptual machinery," to use a phrase that Thomas Senor applies (unironically) to his own rendering of divine/human properties in the service of his kenotic Christology.[27] Against such conscription of theological discourse, Brian Hebblethwaite well notes that even in the midst of our trinitarian and incarnational discussions, we have little ground for suggesting what God can and cannot do (or can or cannot *be*) on the basis of ontological supposition—what matters is what the church has come to believe *has been done in history*, particularly in Jesus.[28]

However, we have noted above that third-wave kenoticists do consistently make reference to the "portrait" of Jesus in the Gospels. In fact, we have seen that they habitually designate this portrait as the very catalyst for their position, moreover claiming an integrated and holistic approach to scripture as an implication of their christological commitments.[29] As Stephen Davis puts it, "[For] many kenotic theorists, the primary motivation for the theory is not logical or metaphysical but biblical."[30] Such a statement from a kenoticist might seem to undercut the point I have raised above about speculative and self-referential argumentation obscuring a clear focus on Jesus's historically manifested, scripturally recounted humanity. To address this, we must examine the kenoticists' use of scriptural material.

---

27. Senor, "Drawing on Many Traditions," 108.

28. See Hebblethwaite, "Jesus, God Incarnate," 24–25.

29. C. Stephen Evans, Ron Feenstra, and Stephen Davis all declare the significant place of scripture in the initiation of their christological and theological investigations, sometimes even radically juxtaposing their advocacy for "the biblical God" over and against "the God of the philosophers" (a view of God they attribute to more-traditional christological thinkers). See esp. Evans, "Kenotic Christology and the Nature of God," 192–94; Feenstra, "Kenotic Christological Model," 158–64.

30. Davis, "Metaphysics of Kenosis," 125; see also 133. The work of Peter Forrest on kenotic Christology, to date, has been almost solely motivated by philosophical concerns with little attention to biblical material. But this is unique to Forrest among the major advocates we are discussing.

Christ's Humanity and the Problem of Scriptural Fragmentation

Don Cupitt once argued that kenotic Christology is "not a theory designed to account for facts about Jesus, but a theory designed to explain how one can go on believing in the incarnation in a time when the old arguments have broken down."[31] Stephen Davis disagrees with Cupitt, responding that "[the kenotic] theory is primarily designed to account for the biblical picture of Jesus, especially the kenosis hymn in Philippians and the human and divine characteristics attributed to Jesus in the gospels."[32] This is not an uncommon move among third-wave kenoticists: when the speculative or abstract nature of their program is highlighted, they claim to be fundamentally rooted in the biblical witness itself, usually with reference to Phil 2:5–11 and the Gospels.[33] This seemingly functions as an indirect claim that their program can resist the charge of speculative abstraction owing to its reliance on, and reference to, the text of scripture. However, the manner in which many kenoticists call upon scripture reflects many of the same problematic tendencies we have already identified. When third-wave kenotic christologians advocates refer to scripture, they nearly always do so by isolating a particularly perplexing or confusing action or saying of Jesus, which is then taken as needing to explained, or rendered intelligible, by reference to the conceptual machinery of kenosis.

For example, proponents emphasize that Jesus admits that "he does not know" the date of the parousia (Mark 13:32);[34] they emphasize the passage that claims Jesus "grows in wisdom" (Luke 2:52);[35] they emphasize isolated passages that portray Jesus's "frustrations."[36] Stephen Davis has commented on how well a kenotic theory "fits" with these isolated, illustrative moments

---

31. Cupitt, "Christ of Christendom," 137.

32. Davis, *Logic*, 128. See also Davis, "Metaphysics of the Incarnation," 133.

33. Gordon Fee provides a nice summary of the biblical basis that is said to underlie contemporary kenoticism: "New Testament and Kenosis Christology," 25–44. Brown notes that biblical scholars, rather than theologians, were the most radical of the early kenoticists; see his representative commentary on both Gess and Godet (*Divine Humanity*, 62–75).

34. Davis, "Is Kenosis Orthodox?", 130; Feenstra, "Kenotic Christological Model," 146–54. Evans, "Kenotic Christology," 199.

35. Davis, "Is Kenosis Orthodox?" 130; Evans, "Kenotic Christology," 199.

36. Evans, "Kenotic Christology," 199.

from the Gospel narratives.[37] However, this sort of treatment of scripture is, at best, fragmentary and instrumentalist; none of these discussions attend to the narratives in question with any sustained depth or contextual detail, and without any of the requisite attention to the historical materiality, lived sociality, personal relationships, enacted decisions, or specific accomplishments of Jesus, rather the passages are treated as providing particular subject matters, or "data," or even puzzles, ripe for analytical investigation and metaphysical resolution (e.g., "the human properties," "the divine attributes," the "unity of the natures," the "divine self-limitation," etc.).

Of significance for the concern of scriptural fragmentation, Stephen Davis declares that even if Cupitt's point, cited above, about kenotic theories not attending to actual facts about Jesus were true, "it would not damage kenotic theories of the incarnation in the slightest."[38] This is a striking statement, for it seems to imply that even if kenotic Christology was not interested in "account[ing] for facts about Jesus," it would remain unhampered in its theoretical power. This seems to be a tacit admission that it is primarily the theoretical or, more precisely, the analytically descriptive power that ultimately matters for this form of Christology. This much we have noted in our foregoing section, but what we are seeing here is the further point that the theoretical focus is pervasive not just in philosophical argumentation pertaining to the divine attributes but also in terms of scriptural hermeneutics and focus.

True, there are some instances where third-wave kenoticists allude to treating the biblical witness to Christ's history in a less fragmentary, more holistic fashion.[39] Most significant among these would be Evans's claim that

37. Davis, "Is Kenosis Orthodox?" 130; see also *Logic*, 129–30 for his brief discussion of "high" Christology passages in John's Gospel, noting that his theory is "consistent with" them. But the passages' bearing on the lived life of Jesus are not discussed at all; the passages function as a simple example of non-contradiction of the varied concepts Davis is employing. Simply stated, this seems backwards—the biblical revelation ought to proceed the philosophical rendering of anything, not afterward merely being found to be "consistent" with such rendering.

38. Davis, *Logic*, 128.

39. The opportunities to present a holistic Christology in a kenotic tenor are often clearly missed. A key example is Evans's book *Historical Christ and The Jesus of Faith*. Though the work is clearly apologetic in tone and focus (its preface mentions the work of Hick and other less-traditional scholars who it intends to counteract), it still claims to be focused on Christ as a historical individual. Given Evans's interest in kenotic Christology, we would expect kenosis to be integrated into this study and into the varied discussions of Christ's acts as a critical, public individual. But this is not the case; kenosis serves a prominent role in only a single chapter, and that chapter is, perhaps predictably, on the

"the idea of Christ's Incarnation as kenotic in character is supported not merely by individual passages of Scripture, but by the character of Jesus' life and death as a whole."[40] (Though, even here it must be noted that Evans is expressly focusing upon "the idea" of the incarnation.) This comment reads as though it is intended to introduce a developed, thorough focus on the alleged kenotic elements throughout Jesus's historical actions and relationships. But Evans offers only a few generalized sentences in this direction[41] before quickly returning to heightened scrutiny of the question of the abstract divine attribute of immutability.[42]

In short, the third-wave kenoticists under consideration have mainly utilized scripture as an avenue for discussion about the abstract *natures of Jesus* (and their alleged attributes) in conceptually definitional terms, rather than focusing on *the historical human Jesus* as a specific, contextual, relational, social, material person. Christ's humanity, as the character and quality of a specific human being in first-century Palestine, must involve consideration of his space-time person, i.e. his actions, his expressed feelings or those he engendered in others, his suffering, agency, decision-making, and accomplishment, arrayed in relation to himself, his family, his disciples, his society, and to the broader cultural forms of life which impressed themselves upon him and with which he interacts through speech and activity.[43] Though kenosis advocates claim to be moving from concrete items in the biblical witness to their theological suppositions, their mode of approaching scripture repeatedly serves to fragment the career of Christ into instances of isolated datum which are ostensibly troublesome to traditional formulations of christological doctrine, and thereby stand to be speculatively resolved.

---

question of "Is the Incarnation Logically Possible?" (116–36).

40. Evans, *Historical Christ*, 196.

41. The rest of the passage reads as follows: "The New Testament portrait of Jesus tells a story of a person who takes no thought for the ordinary interests that dominate most human lives. He has no wife or home, no career or interest in the accumulation of possessions. Instead he gives himself wholly to the proclamation of the kingdom of God and the nurture of his followers. He finally gives his very life as 'a ransom for many,' not shirking a painful and shameful death for the sake of the redemption of human beings" ("Kenotic Christology and the Nature of God," 196). This is one of the best specific passages on the *historically rendered* humanity of Christ in third-wave kenotic Christology discourse. But its isolation and short length simply make it an exception that proves the rule.

42. Evans, *Historical Christ*, 196–97.

43. Representative of such a holistic understanding of anthropology, see Pannenberg, *Anthropology in Theological Perspective*; Shults, *Reforming Theological Anthropology*.

Continuing with a close reading of the kenoticist's own works, we will see in our next two sections that the commitment to Christ's churchly significance is also impaired along similar lines. Though C. Stephen Evans never quite demarcates what he means by the "practical significance" of kenotic Christology for the church, we will on analysis be able to divide the "churchly significance of Christ" into two discrete (but related) subjects: (1) the *ascension of Christ*, which has been discussed at length in third-wave kenotic Christology and which has a great deal to do with how Christ's presence and significance for the church today are understood, and (2) the intersection of Christology and the lived activity of the church, that is, *Christian praxis*.

Ecclesial Significance and the Problem of Kenotic Ascension

Fundamental to the link between Christ and the church today is our understanding of the ascension. In making this claim, I am following a trend of renewed attention to the ascension inaugurated with the publication of Douglas Farrow's landmark *Ascension and Ecclesia*.[44] Throughout his multifaceted study, Farrow acknowledges the various contortions that have afflicted Christian discourse on the ascension, saying that today the doctrine "is something of an embarrassment."[45] But Farrow's most distinctive contribution is found in both his clarion call for a return to a focus on the bodily ascension of Jesus and in his tenacious defense of its key role in defining ecclesial identity:

> It is the divergence of Jesus-history from our own that gives to the ecclesia its character and its name. It is the divergence of Jesus-history from our own that calls for a specifically *eucharistic* link: for the breaking and remoulding, the substantial transformation of worldly reality to bring it into conjunction with the lordly reality of Jesus Christ. The kind of ecclesiology we wish to do is quite impossible, then, without careful attention to the ascension, however difficult and unpromising that doctrine may appear today.[46]

44. Other writings within this trend would include: Kelly, *Upward*; Granados, "First Fruits," Kapic and Vander Lugt, "Ascension of Jesus and the Descent of the Holy Spirit in Patristic Perspective;" Dawson, *Jesus Ascended*; and another, more recent work by Farrow, *Ascension Theology*.

45. Farrow, *Ascension and Ecclesia*, 9.

46. Farrow, *Ascension and Ecclesia*, 10.

The bridge from Christ to the church (as well as for understanding Christ "with" the church) is instantiated by the ascension; Farrow's detailed work shows that ecclesiology has always been deeply affected by whatever view of the ascension (or lack thereof) was most operative.[47] Therefore, it should come as no surprise that kenoticists' thinking on Christ's ecclesial significance will take much of its coloring from how Christ's kenosis is seen to relate to his ascension.

The first and second waves of kenotic Christology focused substantial energy on the exalted state of Christ. Thomasius, after all, was a strongly confessional Lutheran and was adamant that the assumed humanity of Christ was glorified in its post-resurrection state and borne into a heavenly existence, entailing the acquisition of ubiquity which Christ retains forevermore.[48] But the exaltation presents difficult issues for kenotic thinkers. Many of them have regarded the ascension (or even the resurrection) as the *conclusion of Christ's kenosis* and thus the re-instantiation of any previously emptied or limited divine attributes.[49] Again, Thomasius is representative of such a viewpoint.[50] But, the critical question then arises: if Christ is able to retain his true humanity and re-assume all of the divine attributes to his person, then it seems that the divine attributes in their fullness are compatible with human nature after all,[51] and this raises a question over the whole claim that an ontological kenosis was necessary to enable Christ's human incarnation in the first place.[52] Otherwise stated, if the kenosis is that necessary divine movement which facilitates the union with humanity, then the

---

47. See Farrow, *Ascension and Ecclesia*, 41–164; also Farrow, *Ascension Theology*, 16–49.

48. See Feenstra's apt summation of Thomasius on this: "Reconsidering Kenotic Christology," 131–32.

49. Law, *Kierkegaard's Kenotic Christology*, 61.

50. Thomasius, *CPW*, 78. Feenstra, "Reconsidering Kenotic Christology," 132; Thompson, "Nineteenth Century Kenotic," 84.

51. Law's statement is representative: "If the ascended Christ retains his human nature and receives back the divine attributes he renounced during his earthly ministry, does this not mean that divine and human attributes can indeed exist together?" (*Kierkegaard's Kenotic*, 62, see further 62–63).

52. See Law, *Kierkegaard's Kenotic Christology*, 62–63. Feenstra thinks that Stephen Davis has fallen into a conceptual trap of sorts here in his kenotic Christology; see Feenstra, "Reconsidering Kenotic Christology," 145–46. Thomasius, for his part, is insistent that it is the Christic transformation of Christ's assumed human nature—through his obedience and glorification—that "enabled his human nature to become the locus of the full glory of God" (Thomasius, *CPW*, 79). Cf. Brown, *Divine Humanity*, 46–48.

termination of the kenosis would seemingly also be the termination of the humanity in the glorified Christ.[53] How have third-wave thinkers addressed such thorny issues surrounding Christ's ascension?

David Brown had suggested that the ascension question could be resolved by foregoing the humanity of Christ altogether at the exaltation, putting forth the exotic claim that the humanity could legitimately be preserved as "a remembered experience of the Second Person of the Trinity."[54] (Brown has since moved away from this position in light of critiques.[55]) Ron Feenstra finds such a solution problematic on numerous grounds,[56] agreeing with Lutheran, Reformed, and Catholic confessional traditions that Christ's humanity must be retained in his glorified state[57] (a point that is also resolutely and importantly affirmed by transformation theology; this will occupy us in later chapters[58]). However, Feenstra does recognize that the ascension poses conceptual problems for a kenotic outlook, and so he separates the incarnation from the kenosis. To wit, although the incarnation and kenosis of Christ coincided in their initiation, Feenstra thinks that the Logos could have become incarnate with no self-emptying involved, and thus could have still retained full expression of the divine attributes (though how those attributes would have functioned in union with the human nature is not explained). Feenstra says that the Logos *chose* to undergo kenosis during his earthly life in order to "share our lot or condition during his life on earth."[59] But what exactly this "sharing" consists in, and why kenosis is necessary for it, and why such a sharing is no longer important following Christ's ascension, Feenstra does not address.[60]

53. This form of the critique was made famous by D. M. Baillie's promulgation of it in *God Was in Christ*, 97–98.

54. Brown, *Divine Trinity*, 234. Further: "The divine attributes apply [to Christ] exclusively before the Incarnation, the human attributes exclusively to the period of the Incarnation, and divine attributes again exclusively to the post-Incarnation period" (257). It should be noted that these are suggestive points by Brown, detailing strategies for showing the "coherence" of incarnational doctrine. Brown's more recent work on kenosis does not pursue such lines on the ascension in any clear way: *Divine Humanity*, 259–63.

55. Brown, *Divine Humanity*, 244.

56. Feenstra, "Reconsidering," 147.

57. See Brown, *Divine Humanity*, 245–47; also Forrest, "Incarnation," 232.

58. Davies, *Theology of Transformation*: "We cannot deny the fullnesss of his humanity if we assert that he lives" (18).

59. Feenstra, "Reconsidering," 148. See the critical discussion of Feenstra on this point in Zachariades, *Omnipresence of Christ*, 71–72.

60. Peter Forrest, for his part, mentions two things that Christ needed to be able to

Such a vague rendering of the issues does little to dispel them. Again, the whole logic of kenosis, from Thomasius onward, has been that to live a truly human life, divine attributes must be "emptied" or somehow relinquished. C. Stephen Evans seeks to concur with Feenstra and also clarify the position somewhat by focusing on *the kind of body* that Jesus takes on in the incarnation: "I suggest that we understand Feenstra's suggestion to be the claim that becoming incarnate in an *ordinary* human body requires a kenosis."[61] The point of this modification is to argue that, since Christ's post-resurrection body "differs dramatically from our ordinary human bodies," the kenosis of the divine attributes is no longer necessary and Christ can therefore receive all of them to his glorified self without annihilating his true humanity.[62]

Regardless of these arguments, the overarching ascension theology for both Feenstra and Evans dictates that, though the humanity of Christ continues in his ascended state, the *kenosis* of Christ is long concluded.[63] The kenosis *per se* was a thirty-year experience in the historically human life of the Logos.[64] It was an "exception" to the normal divine mode of operation. Stephen Davis also agrees with this, saying that Christ is still human, but no longer kenotic in any sense.[65] And, more recently, Peter Forrest, though a very different thinker than the others, still concludes that "the kenosis did come to an end."[66] By retaining the notion of the kenosis mainly as an incarnation-effectuating ontological episode, all of these theologians follow in the wake of Thomasius by terminating the kenosis at Christ's exaltation. This means that there is, in fact, no view of the kenosis as a continuing

---

embrace in his earthly ministry that required kenosis: horrific suffering and genuine temptation ("Incarnation," 233). With this every kenoticist would agree. But it is still not clear why the cessation of suffering and temptation means that the kenosis itself would be concluded (since no kenotic christologian limits the kenosis to only these two things), nor is it said why it is assumed that the ascended Christ no longer suffers (or should no longer be enabled to suffer), nor is it clear on Forrest's account how this alleged cessation of suffering (and temptability) could be included in the truly human, ascended person.

61. Evans, "Kenotic Christology," 201.
62. Evans, "Kenotic Christology," 201–2.
63. Also Forrest, "Incarnation," 232.
64. Feenstra, "Kenotic Christological Model," 153.
65. Davis, "Is Kenosis Orthodox?", 114.
66. Forrest, "Incarnation," 232–(33).

reality for Jesus Christ, and thus kenosis plays no ongoing role in Christ's presence and acting in the world today.[67]

The issues here are manifold. Despite the tacit admission that kenosis is serving as a *conceptual* maneuver for "making sense" of Jesus's human qualities in the Gospels, this sort of earthly-only kenosis also leaves wholly undeveloped the ramifications for a continuing kenosis in the Christic life. If kenosis were the manner in which the greatest act of divine humiliation and grace was undertaken, should it be seen only as an "exception" and only to characterize a single thirty-year period in the eternal life of the Son? What then would Christ's kenosis mean for the contemporary church, except as a past element of the earthly ministry, a dogmatic utterance, an ontological "fact" of history?

Moreover, another question is provoked: why would it be *necessary* for the kenosis of Christ to end? These questions remain relatively unexplored in third-wave literature, leaving underdetermined a vital aspect of their discourse: *Christ's contemporary presence*. In fact, there is little third-wave commentary on the *Christus praesens*, nor interaction with sacramental theology, nor thinking on how Christ is currently relating to his church.[68] Questions abound, centering on either the necessity of the kenosis in the first place or the reality of the ascended Christ's humanity.[69] This mode of Christology has focused to such a degree on a coherent rendering of incarnational doctrine that these other aspects of Christology, which have great bearing on ecclesiology and Christian identity, have been neglected. This trend continues when we consider the relation between the kenosis of Christ and Christian praxis.

---

67. See Forrest's discussion of the sacraments for an example of how this plays out in philosophical reasoning: *Developmental Theism*, 180–83.

68. Forrest provides only a slight exception to this trend in his discussion of the "real presence" of Christ, but that discussion actually makes very little of kenosis (*Developmental Theism*, 180–84).

69. Farrow is careful to underline the fact that Christ's humanity must be maintained when considering the ascension: "It is frequently said that the humanity of Christ used to be the great problem for theology but that today it is his divinity which is distracting and difficult. Our study suggests that the case is otherwise. It is still the humanity of Christ over which we are prone to stumble, and what is required today more than ever is a doctrine of the ascension that does not set his humanity aside" (*Ascension and Ecclesia*, 13).

Ecclesial Significance and the Problem of Missing Praxis

Third-wave kenotic Christology has not articulated anything like a defined praxiological dimension, despite the potential that is seemingly latent for such in the wider context of the Phil 2 "kenosis hymn."[70] This lack of attention to Christian praxis is reflective of the scant focus on the Christic implications for ecclesiology overall. For example, none of the essays from leading kenoticists in the volume *Exploring Kenotic Christology* relate their ideas on Christ's kenosis to ethics, praxis, ministry, or to broader church-society relations.[71] Given that, as we have seen, kenoticists proclaim a stated commitment to "practical significance," which implies some measure of influence which flows from the christological suppositions into the practical life of Christians, this appears as a deficiency, or at least as a shrouded area of thought where that commitment stands to be more markedly fulfilled. Kenotic Christology, with its intonations of humility, sacrifice, other-seeking love, and obedience, certainly calls out for praxiological implications in the life of the church, and it is at the very least mysterious that third-wave thinkers have not ventured more obviously in this direction.[72] This praxiological lacuna, when viewed in light of our foregoing analysis in this chapter, could in fact be seen as a necessarily derivative consequence of third-wave kenotic Christology's analytical and conceptual orientation.

Evans and Davis, in a jointly written essay, briefly move toward some articulation of christologically rooted praxis when they offer a description

---

70. See Phil 2:2–11. There is a marked line of biblical scholarship arguing for an *imitatio Christi* in this passage and throughout the epistle: See Tsui, "Kenosis in the Letter of Paul to the Philippians," 242–52. Heil, *Philippians*, 113; Reumann, *Philippians*, 317. Kurz, "Kenotic Imitation of Paul and of Christ in Philippians 2 and 3," 103–26. A minority voice does exist that reads against the *imitatio Christi* in this passage, e.g., Wannenwetsch, "Whole of Christ and the Whole Human Being," 88.

71. With some minor exception in the essay of Ruth Groenhout ("Kenosis and Feminist Theory," 303–12), though even there the comments are vague and conceptual, rather than specific and concrete.

72. Not that kenosis is never employed in praxiological or ministerial contexts; my point here is that these uses of kenosis are not derived clearly or rigorously from specifically kenotic forms of Christology, and that the proponents of third-wave kenotic Christology do not move significantly from their christological points to praxiological ones. A recent article that provides at least a slight exception to this trend is Purves, "Relating Kenosis to Soteriology," 70–90. But Purves's article is only generally ethical and quite abstract, and thus falls short of concrete directives for churchly praxis grounded in the kenosis of Christ.

of how Christ's kenotic relationship with the Father and Spirit can be meaningful for the life and actions of the Christian today:

> The kenotic account highlights . . . the way a truly human Jesus as the Son of God provides a model for us of how human life is to be lived. For we too can live our lives in dependence on the Father and in union with the Spirit, and thus be united to Christ as well. Even the miracles Jesus performs do not separate him from humanity; in fact, he explicitly tells his disciples that if they have faith they will have access to the same miraculous power he himself has shown.[73]

Such a line of discourse seems resolutely aimed at a vigorous delineation of ecclesial significance, with the potential for focused and specific attention on the practices of the church in the world. However, Evans and Davis do not expound the implications of Christ's kenosis for praxis in any more detail than this, and the passage itself is quite isolated in the writings of the principal third-wave proponents I am here considering.

On balance, however, I should raise a point that both acknowledges the more fundamental issue at-play in this particular deficiency (and anticipates one of the key contributions of transformation theology to the project of this book). The point, rendered in its most basic expression, is that a clear praxiological connection between theological *narratives* and specific Christian *acts* is notoriously elusive. Narrative forms of theology encourage us to "live within" communities that are shaped by the biblically and theologically conveyed "story" of God's dealings with the world; the narrative theology of Stanley Hauerwas is a resonant current example of such reflection. Yet, as Oliver Davies trenchantly acknowledges, "the Christian narrative does not, in general, tell us what to do in *this* particular situation."[74] Charles Taylor, in his helpful discussion of "the self in moral space," indicates that our identity is most fundamentally rooted in our *commitments* which allow us to "take stands" in the midst of complex ethical situations.[75] This critical moral space "between narrative and act," which is occupied by living selves in space and time, must be "traversed in the moment of free judgment"—this is praxis at its most basal level, in the complexity and small spaces of real-world encounters.[76] Since kenosis has

---

73. Evans and Davis, "Conclusion: The Promise of Kenosis," 320.
74. Davies, *Theology of Transformation*, 73.
75. Taylor, *Sources of the Self*, 27.
76. Davies, *Theology of Transformation*, 73–74.

a narrative character inherently,[77] and since this colors a good deal of its theological applications, it becomes very difficult to ascertain specifically *how* kenosis relates to specific Christian activity as such. While this difficulty is significant, transformation theology, as an expression of theological questioning directed, fundamentally, to the nature of the human acting itself, will serve to helpfully highlight some ways in which kenotic Christology might be helpfully reconceived.

Conclusion: Toward the Furtherance of Kenotic Commitments

The plot of this chapter should not be misconstrued. It does not consist, as many interactions with kenotic Christology do, in a critique of the notion of divine kenosis (or kenotic incarnation) as such. This study is fundamentally interested in the exploration of kenosis in Christology. Rather, this chapter has contextually analyzed the claimed christological commitments of that movement and then critically interrogated the difficulty the movement has manifested in fulfilling those commitments. By focusing this interrogation via the notion of christological attentiveness, kenotic Christology's overriding focus on intellectual coherence has been unveiled and shown to imperil its other christological commitments: namely, Christ's historical humanity and his ongoing churchly significance.

As noted in the Introduction, the final chapters of this thesis will point-up how the unique kenotic Christology of Jürgen Moltmann presents a path which may more readily deliver on these salient commitments. That is, by presenting a christological program that more addresses some of the issues of *christological attentiveness*. But the notion of attentiveness, though it has been introduced and utilized thus far in this study, stands in need of greater elucidation and refinement before its full force can be applied in the shaping of kenotic explorations.

---

77. See e.g., Fisk, "Odyssey of Christ," 45–73.

5

Refocusing Kenosis (I)

Framing Christological Attentiveness

THE PRESENT CHAPTER IS strategically focused on three closely related tasks: (1) arraying some of the major themes of transformation theology's theological attentiveness generally; (2) exhibiting its principal statements on Christology specifically; (3) and constructively disposing those statements into what I will call "transformational questions for christological attentiveness." These questions will function as a heuristic in christological method and will be applied to the Christology of Moltmann in the book's final chapters. To anticipate, the heuristic questions will center on three major subjects, pertaining to (respectively), the historical *achievement* of Jesus, Christ's current *presence*, and the forms of *praxis* enabled by Christ's lived (and ongoing) accomplishments and relationships.

Along the way, Paul Janz and Oliver Davies will be taken as the principal articulators of transformational thinking (that is, method and questions derived from transformation theology), though at key junctures similarly oriented insights will also be pointed up and synthetically absorbed from Dietrich Bonhoeffer and Donald MacKinnon—each of them being important interlocutors for of transformation theology, particularly as concerns Christology.[1]

The "Rerouting" of Theological Attentiveness

Transformation theology (henceforth largely to be designated in its force and effects by use of the adjective "transformational") presents an orientation

---

1. Bonhoeffer and Mackinnon feature prominently in Janz: see his interactions with Mackinnon in *Command*, 33, 102, 148 and Bonhoeffer in *Command*, 50-53, 145-46, 163-73. Davies expresses key agreement and dialogue with Bonhoeffer throughout *Theology of Transformation*, e.g., 27, 67-68, 142.

which speaks on a primarily methodological and hermeneutical level.[2] In essence, transformational thinking calls Christian reflection, the lifeblood of theology, to give greater place to the specific, experiential, sensible, and spatio-temporal *ground* of the Christian faith. Revelatory events, occurring, witnessed, and experienced in the thick of history, are the fundamental basis for Christian self-understanding and the life of faith.[3] As such, any theological reflection which fundamentally orients itself to an abstract program of analyticity or speculation as the basis of its truth claims (as we have seen, for example, in certain articulations of third-wave kenotic Christology) risks divorcing itself from its indispensably historical ground. And the center of this very ground of theology and Christian identity is Jesus Christ, who is only to be *encountered* in the world of embodied life, not in the domain of discursive propositions or ideas.

Transformational theological method is, in the words of its chief architects, "[An] endeavour which finds its points of theological reference never anywhere else but in and through the world, which is to say incarnationally, just as the ongoing and living reality of the incarnate Christ himself demands."[4] Concerning theological attentiveness specifically, transformation theology pursues a twofold program consisting in (1) a "rejuvenat[ion] of causal and sensible attentiveness" and (2) a "reinvigoration of practical and motive attentiveness."[5] I analyze each of these aspects of attentiveness in turn below.

Causal and Sensible Attentiveness

Transformation theology emphasizes that there are two broadly construed methods of accounting for objects, events, and phenomena. These can be designated as (1) *causal-sensible* accounting and (2) *conceptual* accounting.[6] The first of these proceeds through describing causes that are experienced in sensible terms, that is, in the everyday world of life, understood and encountered spatio-temporally. The second sort of accounting operates on the level of discursive mental activity such as logical deduction, abstraction, and ratiocination. Transformation theology holds, quite simply, that much

---

2. See "Prologue" in Davies et al., *Transformation Theology*, esp. 2–6.
3. See esp. Janz, "Revelation as Divine Causality," 63–64, 67–69.
4. "Prologue," in Davies et al., *Transformation Theology*, 4.
5. Janz, *Command*, 34 and 80 respectively, emphasis added.
6. See Janz, *Command*, ch. 2, esp. 21–22; see also Janz, "Divine Causality," 64–66.

present-day theology (especially theology concerned to defend traditional doctrines) has too often neglected the first of these and privileged the second.[7] Theology thus suffers from a deficiency of causal-sensible accounting.

The hard sciences, and even the social sciences, have remained attentive, by and large, to *both* causal-sensible and conceptual accounting, but when we look to theology

> over the past two centuries, we find that for an array of reasons this twofold kind of attentiveness has with a few exceptions almost entirely disappeared from view. Or more exactly, we find that the question of causal explanation based on the dynamic interactions between bodies in space and time has in one way or another become entirely subsumed under the mental authority of conceptual explanation.[8]

Paul Janz designates this one-sided mode of accounting as "conceptually cognitive mono-vision"[9] and perceives within it far-reaching effects for theology: namely, that academic reflection and systematization of doctrine thereby become less concerned with the "world" as such and more concerned with only intellectual schemas that are overtly abstract in form and reasoning, thus neglecting to impact or draw upon the actual events and experiences in time and space that are the true causal foundations of the Christian faith.[10] As Janz puts it: "[If] God is truly alive in his revelation at the center of life today . . . [then] theology must be attentive through all human faculties and may not confine itself to the discursively mental."[11]

In the thought of MacKinnon, a related point is promulgated specifically in the context of christological accounting.[12] There, MacKinnon enforces the demarcation (originating in philosophy of logic) between first-order and second-order propositions. In relation to Christology, first-order propositions "are 'about' Christ" whereas second-order ones "are about *propositions*

---

7. The most pronounced discussions to this end emerge in the work of Janz, e.g., "Divine Causality."

8. Janz, *Command*, 21.

9. Janz, *Command*, 21; see also Janz, "What is Transformation Theology?" 12.

10. On the point of "causal" vs. "conceptual" ways of accounting, see Janz, "Revelation as Divine Causality," 70–73.

11. Janz, "What is Transformation Theology?", 34.

12. Kenneth Surin designates MacKinnon's focus on "how" theologians speak and think about Christ (that is, "how" they "do" Christology) as "meta-Christology", and says, rightly, that MacKinnon inclines more to these christological discussions than he does to doctrinal Christology as such; see Surin, "Grammar," 107n2.

'about' Christ."[13] To recapitulate this with language of our own, we would say that first-order propositions about Christ concern the embodied, historical reality, relationships, and activity of Jesus—these are, broadly speaking, christological statements, but we will also refer to them as "Christic" statements in order to convey their proximity to the actual embodied person of Christ, and to distinguish them from second-order *christological* propositions which encompass more broadly doctrinal language that systematizes and thematizes the Christic categories, including doctrinal and conceptual language relating to ontological questions.

MacKinnon recognizes, of course, a certain unavoidable and even necessary role for ontological thinking in Christology; e.g., in simply considering the relation between Jesus and God the Father, we verge on questions of an implicitly ontological nature (the relation of two "persons"), and such questions are helpful tools for "advancing our understanding to enable us to see what it is that is at issue in the simpler, more direct, more immediately moving christological affirmations of the gospel."[14] Alongside this, and with corresponding incisiveness, Janz emphasizes a strong opposition to anything like an overarching "theological ontology," for such an extension of controlling ontological conceptions inevitably draws God onto the same "level" of (conceptually reified) "being" as that of worldly beings.[15] In summing the sentiments of Mackinnon and Janz on these scores, we can emphasize that both first- and second-order propositions must exist in discourse about Christ, but they must retain a critical balance with one another, wherein those of the first-order are primary in christological attentiveness, so that the concrete life of Christ is not dimmed by overriding attention to the christo-*logical*.[16] It is upon actual historical and spatio-temporal reality, the embodied (and continuing) life of Christ, that the church depends

---

13. Surin, "Grammar," 96(–97). See Mackinnon, "'Substance' in Christology," 246–47, 251 and also, "Does Faith Create Its Own Objects?" 221.

14. Mackinnon, "'Substance' in Christology," 246; on the inescapability of ontological categories (whether explicit or implicit), see 244–47. Janz allows for "the importance and value of a properly modest and rigorous ontology" (*Command*, 59), but is especially wary of its employment in christological questions, for reasons we've seen.

15. Janz, *Command*, 58–60.

16. Again, MacKinnon: "To recognize the use of ontological categories as something indispensible in theological work is not for one moment to identify that work with the use of such categories in *rebus divinis*. *The part is not the whole*" ("Substance in Christology," 245, emphasis original). Janz likewise will refer to the necessity of a "twofold attentiveness" in "Divine Causality," 75–76.

and by which Christology should be directed.[17] Theology needs to cultivate an attentiveness to this fundamentally "incarnational ground,"[18] that is, the historically-attested events which form and animate the Christian community. Such a transformation of method pushes the theologian to ask, in approaching and appropriating scriptural content, *what happened in embodied history?*[19] And what does the sort of accounting which results from this question mean, concretely, for the work of God in the midst of embodied existence today? As MacKinnon bluntly puts it: "Christians are [those] who believe that, as a matter of fact, *certain events happened.*"[20] Christology should be the last of all theological disciplines to seek a speculative retreat from contingent and particular history.[21]

It should be noted clearly here that transformation theology is not opposed to the deployment of abductive or even deductive reasoning within certain bounds, so long as such reasoning is thoroughly grounded in real-world happenings and does not verge into self-referential tautology.[22] In terms of epistemology, the transformational orientation on the use of "reason" is effectively Kantian (on a particular reading of Kant's epistemology, presented most forcefully in the work of Janz[23]) insofar as it advocates a "humble" or chastened place for speculative reasoning and encourages its necessary grounding in empirical realities. Ontology *per se* cannot and should not be avoided, but what Kant calls a "proud ontology," conducted via the operations of allegedly "pure reason," which does not recognize the anchoring authority of sensibly encountered life, can only produce "certain rational illusions" which, if ontologically reified, overleap the limits which must attend reason as a conceptual and abstract endeavor. Such a critical

---

17. Janz, "Divine Causality," 89–94.

18. Janz, *Command*, 39.

19. Especially in reference to Christ: Janz, *Command*, 134–35, 137–38; "Coming Righteousness," 89–90.

20. Mackinnon, "Our Contemporary Christ," 83, emphasis added.

21. Janz employs the "retreat" metaphor also in this context (theology retreating from embodied history and toward abstraction): *Command*, 3, 33, 164. Janz likewise frames the movement toward analytical self-definition in terms of a seduction ("the selfsecuring lures of analyticity", 43). MacKinnon similarly bemoans the constant temptation to move theologically away from the true contingency and risky history of Jesus of Nazareth ("Contemporary Christ," 83, 86–87).

22. Janz, "Divine Causality," 71–73.

23. At greatest depth in Janz, *God, The Mind's Desire*, 123–67.

orientation resides at the heart of Kant's first Critique.²⁴ There, Kant levels his attack at what he refers to as "dogmatism," by which he means at least partly the groundless reification of pure ideas which claim jurisdiction over the whole enterprise of human knowing, beyond the limits of experience. Any such dogmatic pursuit of cognition via "pure concepts" illegitimately assumes sovereignty over what Janz describes as the causal "authority" of the given external world, or, more specifically "the causal dynamism of the embodied world."²⁵ Janz sums the key outcome of this Kantian limit to speculative reasoning by declaring that "discursive reason must always, *for its own very integrity,* hold itself to account before the tribunal of the real empirical world in space and time."²⁶

But unbridled speculation via the conduits of abstract concepts is not the only way in which Christian theology can "point away" from the world of real, experienced life. Oliver Davies, for his part in formulating the epistemological and hermeneutical basis for transformation theology, discusses the related theological tendency to rely on *metaphor*, especially indexical metaphors relating to distance or time,²⁷ to describe the human relationship to theological realities:

> Indexical reference to what is not in space and time is not reference at all, and thus, by implication, can have no real meaning. . . . If the object pointed to is not in fact in space and time, and has no referential existence, then what we are left with is the act of pointing itself: the act of pointing *away* [from the world]. . . . But the Christian, like anyone else, lives only in the world of space and time. And so by the internalization of such a metaphorical conceptual paradigm which points *out* of the world, the Christian self is drawn to live under alienation *within* the real world, of where there can be no real 'outside'. Thus we Christians

---

24. E.g., "[The] understanding can never overstep the limits of sensibility within which alone objects are given to us. Its principles are merely rules for the exposition of appearance; and the proud name of an ontology that pretends to provide, in a systematic doctrine, synthetic a priori cognitions (e.g., the principle of causality) of things in themselves must give way to the modest name of a mere analytic of pure understanding" (Kant, *Critique of Pure Reason,* A247/B303).

25. Janz, *Command,* 25–26. See Janz's related and important discussion on the Kantian critique of "subreption" in *Mind's Desire,* 154–56.

26. Janz, *Command,* 26.

27. The specific target on which Davies focuses in order to make his larger point is T. F. Torrance's use of the metaphor of "height" and his indexical use of geometric concepts to discuss the incarnation in *Space, Time, and Incarnation,* in which see esp. 67–75.

who live by this paradigm, may find that we live but poorly in the world, and not at all in any other.[28]

At the root of this fundamental axis of attention, then, transformation theology echoes the dictum that "because in the reality of Jesus Christ the reality of God has entered into the reality of the world fully, therefore theology may not look away from the world but nowhere else than the world of real embodied life to engage with the revealed reality of God."[29] Such a statement on theological method opposes any route by which empirical reality might be evaded, whether that be unbridled abstract cogitation or obstructive metaphorization. In this register, transformation theology stands alongside, and takes further, some of the powerful ideas adumbrated by Bonhoeffer in his ethical writings: "One does not have to choose between Christ and the world. Belonging completely to Christ, one stands at the same time completely in the world."[30]

Motive and Practical Attentiveness

Since the strong focus on causal-sensible attentiveness is a basic feature in the redirection of attentiveness advocated by transformation theology, we will be able to address the closely related topic of motive-practical attentiveness in shorter order. In so doing, we direct attention principally to Janz's distinct emphasis on what he calls "appetitive" or "motive" reasoning, which he discusses in contrast to "conceptual" or "discursive" reasoning. The latter is "a formal exercise of reason" that transpires within "the cognitive domain;"[31] in short, it is used in the "ordering of *percepts and concepts* for thinking."[32] The former, however, refers to that form of reasoning employed in the "ordering of *appetites* (or desires) and *motives* for bodily action,"[33] and it is attention to this form of reasoning that Janz sees to be lacking in many forms of theological discourse today. More precisely, when desire and appetition do feature in contemporary theological discussion they are still often treated essentially discursively as themes under

28. Davies, "Interrupted Body," 43.
29. Janz, "What is Transformation Theology?" 11.
30. Bonhoeffer, *Ethics*, 62.
31. Janz offers as examples the sorts of intellectual cogitations that accompany mathematical operations, literary interpretation, ethical judgments, etc.
32. Janz, *Command*, 78–79.
33. Janz, *Command*, 79.

the remit of conceptual reasoning, and thus without breaking through to a proper attentiveness to the fundamentally different kind of reasoning actually involved at the first-order level in the relation of human desires and motives to decision and action.[34]

Drawing on Aristotle, Aquinas, and Kant, Janz develops and makes central the ways in which our desiring faculty manifests itself in embodied action—or, more specifically, in the "free causal agency of enacted decisions,"[35]—and moreover how such action is that which animates the progression of human life and history, as desiring beings enact their will upon the material, space-time world.[36] According to Janz, everything human beings do, even cognitive reasoning itself, is ultimately "organized on the basis of some motivating *desire*."[37] With the aid of insights from Kant's work on "practical reason," he pinpoints that the ordering of many of our desires, when dealing with issues of moral value and not mere pragmatic execution, is determined by something else, something which immediately emerges in our deepest self as a kind of "law." Janz refers to this judging faculty as "ought-consciousness" or "moral consciousness."[38] This inner law which confronts us with a sense of moral obligation is what motivates our will to enact our desires in the world, thereby affecting the world in particular, morally-colored ways. As Janz sums this relation:

> The whole force of free causality is that as embodied beings, humans can through the *will* bring their own *rational* law of desire to bear on the laws of the nature mechanism [the deterministic world of natural laws] in a causal 'making real' of desired ends in embodied life through enacted rational decision.[39]

Now, this sort of reflection on human desiring and acting, while instructive, does not as yet reflect any clear christological significance. But its

---

34. There are notable exceptions to this neglect, of course. Aside from transformation theology, the work of James K. A. Smith is resonantly focused on the themes of desire, formation of appetites, and enacted life: e.g., *Desiring the Kingdom*. Intersections with overtly "postmodern" forms of philosophy and theology have generated work on desire as well, e.g., Shults and Henriksen, *Saving Desire*.

35. Janz, *Command*, 144.

36. Also referred to as the "faculty of appetition", "desire," "will," etc. See, e.g., Janz, *Command*, 9–10, 81–85, 100–111, 141–43. The most pronounced and important discourse appears in ch. 5 of *Command*.

37. Janz, *Command*, 86, emphasis added.

38. Janz, *Command*, 94.

39. Janz, *Command*, 143.

implications for such become clear when Janz proceeds to argue that our ought-consciousness—indeed our whole activity of rational moral judgment—is in fact reflective of our sinful state before God.

Hereby Janz emphasizes that the plight of unrighteous humanity is not simply a matter of believing the wrong things about God or a deficient intellectual capacity, but that it is also deeply entangled in the biblically derived notion of "*covetous* desire"[40] or, indeed, the "deceitful desires" of our "old self" (see Eph 4:22). For Janz, this *cor curvum in se*—Augustine and Luther's "turned-inward heart"—is what alienates human beings from righteous obedience to the will of God;[41] it is "a radical alienation from God by a corruption of desire."[42] Human sinfulness, on this rendering, manifests itself via the operation of our moral judgments. The story of "the fall" in Genesis 3 conveys humanity's acquisition of the knowledge of good and evil—that is, moral consciousness. Janz thus takes this to illustrate that humanity's fall was a "fall into moral consciousness,"[43] and he agrees with Barth in saying that "when [Adam] sinned . . . he became 'ethical man.'"[44] Once human moral consciousness was inaugurated, we became a "law unto ourselves," rationally judging the world and bringing it under the jurisdiction or our own covetous desire through the imposition of our own autonomy.[45] This character of our practical or motive reasoning is so humanly pervasive and powerful that even the Mosaic law, which comes from God, cannot be received as the divine law that it is but will instead invariably be "misread as essentially a moral code."[46]

There are several points at which such an "appetitive harmartiology" could be expounded at greater depth or debated, and I do not necessarily

---

40. Janz, *Command*, 144.

41. Janz, *Command*, 132. Janz well notes that, biblically speaking, humanity is not separated from God's love, but from his *righteousness*.

42. Janz, *Command*, 107.

43. Janz, *Command*, 113.

44. Barth, *Church Dogmatics*, II/2, 517; quoted in Janz, *Command*, 113.

45. "[In] the fall away from God into the knowledge of good and evil through a corruption of desire we have become a *law unto ourselves*. This law unto ourselves which we have become, in other words, is an autonomous (self-regulating) moral law by which we bear our own measure of righteousness irremediably within us, in the immediacy of our desiring and motivating intellect for the question of how shall we live" (Janz, *Command*, 114).

46. Janz, *Command*, 120. Janz offers further argumentation to this point in chs. 6 and 7 of *Command*.

follow Janz's framing of a foundational hamartiology as such.[47] But we are here only briefly summarizing it in order to underscore transformational attentiveness to *desire, will,* and *action.* This aggressively pursued attentiveness provides a counterbalance and corrective to any system of theology which only (or even primarily) emphasizes humanity's problem as one confined to intellect or thought, "wrong thinking" or "disbelief." Fundamentally, transformation theology says, we sin because we do not "will" as God wills. We want our will to be done, and so we ignore our fellows and try to control our world, defusing and avoiding any complexity or contingency which threatens us. As Davies puts it: "We reason as an agent when we seek to get our way in the world. . . . [We] reduce the complexity of the world . . . through the active pursuit of our own self-interest."[48] If this sort of disordered, grasping, autonomous desire is the plight (or at least a significant part of the plight) of humanity in its alienation from God, then attentiveness to it will have a significant bearing on transformational christological reflection.

Implications of Transformational Attentiveness

A perceptive question at this point would be: what follows? What follows from such a refocusing of theological attention along these causal-sensible and motive-practical lines? Not surprisingly, with its concentration on embodied realities as attested in the scriptures and manifested in the church and world through desired ends and enacted decisions, transformation theology has distinguished itself through an acute focus on both ethics and praxis.[49] Thus, it is not only concerned with the transformation of theological attentiveness along methodological and hermeneutical lines,[50] but it is also deeply concerned with giving a richly theological account of the transformation of the world itself, in line with the redemptive transformations

---

47. Most crucially, Janz locates the origination of "ethical" human thinking, and thus "sinning," within a framework of basal covetousness. I would, however, go further than this and ground said covetousness in a fundamental psychological adaptivity, driven by fear of scarcity, pain and, ultimately, death. Sin, in this case, is rooted in fear and the imperiled nature of the human situation, subjected as it is, to frailty and death. See Beck, *Slavery of Death.*

48. Davies, *Theology of Transformation,* 170.

49. See e.g., chs. 5 and 6 in Davies et al., *Transformation Theology.*

50. "Prologue," in Davies et al., *Transformation Theology,* 2–4; Janz, "Divine Causality," 64.

wrought in Christ.⁵¹ It is this focus on Christian acts *as acts* that animates a transformational ethical focus and highlights its unique contours: "Ethics is a project of transformation, a project of disrupting our concepts and theories and the ways we act."⁵² The ethical edge here summons us to be attentive to the ways in which our contemporary world cries out for transformation—in the face of endemic poverty, oppression, trauma, and grotesque evil. These realities confront us and call for response; human suffering is a "given" of worldly experience, in the face of which any retreat into abstraction can be most pernicious; a non-dogmatic epistemology here has direct *ethical* implications.⁵³

But this ethical attentiveness does not stop merely by attending to the plight of the world; theology, as a distinctly ecclesial practice, should also maintain focus on the church's post-resurrection and post-Pentecost *kairos*. The broken world and the transforming ways of God do not stand wholly apart from one another; Christ and the Spirit work redemptively through ecclesial realities to bring about change. Transformation theology is committed to what it calls the "incarnational reality" of Christian existence, and we will see in our next chapter that this orientation is dependent on a strong reading of Christ's ascended state and heavenly session.⁵⁴ Hereby we are encouraged, via the critical use of reason, to pay attention to God's revelatory acts *within* the world and especially to Christ's continued lordship over the world in his glorified state.

All of this has strong praxiological implications. Incarnationally grounded theology operates with its face turned toward the world,⁵⁵ pursuing participation in Christic realities in the midst of an ecclesially formed intelligence that sustains and informs Christian acts.⁵⁶ The church's mis-

---

51. "Prologue," 2–6. See also Davies, *Theology of Transformation*, Part III.

52. Sedmak, "Disruptive Power of World Hunger,"136.

53. Janz, *Command*, 31–32.

54. Relatedly, see Doug Farrow's discussion of "The Politics of the Eucharist," in his *Ascension Theology*, 89–119.

55. "Transformation Theology at its heart is resolutely and uncompromisingly a *theology in the world*" ("Prologue," 4).

56. As Davies puts it, "If the *imitatio Christi* or following of Christ in the pattern of enacted love in his name, is the foundation of our discipleship in him, and if this is a Christian calling and so the basis of our ecclesial belonging in the ground of the Church, then Transformation Theology . . . will provide a more fundamental mode of ecclesial thinking which can point to the foundations of our faith and to the ways in which we belong to one another in Christ" (*Theology of Transformation*, 143).

sion—under the continuing lordship of the Son and the enduring power of the Spirit—is an ongoing mission, and thus theological accounting must show resolute awareness for what can be called "ecclesio-experiential" input. What are the church's current struggles and contexts, in the thick of particular places and specific times, in the warp and weft of material, embodied existence? Theological reflection cannot stand apart from these inputs as a detached academic discipline—it must be thoroughly grounded by and bound to the world, directing its attentions to the center of actual life—in Janz's words, there must be "a certain dependence on and therefore a certain subservience . . . to the causal dynamism of the reality in which we find ourselves alive."[57] Transformation theology's shared ground with certain forms of liberation theology here becomes apparent, as there is agreement between this dimensionality and Gustavo Gutierrez's famous designation of theology as "critical reflection on praxis" which then informs further praxis.[58] For both liberation and transformation theologies, theology comes *after* praxis and proceeds *alongside* praxis.[59] It is in this steadfastly "world facing" sense that Davies has compellingly suggested that true transformation theology is in fact "first-order" theology—it is a "theology of the act" and involves Christian acting in the world first, and academic reflection on that action second.[60]

If true, then the efforts of professional theologians would be for the distinctly ecclesial purpose of helping to effectuate understanding and awareness in order to empower further ecclesial activity and reflection. Doctrinal intellection alone cannot be the theological enterprise:

> In other words, theology—academic theology—is called to help us to recognize [Christ] there, at the turning points of the historical world in our own 'everyday' situational reality, more quickly and more fully. It is called to create a Christian culture in which this

---

57. Janz, *Command*, 33.

58. Gutierrez, *Theology of Liberation*, 5–8.

59. Janz, *Command*, 9. See Davies's nuanced and largely sympathetic interactions with liberation theology in *Theology of Transformation*, 24–25, 86–88, 142.

60. Davies, *Theology of Transformation*, 139–43. Further: "Theology of transformation is distinctive as a theology to the extent that—as an act-oriented theology—it *knows its own limits*. . . . [Theology] needs to rediscover its own proper nature as being in service to the Christian act. We need to relearn a certain humility, but also a certain wisdom in the recognition of the distinction between second- and first-order theology. [F]irst-order theology belongs to the act itself. First order theology is the Christian intelligence that grounds our Christian acts" (142).

recognition itself becomes embodied as a central part of what it is to be a Christian in today's world.[61]

It is along these wavelengths that even the more radical statements of Bonhoeffer resonate: "[The] reality of God is disclosed only as it places me completely into the reality of the world."[62]

Conclusion—Getting Attentive with Christology

It should now be quite evident how the outlook—the *attentiveness*—that is pinpointed by transformation theology is useful for the agenda of this book, in both a critical and constructive dimension. First, transformation theology's critical edge compellingly targets the sort of deficiency in "christological attentiveness" which I have diagnosed in third-wave kenotic Christology, providing more insight and lines of reasoning on that score. Second, transformation theology's constructive stance—that is, the sort of attentiveness it *advocates* rather than censures—establishes principles and criteria which dynamically frame the ecclesial relevance to which a program of Christology attains, and this it does by critically disallowing any retreat into speculative abstraction when the questions of embodiment, concreteness, or action-in-the-world are pressed.

---

61. Davies, *Theology of Transformation*, 55.
62. Bonhoeffer, *Ethics*, 59.

6

Refocusing Kenosis (II)

Christ in "Transformed" Key

IN WHAT FOLLOWS I will be aiming to examine the major christological statements of Janz and Davies, while also turning to MacKinnon and Bonhoeffer on occasion to elucidate further the fundamental nature of certain christological points. The whole exploration will be in the service of clearly arraying a christological attentiveness that is more focused on Christ himself and less on Christology-as-concepts (though not, certainly, to the complete neglect or refusal of the latter).

The Accomplishment of Jesus Christ

Janz's discussion on "Christ, Reality, and History,"[1] begins with a characteristically transformational question: "What *actually happens in the world* when in the revelation of God in Jesus of Nazareth 'the Word became flesh', or when 'God becomes man'?"[2] In setting out an answer, act-oriented theology looks to the biblical accounts to see what *happened* and what was *achieved* in the particular embodied life of Jesus and to be affected by it in the center of the lived life of the church.[3] This stance provokes an intense focus on

---

1. Janz, *Command*, ch. 8. Cf. also Janz, "Divine Causality," esp. 79–83; Janz, "Coming Righteousness," esp. 89–94.

2. Janz, *Command*, 137, emphasis added.

3. Janz, "Divine Causality," 63–64. Hebblethwaite provides a summary of the "particularity" of the Incarnation which accords well with this point in TT: "The particularity of the Incarnation, the fact that if God was to come to us in person it would have to be at a particular time and place in history, certainly, as I say, [. . .] means that we . . . cannot enjoy precisely the same face-to-face human encounter with God incarnate . . . Our personal commerce with God is through the spiritual and sacramental presence of the one who did tread the hills of Palestine, whose character and acts we read about in the Gospels" ("Jesus, God Incarnate," 24).

the historical texture and concrete, enacted progressions of Jesus's life.[4] It is the historical actions—or, the "enacted decisions"[5]—of the man Jesus of Nazareth which give shape to a transformationally attentive Christology. If it is the entirety of Jesus's life that matters (and not just the first and final chapters of the Gospels—the birth, the death, and the resurrection), then the habitual compartmentalizing of the gospel history which often transpires in theological discourse must be avoided. Janz makes this clear:

> It is not right, in other words, as we can be apt to do in doctrinal theory, to treat "incarnation", "cross" and "resurrection" collectively as the three thematically central Christological loci without equally acknowledging that the real power and efficacy of these events hangs inalienably on what the man Jesus accomplishes in his mortal life.[6]

Importantly, as we will see later in this study, Moltmann makes a very similar sort of point central to his own christological work.[7] Jesus's life should not be considered in discrete and unrelated sections—it is the *full* accomplishment or achievement of his life and his faith which should direct our theological thinking and categories. And this accomplishment will be colored, inevitably, by the distinct historical context and contingent sociality of Jesus as a Jewish man, in his own time and space, as recounted in the biblical materials. Knowledge of Christ in this register is therefore, in MacKinnon's words, "[knowledge that] inevitably draws on one's own experience of human life . . . together with . . . awareness of the cultural and historical particularities of the society in which Jesus lived and whose needs

---

4. Note Mackinnon's words: "[In the gospels, we] notice a deep concern with the texture of every situation in which [Jesus] is involved" ("Tomb Was Empty," 259).

5. Janz, *Command*, 141–46.

6. Janz, *Command*, 147. N. T. Wright makes a similarly concerned point from the perspective of his New Testament and early Christianity scholarship: "It would not be much of a caricature to say that orthodoxy, as represented by much popular preaching and writing, has had *no clear idea of the purpose of Jesus' ministry*. For many conservative theologians it would have been sufficient if Jesus had been born of a virgin (at any time in human history, and perhaps from any race), lived a sinless life, died a sacrificial death, and risen again three days later" (*Jesus and Victory of God*, 14, emphasis added).

7. Moltmann argues for an implicit expansion of the Nicene and Apostles Creeds so that they more holistically capture *the full spectrum of the life* of Jesus, see *Way of Jesus Christ*, 150 (more broadly, see the entirety of ch. 3 in that work).

he immediately addressed."⁸ (Such a transformational outlook accords well with what Moltmann refers to as a "holistic Christology."⁹)

What, then, is the *accomplishment* that Christ lives out? In MacKinnon's rendering, it is his "faith," which can only be articulated as something *achieved*, for faith is not a concept but a form of human *activity*, a thing that is *done*, and therefore it is an occurrence that is actualized in temporal life: "If Christ has faith, and if that faith is uniquely creative, it has to be understood as something *achieved*, an affirmation of God in relation to mankind not in word only but in *deed*."¹⁰ Similarly themed is the thinking of Janz, who identifies Christ's accomplishment as his lived righteousness, that is, his accomplishment of faithfully living in full obedience to the will of God.¹¹

We will recall from our earlier discussion that transformation theology promulgates what we might call an "appetitive understanding of sin," wherein sin is not described in terms of a distortion of the intellect, or in simple willful rebellion against known standards and proper motives, but rather as a fundamental distortion of desire.¹² The effect of this on christological reflection now becomes apparent: on a transformational reading, human reconciliation to the righteousness of God requires a human will that aligns its desires completely with divine prerogatives for human existence. It is here, then, at the intersection of a "covetously desiring" human being and the "lived righteousness" of God (a "better righteousness," to use Bonhoeffer's phrase¹³) that Janz locates the specific, historical accomplishment of Jesus Christ. For Jesus, by entering into the finite human situation, "inhabit[s] the law of covetous desire," and yet neverethelesss he succeeds in living his life "in the perfect unity and obedience of a fully human will with the perfect will of God."¹⁴

---

8. MacKinnon, "Does Faith Create?", 221.

9. See *Way of Jesus Christ*, 3, 119.

10. MacKinnon, "Does Faith Create?", 214, emphasis added.

11. Janz also quotes MacKinnon's reference to Jesus's "historically achieved innocence" in this same vein (*Command*, 148). See further MacKinnon, "Irreversibility of Time," 97.

12. Janz, *Command*, 109–16. It is worth noting that the extreme moralism of an Augustinian appetitive hamartiology is missing from transformation theology, an important distinction biblically and pastorally.

13. E.g., Bonhoeffer, *Discipleship*, 85–89, 114–17.

14. Janz, *Command*, 144, 148.

When it comes to discussing the person of Christ, the focus need not fall on metaphysical minutiae or a balancing of ontological properties in the midst of two abstractly-conceived "natures." Christ, in his historical activity, demonstrates who he is by enacting God's righteousness in the midst of human embodiment, human activity in space-and-time, which fundamentally entails the operation of human desire:

> The oneness of Jesus with God, that is, the full divinity of the man Jesus, is not the unity of two speculatively generated suprasensible essences coming together abstractly in an ideal realm of 'substance', as reassuring as such false dogmatic securities may be for the demands of a purely cognitive understanding of this oneness. . . . [It is in] the perfect unity of real embodied human will with the will of the Father, and not on the level of metaphysical 'essences' or philosophically abstracted and thus purely speculative 'substances', that Jesus is 'the image of the invisible God' (Col. 1.15) and 'the exact imprint of his being' (Heb. 1.3).[15]

Janz avers that Christ did not come to teach about the "essence" of God or abstract metaphysical axioms pertaining to a divine "nature," but rather he consistently directed attention to the *will* of God.[16] To borrow a phrase from Dale Allison, Jesus is "the embodiment of God's will."[17] This reflects the holistic testimony of the Gospel narratives; they do not speak in terms of two mysteriously united pieces of ontology but of a first-century man, chosen by God to carry out God's righteousness on earth and to bring that righteousness "into death, thus destroying death."[18]

This certainly attends to the Gospel sources with both sensible-causal and practical-motive attentiveness, focusing on embodied realities and

---

15. Janz, *Command*, 148, 149.

16. See Janz, *Command*, 149–50; Janz, "Coming Righteousness," 90–91. Some of the most pertinent passages referred to by Janz are: Jesus comes to reveal and do the Father's *will* (John 4:34, 5:36, 6:38); Jesus comes to enact the Father's *commandment(s)* (John 12:49–50, 14:31, 15:10); those "who resolve to do the *will* of God will know whether my [Jesus's] teaching is from God" (John 7:17); not all who call Jesus "Lord" will enter the kingdom, but only those that "do the *will* of my Father" (Matt 7:21); all who "do the *will*" of the Father are Jesus's brothers and sisters (Matt 12:50); and, of course, the Lord's prayer, which prays that the Father's "*will* be done on earth as it is in heaven" (Matt 6:10).

17. Allison, "Embodiment of God's Will," 117–32.

18. Janz, *Command*, 147. Cf. the first sermon following the ascension of Christ, especially the language applied by Peter to Christ: "Men of Israel, listen to these words: Jesus the Nazarene, a man attested to you by God with miracles and wonders and signs which God performed through Him in your midst" (Acts 2:22).

enacted desire. But, it may be asked, does this articulation not impoverish the Christ of the church to some extent? If Jesus is "the only man who has ever lived in full obedience to God," then this makes him highly unique, but seems to possibly resemble a "degree Christology," or possibly a resuscitation of Schleiermacher's *Urbildlichkeit* with its "absolutely potent God-consciousness."[19] To pose the issue a different way, we might return to the classic division between Christ's person and work: If a major part of the *work* of Christ is his historically realized righteousness, conforming his will as a man to the will of the Father, what is it about his *person* that is unique enough to establish and accomplish such an achievement?[20]

It can be rightly surmised that transformation theology will answer this important question in a different manner than forms of Christology which focus on an analysis of the classical philosophical concepts (*ousia, physis*, etc.). Any such recourse to an in-depth speculation about two natures and their variegated, analytically conceived properties would be beyond the hermeneutical and rational limits that transformational discourse sets for itself, as we have seen.[21] What then does it do with Chalcedon? Both Janz and Davies are nuanced in their handling of that tradition. They have both evinced an affirmation of the creedal language, in tandem with an explicit avoidance of theorizing intended to "resolve" the conundrum of the two natures, nor even to give any positive content to those natures as such. Janz, in fact, proposes that all of the most distinctive "revelational claims" of Christian theology[22] are united precisely in the fact that "they derive the *basis* of their authority explicitly from their *inability* or indeed refusal to be 'resolved' into broader systems of explanation."[23] Significantly for this present work, Janz targets the resolution-seeking, abstract mode of many "kenotic approaches" to Christology. He sees such christological programs often functioning as

---

19. E.g., Schleiermacher, *Christian Faith*, 364, 367. On which, see Kelsey, *Thinking About Christ with Schleiermacher*, 51–56.

20. Catherine Kelsey rightly draws attention to the need for such a unity in the person and work of Christ (on the basis of Schleiermacher's own incisive analysis of this relationship), *Thinking About Christ with Schleiermacher*, 69–74.

21. On the "limits" of transformation theology, see Davies, *Theology of Transformation*, 142; see also "Prologue," 5.

22. He lists these claims as "incarnation, resurrection, Ascension, creation *ex nihilo*, eschaton" (Janz, "Divine Causality," 79).

23. Janz, "Divine Causality," 79. See relatedly, Janz, *God, the Mind's Desire*, 173–85.

mechanisms which purport to be able to draw the authority or finality of the incarnation and the cross more fundamentally into a doctrinally analytical system of resolution, and to 'validate' it within such an ideality. [Such] approaches are . . . an illegitimate tautological shortcut . . . The essential point here is that kenosis, in its causally embodied *reality*, in no way *solves* the theological problem of God's relation to the world on the cross, it rather *defines* the problem in its full and sheer intractability.[24]

Janz elsewhere praises theologies where "kenosis . . . is precisely not viewed as an opportunity for semantic resolution within structures of meaning, even doctrinal meaning."[25] He notes examples of this less-speculative kenotic approach in Rowan Williams, Schleiermacher, Bonhoeffer, Rahner, and MacKinnon, and he critically juxtaposes these with the use of kenosis in Jüngel and Moltmann.[26] While Janz's point here may hold good for Moltmann's use of kenosis as a broad principle of theological conceptuality, this present book will show that Moltmann's use of kenosis *in his Christology specifically* is very much focused on causal, embodied, historical, and relational categories, and as such does not fall into the "resolving" procedure of essentially christological apologetics. But this is to anticipate the book's later work.

In short, it is evident that Janz's stated critique above comports with and furthers our concerns about third-wave kenotic Christology: *the focus on a resolution to the "problem" of the two natures results in a misplaced attentiveness and effectively trammels potential contributions to other, vital christological commitments.*[27] To avoid such a predicament in its own christological attentiveness, it has been the standard move of transformation theology to focus on the historical person (i.e., the *hypostasis*) of Jesus, and also on the continuing endurance/presence of that Christic existence in concrete terms.[28]

But in attending to the *material*, rather than the motive or appetitive, dimension of Christology, cannot something about the unique *person* of Christ be said? Transformation theology has answered this in the affirmative. If in Janz we see the development of an appetitive (that is, action

24. Janz, "Divine Causality," 84.
25. Janz, *Command*, 45.
26. Janz, "Coming Righteousness," 105.
27. Janz, "Coming Righteousness," 105–7, esp. 106.
28. See e.g., Janz, *Command*, 146–47; Janz, "Divine Causality," 79–80; Davies, "Interrupted Body," 45–46; Davies, *Theology of Transformation*, 59.

motivated by desire) understanding of the work (accomplishment) of Christ, it is in Oliver Davies that we discover a complementary material understanding of the person of Christ, or "a new Christological reading of the body of Jesus."[29]

The Embodiment of Jesus Christ

Davies offers a striking thesis: "the body of Jesus is itself the site of a cosmic drama."[30] It is important to take full measure of this assertion; it is not any repetition of *Christus Victor* atonement motifs—it is not saying that Jesus wins a victory on the cross in the midst of a cosmic drama (though this is not ruled out). Rather it is claiming that his very *hypostasis*, his very embodied existence, is *itself* the site of a cosmic drama. Davies assumes Chalcedon as normative for establishing the unity of what the church has called the "divinity" and the "humanity" of Jesus, but he proceeds to describe this unity on the basis of a historical coinherence that changes through a process of intensifying transformation. In short:

> While the historical body of Jesus manifests all the properties which we associate with our own bodies, it is also the case that it is an extraordinary body.[...] [In Jesus, we see a] progression from an embodiment which is primarily human (though within the context of the hypostatic union of the two natures) to an embodiment which is primarily divine (though still within that same union) [and] we can point to the Easter period as the focal point in that transition.[31]

What such a schema allows Davies to argue, firstly, is that the embodiment of Christ is perpetual once begun.[32] Once materiality becomes an aspect of the life of God through the incarnation of Jesus Christ—once God has drawn near as "God with us"—this means that though the embodiment of Jesus *changes* (in striking ways[33]) it never *ceases*. Following the resurrection and the ascension, Jesus's body has "a new relation to space and time" and

---

29. "Prologue," 6.
30. Davies, "Interrupted Body," 46.
31. See further Davies, *Theology of Transformation*, 110–18.
32. Davies, "Interrupted Body," 43–47.
33. We can highlight the retaining of wounds/scars, as well as the ability to pass through walls and cover great distances nearly instantaneously, as just some of the distinctions of Christ's "resurrection body" (see e.g., John 20:19, 26–29).

remains fundamentally related to it. As the glory of Christ becomes more revealed in the course of his earthly life,[34] he is then taken from view—the body ascends and vanishes amidst the clouds, withdrawing its visible presence. It is at this point, says Davies, that Christology has often erred, seeing Christ and his redemptive work today as "figurative and detached from the senses: from our here and now." But he goes on to claim that "it is the exact opposite which is the case."[35]

But what can this mean for the church? How is Christ "here and now" with us, post-ascension? It is at this point that transformation theology calls upon a robust pneumatology; it is claimed that the Spirit "makes real to us the body of Christ." More fully: "[It is] through the advent of the Spirit that the presence of Christ in the fullness of his humanity becomes universally possible to those to whom he is known in the Spirit through faith."[36] In many ways, Davies builds on John Calvin's proposed relationship between the ascended Christ and the present Spirit; Christ's heavenly embodiment is still local (rather than ubiquitous, as in Luther's thought) and made presently and materially accessible to us by the Spirit (rather than available to us by memory, as in Zwingli).[37] Davies claims that though Christ is no longer visible, he is still "available to the senses" albeit "in an entirely new way."[38]

Davies emphasizes that the Johannine tradition clearly relates the advent of the Spirit with the absence of Jesus,[39] and Paul's writings further develop "a profoundly intimate link between the Holy Spirit and the body of Christ."[40] We must remember that, foundationally, transformational thinking is concerned to produce theology that is "turned toward the world."[41] As discussed earlier, theology as a discipline has an "object" of

---

34. Something that is previewed by the Transfiguration: Luke 9:31–32; Mark 9:2–3; Matt 17:2.

35. Davies, "Interrupted Body," 50.

36. Davies, "Interrupted Body," 50.

37. E.g., Calvin, *Institutes*, 4.17.18,29. See Doug Farrow's perceptive discussion of the differences in the dominant Reformation theologies of the ascension: *Ascension and Ecclesia*, 172–80. For Davies's commentary on Calvin: Davies, "Lost Heaven," 19–21; Davies, *Theology of Transformation*, 9–10, 140, 251.

38. Davies, "Interrupted Body," 50.

39. Davies, "Interrupted Body," 49, 50–51.

40. Davies, "Interrupted Body," 51.

41. Davies will use the substantival phrase "Theology in the World" to simultaneously designate and describe the critical theological directionality of this line of thinking. See

its study—it is after all the object within study of a given discipline that determines that discipline and forges its unique concerns. On this basis, Davies poses the following key question:

> But what determines us [in Christian theology]? What is our present material object? We have ... presented the case that this must be the living or exalted Christ who is our present material as well as formal object. It is not only the idea of Christ who is our object but also his reality. This is not only a past reality (as recorded in Scripture for instance), but also a present one. And so we can speak of Jesus Christ as the present material and formal object of our thinking.[42]

Thus, in this sense, all of theology is determined by Christ(ology), which is both its object (focus) and proper "ground" (basis). This is the definitive statement on christological attentiveness. Importantly, this means that transformation theology is not only concerned to speak about christological "ideas" but also about "Christic" realities.[43] The exalted Christ, including his exalted body, now has a unique but real Christic relationship to the world, and this relationship is said to be *mediated by the Spirit*. Davies takes great pains to discuss what he sees as an unfortunate trend in theology whereby the Spirit is seen to "substitute" for the now-ascended Christ.[44] Rather than substitution, Davies sees in the New Testament a portrayal of pneumato-christological mediation.[45] Such a notion is certainly not unique to Davies; it underlies many sacramental theologies (with the notion of *epiclesis*, etc.) and of course, as noted, the thought of Calvin.

However, the idea of pneumatological mediation does seem to resist a clear *prima facie* understanding, and so begs the question: what does it mean, precisely, to say that the Spirit "mediates" the presence of the exalted Christ? A full exploration of this question is beyond the scope of the present chapter, but in the thought of Davies, at least, the point seems to be that Christ's literal presence is brought into our sensibility through

---

Davies, *Theology of Transformation*, ch. 2, esp. 52–7; also Davies, "Interrupted Body," 56.

42. Davies, *Theology of Transformation*, 54.

43. I'm employing the christological/Christic distinction because it very helpfully conveys one of the major points of transformational reflection on Christ's current reality. However, the major transformation theology proponents have not widely employed the term "Christic" in their writing to date.

44. Davies, "Interrupted Body," 44.

45. See Davies, *Theology of Transformation*, 26, 88–93; Davies, "Interrupted Body," 50–54.

the work of the Spirit (in Calvin's words, the Spirit "truly unites things separated in space"[46]). That is, we can encounter Christ in a genuinely perceptual way that is beyond the standard epistemological distinction between "subjective" and "objective." Said yet another way, the pneumatically enabled perception of Christ is not in the form of a concept developed within human cognition (subjective) nor as an object in continuity with the created order (objective). It is something truly new—Christ is the new creation in embodied and transformed person—and as such he can only be encountered in the experience of the "powers of the age to come" (Heb 6:4), that is, the power of the Spirit.

As an attempt to present a tangible (and famous) example of this sort of real Christic encounter, Davies returns many times to the Damascus Road experience of Paul and its varied recountings in scripture.[47] He makes much of the key role of the Spirit in Paul's encounter with Christ: Paul's ordinary sensate organs (eyes, in this case) are overwhelmed to blindness by the Christic presence (Acts 9:8–9), and it is only by the impartation of the Spirit by Ananias that he regains his capability of visual perception (Acts 9:17–19). Though not highlighted by Davies, a redolent parallel is present in Acts 8, where Stephen can "see" Jesus "in heaven" but only *after* the text informs us that he is "full of the Holy Spirit" (Acts 7:55–57).

It should not be missed that what transformation theology wants to posit here is the current universality of Christ (he can be present by the Spirit "at any place and at any time"), and that this universal and embodied relationship to the spatio-temporal world is a direct result of his exaltation.[48] What this means is that it is in the midst of Spirit-mediated, Christic transformations of *this world* that theology must operate and upon which it must focus. Praxis must command our attention.

---

46. Calvin, *Institutes*, 4.17.10. This spatial unboundedness is a radicalization of the spatial ambiguity which characterizes the resurrection accounts of Christ's body, wherein Christ passess through walls, covers vast distances instantaneously, etc.

47. Davies, "Interrupted Body," 44–45, 52–54; Davies, *Theology of Transformation*, 122–31.

48. Davies, *Theology of Transformation*, e.g., 130.

The Worldly Place of Jesus Christ

The praxiological emphasis of transformational Christology can be seen perhaps most clearly in Davies's "ontology of Christological encounter."[49] Christ's being now inhabits a sphere that we cannot circumnavigate—it resists our current cognitive apparatus. Directly related to the points in our foregoing section, transformation theology emphasizes that when Christ is presently "encountered" in the life of the church, it would be a mistake to see this merely as a subjective, inward experience (as in some pietistic traditions) or an objective, outward event (as in some charismatic traditions). Calling attention again to the post-ascension "appearance" of Jesus to Saul on the Damascus Road, Davies argues that this appearance contains numerous ambiguities which are suggestive of a sort of dual-perceptibility that resembles both objective event and subjective experience, yet simultaneously repels each categorization:[50]

> If, therefore, in his 'Damascus road' embodiment, Christ was neither 'objectively present' in the ordinary sense of the term, but neither was he 'subjectively present' in the ordinary sense of the term, then it appears on the basis of the account in Acts that his exalted form defies the normal categories of subjectivity and objectivity altogether.[...] The suggestion here then is that the 'non-objectifiability' of the exalted body results not from its failure to be real, or from its being only partially real, but rather from our own incapacity as creatures to grasp the full depth of the reality that is disclosed in it.[51]

This outlook provokes a major, orienting, and critical question: "Where is Jesus Christ in the world today?"[52] The answers of transformation theology to this question are resonant: Christ is in "[the] poor and vulnerable, the sacraments, the Church, and in the Bible."[53] Davies unpacks these aspects of Christic presence in the following important piece of theological reasoning, worth quoting at length:

---

49. Davies, *Theology of Transformation*, 130; see further 129–33.
50. Davies, *Theology of Transformation*, 127–31; "Interrupted Body," 44–45, 52–53.
51. Davies, *Theology of Transformation*, 129.
52. See Davies, *Theology of Transformation*, ch. 1, esp. 4–5; see also 61–64.
53. Davies, *Theology of Transformation*, 58; see also Davies, "Interrupted Body," 56–57.

> As exalted, he cannot be directly present, since—according to Scripture and tradition—the created order has not yet been transformed in accordance with the transformation effected in the body of Jesus in such a way that it can sustain such an immediate presence. The presence of Christ has to be mediated, therefore, by created materiality; it has to be hidden. This mediation takes place through divine rather than created agency, however, and rests within the regenerative purposes and power of God. It is something that we specifically associate with the agency of the Spirit in the power of God.[54]

This is why the ecclesiological and experiential dimensions of transformational thinking become so important: Christ is the formal and material object of theological concern, and this means, on Davies' argument above, that Christology must look to this-worldly locales, environments, situations, and interpersonal dimensions in an effort to perceive the hidden presence and activity of Christ. Scripturally speaking, Christ uses direct language to radically identify himself with the poor, needy, and suffering (see Matt 25:34–40) as well as with the church (see Acts 9:4–5). He exists in solidarity with the poor,[55] and he commissions, suffers with, and works through the church.[56] These are among the "modes" of his presence today. It is a presence which is only effectuated via his exalted (transformed, mediated, world-encountering) self and the power of the Spirit to "make this real" for us "in the actuality of our sensible living."[57]

The arena of praxis is the arena of enacted decisions, motivated by our desiring, appetitive reasoning. To quote Janz again: "passional desires most essentially *are . . . motivations for action*."[58] This means that the praxiological force of transformational Christology is perceived most acutely when the link between Christ's presence today and the mode of Christian acting in the world is made explicit, as in Davies:

> Life in the church is always temporal, of course, structured between past and future. But it is also fundamentally *present*, where presence is the presence to sensibility of the risen body of Christ,

---

54. Davies, *Theology of Transformation*, 125.

55. On this, see also the important essay by Coakley, "Identity of the Risen Jesus," 301–22.

56. For the poor, see Davies, *Theology of Transformation*, 5, 63, 85–86; for the commissioning of the church, e.g., Davies, "Interrupted Body," 54–55.

57. Davies, "Interrupted Body," 57.

58. Janz, *Command*, 89, further 88–91.

made fully particular and universal through its ascended state, in a way that changes our experience of the world. To be a Christian then is to live within or from out of this entirely unique relation, which is expressed as a 'following', or discipleship of church practice and concern . . . as we enter into the givenness of the sensible real: of the 'everyday'.[59]

Pivotally, then, transformational discussions of Christic presence are irreducibly discussions also about Christian action even in the most mundane contours of worldly situatedness. Davies' thoughts here display deep parallels with Bonhoeffer's radical equation of the church with the worldly presence of Christ's exalted self: "Between his ascension and his coming *the Church is his form and indeed his only form.*"[60]

Critical Considerations for Transformational Christological Attentiveness

Conversations about doctrinal Christology tend to follow well-worn pathways. In many respects, transformation theology departs from those pathways and raises vital issues in a refreshing way. However, the strategy and intended contributions of our study beg us to ply transformational thinking with two concerns, and these concerns hinge around the tightly related topics of incarnation (as a metaphysical idea) and Chalcedon (as a creedal parameter for christological orthodoxy). Does transformation theology's stand against abstraction inhibit it from affirming the incarnation as a doctrine or Chalcedon as a framework? The reason for pursuing these concerns is simple: if our study hopes to rehabilitate kenotic Christology via alleged correctives offered in Moltmann's understanding of Christ, and if those correctives are going to be framed in critical terms proffered by transformation theology, then we need to be sure that transformation theology is not transmitting its criticisms and ideas from a place which lacks commitment to orthodox christological frameworks.[61] For properly kenotic Christology is fundamentally concerned to show a kenotic reading of Christ to be both orthodox in a broad sense as well as ecclesially

---

59. Davies, "Interrupted Body," 56.

60. Bonhoeffer, *Christ the Center*, 58, emphasis added. As we have noted, transformation theology also finds the "form" of Christ in the poor.

61. Meaning, broadly and with room for nuance of interpretation, the Chalcedonian Definition.

relevant.⁶² So transformation theology must be interrogated along the following lines if it is to be appropriated successfully in the project of rehabilitating a creedal, kenotic, ecclesially relevant Christology.

First, it is admittedly unclear precisely to what extent transformation theology allows for consideration of the incarnation itself. To be sure, the language of incarnation is present, but owing to the concentrated focus on Christ revealing not God's "being" but rather his divine righteousness, the incarnational affirmations take on somewhat ambiguous dimensions, at least in some of Janz's work. This emerges, for instance, in the clear intensity with which Janz affirms the relationship between Jesus and the Father on the grounds of the revelatory obedience of Christ, e.g., "[The] 'being' or reality of God revealed in Jesus Christ is nothing less than the re-advent of the original righteousness of God from which we have become alienated.[. . .] a righteousness which is actually *accomplished* and enacted causally by God himself in embodied history in the real world."⁶³ We will remember that this affirmation is dependent on Janz disbarring any cogitation of the Jesus-Father relation along the lines of supra-sensible "essences" or "speculatively ontological or metaphysical projections."⁶⁴ Indeed, so thoroughly is this line followed by Janz that the "unity" of Jesus and the Father is said to only be addressed insofar as we speak about "what Jesus Christ really accomplishes or achieves" in his lifetime, specifically his "righteousness and innocence."⁶⁵

Now if such declarations are faced squarely and in isolation, it will seem apparent that what is expresssed verges on some variety of a "degree Christology" or "exemplar" model for understanding Christ—he is the righteous man of God, and God's "God-ness" is known in him not because of any unity of metaphysical being (i.e., "consubstantiality") but because he obeys God's will—thus, in the spirit of Schleiermacher's *Gottesbewusstsein* Christology or John Hick's inspiration Christology,⁶⁶ the traditions concerning Christ's virginal conception, his eternality, and his pre-existence would seem to be diminished in favor of a more volitional and praxiological

---

62. See, e.g., Davis, "Is Kenosis Orthodox?" in *Exploring Kenotic*.

63. Janz, *Command*, 133–34.

64. Janz, *Command*, 146–47.

65. Janz, *Command*, 147.

66. E.g., in Schleiermacher, *Christian Faith*, §88–93; e.g., in Hick, "Inspiration Christology for a Religiously Plural World," 18–22.

model.⁶⁷ Importantly, though, it is directly after these implications arise that Janz states "[none] of this is by any means to suggest that Jesus 'becomes' the God-man or that he 'achieves' divinity through what he accomplishes in his life. It is not, in other words, to jeopardize Christ's divinity from his birth[.]"⁶⁸ Valuable as they are, such assurances are only necessary because of the possible implications of what has gone before.

Second, and closely related, is the question of Chalcedon specifically. Certainly Janz and Davies both semantically assent to the divinity of Jesus along Chalcedonian lines, even sometimes using the Johannine language of "eternal Logos" or "incarnate Word."⁶⁹ But it is never quite clear if they are affirming the formalities of such language while filling it with fresh meaning, leaving the (in)famous ontological insinuations of Chalcedon behind, or if they are affirming it in the spirit of Chalcedon itself, but electing to focus on other, long-neglected and underemphasized, aspects of the incarnate life of Christ.⁷⁰ These ambiguities on the part of transformational theologians, however, are perhaps best construed as arising from christological tradition's own obscurities,⁷¹ coupled with the unique methodological reorientation that transformation theology promulgates. As we have seen, much of the transformational concern with abstraction in Christology is that it can often serve to domesticate the true transcendence that confronts the world in Christ as God-with-us.⁷²

Heuristic Questions for Christological Attentiveness

All of the above points have been unavoidably summative, and they have not been able to draw out all the careful nuance and critical circumspection that transformation theology has thus far given to many of its statements.

---

67. Compare Janz's statement that "the oneness of Jesus and God is . . . the utter openness of this one real human being . . . to the divine will" (148) with the classic articulation in Schleiermacher of Christ's "unhindered potency of God-consciousness" (Schleiermacher, *Christian Faith*, 365).

68. Janz, *Command*, 147.

69. E.g., Janz, "Coming Righteousness," 89, 96; Davies, "Interrupted Body," 46.

70. Janz's discussion of Chalcedon in *Command* (147) affirms the "challenge" of Chalcedon, and articulates that challenge as only necessitating that Christian theology grapple with the "person" of Jesus, not the posited two natures.

71. Coakley, "What Does Chalcedon Solve and What Does It Not?" 143–63. Also Brown, *Divine Humanity*, ch. 1; Grillmeier, *Christ in Christian Tradition*, 2:3–14.

72. Janz makes these points with force in *Mind's Desire*, 203, 216–17.

However, we have covered enough territory to be able to formulate a series of three heuristic questions which distill its major emphases for Christology. These questions arise organically from our exposition of a transformational outlook on Christology thus far.

The Question of Christic Accomplishment

"What is accomplished in the world by the life of Jesus?" This question pushes Christology to avoid giving grounding primacy to speculative abstraction regarding the creedally posited "two natures" or their properties. These two natures are affirmed, but they are not discussed apart from their embodiment in history, and that embodiment comes in the one, historical, concrete, actual, and *continuing* person of Christ. As Janz says, discussion about these natures and what properties they may or may not contain, or how they may or may not be fused, or how they may or may not constitute a human mind (or soul or essence or substance, etc.) can tend toward "speculative imaginings"—and as such they can serve to point away from the actuality of Christ as a real, living, self.

In line with its roughly Kantian orientation on epistemology, transformation Christology will "knows its own limits" and thus deliberately keep its discussions from undue speculation.[73] In short, when Christology is plied with this question—"What is accomplished in the world by the life of Jesus?"—it is being tasked with maintaining the integrity of its reasoning by not overleaping the bounds of the empirical, allowing reality itself to exercise authority and even limit its abstractions.[74] Said differently, "what is accomplished in the world" is always an empirical, rather than abstract, question; thus it consistently refocuses Christology on the lived life of Christ and disallows a retreat into metaphysical supposition.

While not necessarily denying the secondary value or even the theological indispensability, within clear epistemological limits, of ontological discussion of the two natures, *the grounding theological orientation to the*

---

73. Davies, *Theology of Transformation*, 142.

74. Janz, *Mind's Desire*, e.g., 145–52, 168–69. Though Janz leans heavily on Kant to sustain the notion of empirical integrity in the use of reason, he does admit that Kant's usefulness to theology is limited insofar as "transcendence in the Kantian scheme of things is precisely *not real*, as theology demands, but purely ideal or purely mental[.]" Mackinnon's use of the tragic as an entry into the transcendent as a finality of non-resolution is appropriated by Janz to ameliorate this deficiency in the Kantian outlook (170–85; 201).

divinity and humanity of Jesus, as well as his relations with the Spirit and the Father, should be articulated along lines that direct attention to the actual, historical life and ministry of Jesus, with a view to these as intrinsically and fundamentally related to the significance of his death and resurrection. This promotes a focus not fundamentally on conceptual considerations of Christ's ontology, but on his lived righteousness—the *historical achievement of his life* and all its varied implications.[75] What does Jesus "live out"? How are the worldly realities that he encounters changed or transformed by him? In short, what is Christ's accomplishment (in the past, in the Gospel histories). Morever, what is Christ accomplishing *now* as a person? This leads immediately to the next heuristic question.

The Question of Christic Presence

"Where is Jesus Christ? This question pushes christological reflection to avoid seeing Christ and the world (that is, present empirical reality) as disjunctive or detached from one another. Christology does not "end" with a substitution of the Holy Spirit after the ascension. The lordship of Christ, as emphasized in all the classic "high Christology" passages of the New Testament, is intimately and foundationally bound up with the world itself and that very world becoming new. Christ continues, and this question is intended to make Christology attentive to our present, space-time reality. The linchpin for this sort of attentiveness is a *refocused understanding of the ascension* and its significance. When Jesus is treated purely in terms of his "past" existence in first-century Palestine,[76] without attention to his living reality today, Christian reflection naturally migrates away from Jesus's lived social and physical contexts in the past and also neglects the materiality of Christ's existence presently and its significance for materiality itself.

Moreover, the living and continuing relationships of Christ must be emphasized, and seen to exist in continuity with his earthly life. The

---

75. Of course, for lived sinlessness to be something that can be meaningfully construed as an "accomplishment," we must entertain, on the apparent witness of the Gospel narratives themselves, that *it was in fact a possibility for Christ to sin*. This has been a consistent emphasis of many forms of kenotic Christology as well, and thus represents one among many areas in which the christological concerns of kenotic thinking and transformation theology align.

76. Admittedly, for some Christology that focus is not solely on the "past" Christ, but also on the "future" or returning Christ. But even this dual emphasis leaves out what we are here emphasizing: *the present Christ.*

ascension is not an addendum to the incarnation and resurrection, but is rather their next and continuing chapter. This means that Christ's earthly accomplishments manifested by his enacted decisions (obedience, healing, solidarity, etc.) will be seen to exist in continuity with Christ's continuing accomplishment in the world, via his Spirit and through his church. A strong reading of the exaltation leads concurrently to *thinking of the church in a Christic way*; the church is the mode of Christic presence and action in the world, as Bonhoeffer rightly emphasized.[77] Thus, Christology automatically entails "christopraxis."[78] And praxis itself animates our final transformational question for Christology.

The Question of Christic Praxis

"What has Jesus Christ made possible in the world?" This question motivates Christology not to remain always in the form of second-order statements about how we conceive and understand Christ and his work, with no specifically derived praxiological implications. If Christ is a continuing reality, and if his resurrected and exalted state contains profound implications for the future of this world and those who live in it, then his righteousness automatically entails a mode of life and a form of praxis, a way of being "Christic" in the world, as a Christian. As Davies states it: "Jesus' entry into heaven makes concrete new possibilities for our embodied existence."[79] Thus, Christology should treat Christ as a continuing reality with a continuous and real affect on the world, in and through the material means of history via the confluence of the divine will and humanly enacted decisions. Whatever is said about Christ, his kenosis, his accomplishments, his relationships to the Father, the Spirit, and to others, will be shown to have direct praxiological implications for the mode of Christ's activity today, that is, his church.[80]

---

77. E.g., "The Church is the body of Christ. Here body is not only a symbol. The Church *is* the body of Christ, it does not *signify* the body of Christ. When applied to the Church, the concept of body . . . is a comprehensive and central concept of the mode of existence of the one who is present in his exaltation and humiliation" (Bonhoeffer, *Christ the Center*, 59).

78. Moltmann, *Way of Jesus Christ,* esp. 41–43.

79. Davies, "Evolution, Language and the Biblical Text," 50.

80. "The Christian affirmation that God has taken flesh and that he still lives among us is one which also has implications for a Christian understanding of personhood and existence" (Davies, *Theology of Compassion*, 9).

Conclusion—Attentiveness Reframed

This chapter has focused on transformation theology. After delineating some of the principal and distinctive elements of its theological venture, our discussion has focused on its specific implications for the framing of Christology, especially in terms of "christological attentiveness." We find much in transformation theology's emphases that augment our critiques of third-wave kenotic Christology and that further sharpen the specific mode of christological attentiveness that would be needed in order to not fall victim to the same deficiencies. In order to array this clearly, we distilled our discussion of a transformational christological outlook into three "heuristic questions" for Christology.

These three questions, which attend resolutely and respectively to the historical, presential, and praxiological dimensions of Christic realities, are intended to serve as a constructive tool in our investigation of Moltmann's kenotic understanding of Christ. As I have argued extensively in earlier work, Moltmann develops and promotes a uniquely rendered form of kenotic Christology.[81] But does it succeed, ultimately, in avoiding the ever-luring pitfalls of excess and abstract speculation? Does Moltmann's Christology "make Christ real," or does it turn Christology into a groundless flight of conceptual imagination? Because transformational christological attentiveness so readily unearths these deficiencies, our three heuristic questions are strategically suited for framing Moltmann's specific christological contribution and distinguishing it from other forms of kenotic Christology. The goal, then, of these transformational critical questions is to help sharpen the exploration and application of Moltmann's specific form of christological attentiveness and what it means for his own unique kenotic Christology.

---

81. See Youngs, *Way of the Kenotic Christ*.

Renovating Kenosis

The Kenotic Christology of Jürgen Moltmann

IT IS NOT UP for dispute: Jürgen Moltmann is one of the most significant theological voices of the past century. History may well judge him to be the *most* influential Protestant voice of the era, possibly even exceeding Karl Barth, at least in terms of global, ecumenical, and interdisciplinary impact. At all stages of his spiritual life and academic career, Moltmann has been compelled to "reimagine" both theological doctrine and the way of the church in the world, to challenge and revise their understandings.[1] And this not out of any particular concern for trendiness or casual subversion, but on the basis of his eschatological commitments.[2] As Ryan Neal has rightly emphasized, for Moltmann theology *is* hope,[3] that is, it is an exercise of the church, and like all Christian activity, it occurs (or ought to occur) in pursuit of a horizon that has not yet arrived, a future that is still-to-come, the "coming" God, not a God of the mere finished and static past, whom we can master, control, or circumscribe, but a messianic God who unseats our knowing with the radically new. Hence, Christian theology always stands in need of revision.[4] The past does not reign, but the future. When theology becomes quiescent, when it petrifies and commits itself to a simple repetitious defense of history and a maintenance of the status quo, then it tacitly denies the eschatological trajectory, the impetus of hope, that ought to throb within all dimensions of the Christian witness.[5]

---

1. See his autobiography, *Broad Place*, especially chs. 7, 8, 16–23, 27.

2. Articulated in his first major work, *Theology of Hope*, but always in dialectical relationship to his Christology (see comments in Youngs, *Way of the Kenotic Christ*, 3–8).

3. Neal, *Theology as Hope*.

4. See Moltmann, "Theologia Reformata et Semper Reformanda."

5. I detail Moltmann's methodology on these fronts at some length in *Way of the Kenotic Christ*, 3–27.

It is on account of these fundamental commitments that Moltmann's thought uniquely aligns with some of the emphases from transformation theology that we have explored. Given Bonhoeffer's significant joint influence on both tranformation theology and Moltmann, this should perhaps be unsurprising.[6] Both Moltmann and transformational thinking are concerned to speak *in the key of reality*, and to thereby perhaps gain a hearing in a "world come of age."[7]

This chapter aims to summarize the kenotic Christology of Moltmann, and in so doing it takes up and highlights various dimensions of my previous book on Moltmann's Christology.[8] Given this, significant portions of both my exposition and argumentation pertaining to Moltmann's views are truncated in this present chapter. Interested readers are encouraged to consult that previous work for a fuller treatment of the unique, robust kenotic thinking which Moltmann brings to bear on his Christology.

Kenosis as Characteristic of Divine Life

Many proponents of the first, second, and third waves of kenotic Christology commit to the same notion: the self-emptying of the incarnation represents an *exception* to the typical mode of divine life. And one can follow this logic, certainly. The whole notion of self-emptying ("emptied himself," Phil 2:7) seems to imply a foregoing fullness of existence that is somehow changed and made different for a time. Under this interpretation, the incarnation does not tell us how God *is*, but simply how God the Son *was*, for a limited duration. Divine kenosis would hereby be *exceptional*, rather than typical. (This reasoning is doubtless at the root of the common tendency to "end" the kenosis at the ascension of Christ, as we saw above in chapter 3.)

Decades ago, Moltmann challenged this understanding of God's relation to the kenosis of the incarnation, saying

> When the crucified Jesus is called the 'image of the invisible God', the meaning is that *this* is God, and God is like *this*. God is not greater than he is in this humiliation. God is not more glorious than he is in this self-surrender. God is not more powerful than he is in this helplessness. God is not more divine than he is in this

---

6. Both are also indebted to important methodological considerations deriving from liberation theology.

7. See Bonhoeffer, *Letters and Papers from Prison*, 324–29.

8. Youngs, *Way of the Kenotic Christ*, 99–143.

humanity. The nucleus of everything that Christian theology says about 'God' is to be found in this Christ event. The Christ event on the cross is a God event.... So [we] must take up the elements of truth [*Wahrheitsmomente*] which are to be found in *kenoticism* (the doctrine of God's emptying of himself).[9]

Rather than seeing the kenosis as an exception in the history of God, Moltmann treats it as revelatory for the true nature of that history. The kenosis of Christ is the climactic expression of the God who has always loved creation and related to it in kenotic, sacrificial, and other-seeking ways.[10] A similar interpretation, though with some important differences, can be found in the commanding exegesis of Phil 2:6–11 provided by N. T. Wright, Michael Gorman, and Richard Bauckham.[11]

In fact, for Moltmann, divine kenosis does not "commence" when the created order comes into being, but rather kenotic relating to the created order is itself an extension of God's own internal kenotic relationships. Moltmann views the Trinity as inherently kenotic, with the three persons mutually self-giving in relation to one another throughout all eternity. His reasoning here takes up and extends similar impulses found in Hans Urs Von Balthasar[12] and resonates with the thinking of Sergius Bulgakov.[13]

Much more can be said about these movements in Moltmann's thought. But we are here concerned with the methodology—and thus, indeed, the Christology—which is produced. How does this rendering of the *grammar of kenosis* renovate the problematic presentation found in third-wave Christology? Put most simply, Moltmann hereby avoids the *competitive ontology* which attends so many kenotic christological treatments. God's kenosis is natural and essential to Godself; it is not something which "must" be done to "effectuate" incarnation. This does not diminish its sacrificial or loving nature (a chief emphasis of kenoticists like C. Stephen Evans[14]); rather, it *radicalizes* our perception of such a nature by making it constituitive of God's trinitarian life in its fullness. The New Testament witness declares

---

9. Moltmann, *Crucified God*, 205 (German: 190).

10. See, e.g., Moltmann, *On Human Dignity*, 42; Moltmann, *Coming of God*, 303–4; Moltmann, *Trinity and the Kingdom*, 59–60, 118–19; Moltmann, *Crucified God*, 270–78; Moltmann, *God for a Secular Society*, 181–85.

11. Wright, *Climax of the Covenant*; Gorman, *Cruciformity*; Bauckham, *God Crucified*; see discussion in Youngs, *Way of the Kenotic Christ*, 55–66.

12. Balthasar, *Mysterium Paschale*.

13. See Bulgakov, *Lamb of God*. See also Youngs, "Wounds of the Emptied God."

14. See Evans, "Self-Emptying of Love."

both that in Christ "the fullness [*plēroma*] of God was pleased to dwell" (Col 1:19) *and* that Christ "emptied himself" and "humbled himself" (*ekenōsen . . . etapeinōsen heauton*). This dual affirmation indicates that the *plerosis* of God is not depleted or interrupted by his *kenosis*. Rather, humility and vulnerability give a genuine and revelatory window into the life of the triune God.[15] Look to the self-emptied One, and you will see the fullness; as Moltmann says above: "This is God, and God is like this."[16]

Though they certainly run athwart certain affirmations of classical theism (especially a commitment to strong immutability[17]), there is clear devotional and even pastoral value to these affirmations. But for this book's project, the theological benefit is also clear: by avoiding a competitive ontology, Moltmann thereby eschews most of the kenotic ontological speculation that alchemizes the properties/attributes of the ostensible two natures of Christ.[18] Moltmann's approach relativizes superficialist renderings of the divine attributes *ab initio*, asserting the biblical primacy given to portraying a dynamic divine identity.

---

15. Moltmann here agrees with Kierkegaard, Gregory of Nyssa, and others in saying that "only God can limit God" (*Science and Wisdom*, 62). See further, Youngs, *Way of the Kenotic Christ*, 72–76.

16. See also his affirmation in Moltmann, *Trinity and the Kingdom*: "[If] the significance of the Son's incarnation is his true humanity, then the incarnation reveals the true humanity of God. That is not an anthropomorphic way of speaking, which is therefore not in accordance with God's divinity; it is the quintessence of his divinity itself [*der Inbegriff seiner Göttlichkeit selbst*]. . . . His strength is made perfect in weakness. The traditional doctrine about God's kenosis has always looked at just the one aspect of God's self-limitation, self-emptying and self-humiliation. It has overlooked the other side: God's inward limitations are outward liberations [*Einschränkungen Gottes nach innen sind Freisetzungen nach außen*]. God is nowhere greater than in his humiliation. God is nowhere more glorious than in his impotence. God is nowhere more divine than when he becomes man" (119; German: 133–34).

17. For which Moltmann has little patience; see, e.g., *Way of Jesus Christ*, 53.

18. Some critics fixate on Moltmann's (metaphorical) appropriation of the *zimzum* motif from Kabbalah as indicative that he is fundamentally beholden to a competitive view of ontology. His commitment to inner-trinitarian kenosis obviates this concern, as, once kenotic love is admitted as an eternal feature of the divine life, God's loving works *ad extra* simply reflect his loving self-relations *ad intra*. As the inner life of God affirms real agency and persons in kenotic interrelation, so too, then, would God's outer life reflect the same, with no necessary competition, but rather a metaphysics of compassion (*com-passio*). On this final point, see Davies, *Theology of Compassion*. See also Polkinghorne, *Work of Love*, particularly the essays by Polkinghorne, Ward, and Fiddes.

Given the alignment between the immanent trinitarian life and the expression of that life in the economy of history,[19] and given that Jesus Christ is seen by Moltmann as revelation of the former via incarnation within the latter, it should not surprise us to find a kind two-leveled reasoning in Moltmann's christological thought. In my past work on Moltmann, I have phrased it in this way:

> When we talk about Moltmann's Christology, we must recognize that we are dealing with a *dual-leveled* kenosis. One level is intra-trinitarian and refers to the continued kenotic relating between the divine persons; this is derived by Moltmann from the way in which Christ relates to the Father and the Spirit in the course of his earthly life.... The other level of the kenosis is the relationship between Christ's divinity and humanity, and it refers to the humiliation and lowliness undertaken by God in becoming human.[20]

In short, Moltmann's kenosis is relational and concerns relationship.[21] Thus, it does not retreat into tauto-theology, but remains at the level of the empirical, in which observations can be made regarding the confluence of relationality and agency in human history. Fundamentally, the limitation indicated in the *self-limitation* of kenosis is the self's willing ceding to another. Hence, *kenosis cannot exist without an other*. Kenosis depends on relationship, and relationship entails kenosis.[22] Moltmann's *relational* kenosis shares the sort of attentiveness championed by our transformational hermeneutic for Christology. In the remainder of this chapter, I will briefly circumscribe the *kenotic relationships* of Christ as they emerge in the Christology of Moltmann.

Moltmann's Relational Kenosis (I): Father

The self-emptying of Christ in relation to the Father—we could call this the "Christic patriological kenosis"—consists most overtly in Christ's loving *obedience* to the Father. It is fundamentally a kenosis, a self-limiting

---

19. Moltmann famously adopts and doxologically modifies Rahner's Rule: see *Trinity and the Kingdom*, 153–54.

20. Youngs, *Way of the Kenotic Christ*, 87.

21. His view of intra-trinitarian kenosis is carried forward systematically in his appropriation of *perichoresis*; his extra-trinitarian kenosis is biblically framed via his reflections on the divine Shekinah; see Youngs, *Way of the Kenotic Christ*, 83–95.

22. E.g., Moltmann, *God for a Secular Society*, 145–50; *Passion for Life*, 21–22.

or self-exposure, in regard to the Son's *will*. The incarnate Son submits to the Father, implictly in his actions and overtly by his own attestions, recounted with regularity in the Gospel of John: "When you have lifted up the Son of Man, then you will realize that I am he, and that *I do nothing on my own, but I speak these things as the Father has instructed me*. And the one who sent me is with me; he has not left me alone, for *I always do what is pleasing to him*" (John 8:28–29).[23] Again, this obedience is an *extension* and *realization* of the intra-trinitarian relationship between the Father and the Son; as Moltmann has it: "There is no imaginable condition of the Son of God in which he would not exist in this self-emptying surrendering [to the Father]."[24]

Kenosis, on Moltmann's understanding, does not necessarily include suffering; however, it does necessarily entail *vulnerability to suffering*. Since kenosis is a relational (rather than abstract ontological) category, it ensconces the possibility of being wounded by the agency of the other or of self-imposed wounding for the sake of the other. In terms of the kenotic obedience to the Father, the Son's vulnerability is most clearly seen in the Gethsemane pericope:

> They went to a place called Gethsemane; and he said to his disciples, "Sit here while I pray." He took with him Peter and James and John, and began to be distressed and agitated. And he said to them, "I am deeply grieved, even to death; remain here, and keep awake." And going a little farther, he threw himself on the ground and prayed that, if it were possible, the hour might pass from him. He said, "Abba, Father, for you all things are possible; remove this cup from me; *yet, not what I want, but what you want*" (Mark 14:32–36).[25]

This tortured prayer, this enactment of expressed surrender which is not coerced but willingly entered, portrays the depth of the patriological kenosis more intimately than any syllogism or ontological arithmetic. Moltmann is stark is his understanding of this event in the life of Christ: "It is only by firmly *contradicting his very self* that Jesus clings to fellowship with the God who as Father withdraws from him[.]"[26]

---

23. Emphasis added. See also John 4:43, 5:19–25, 5:30.
24. Moltmann, "God is Unselfish Love," 119.
25. Emphasis added. Parallels in Matt 26:36–39; Luke 22:39–44.
26. Moltmann, *Trinity and the Kingdom*, 76, emphasis mine.

Moltmann's Relational Kenosis (II): Spirit

The self-emptying of Christ in relation to the Spirit—we could call this the "Christic pneumatological kenosis"—consists most overtly in Christ's loving dependence on the Spirit. It is fundamentally a kenosis, a self-limiting or self-exposure, in regard to the Son's *power*. And we should not think of power here solely in terms of "miraculous power" (though this is included), but in power as "power for acting," the engine of agency, the catalytic force of Jesus's acts. For Moltmann, Jesus is "the Spirit-imbued human being who comes from the Spirit, is led by the Spirit, acts and ministers in the Spirit."[27] The four Gospels all bear witness to the baptism of Jesus with the Spirit;[28] Jesus himself attests that he has been given the Spirit "without measure" or "measurelessly" (*ou gar ek metrou*, John 3:34); and the kerygma of the early church preserved this dimension of his public person as a pronounced detail: "God anointed Jesus of Nazareth with the Holy Spirit and power, and he went around doing good and healing all who were under the power of the devil, because God was with him" (Acts 10:38). Indeed the whole course of Jesus's lived ministry is "thrust along" by the Spirit.[29]

The vulnerability entailed in this dimension of the Christic kenosis is the exposure of weakness, of inability; Moltmann's Christology presupposes that there are numerous facets of the messianic mission that could not have been carried through on Jesus's own power or resources. At least four such facets can be highlighted in short order: First, predictably, Moltmann's kenotic Christology teaches that the Spirit is the working force behind Jesus's miraculous acts.[30] Second, Jesus's prophetic activity and ministry to the poor is animated by the Spirit—indeed, the whole of Jesus's obedience to the Father is itself empowered by his reliance on the Spirit.[31] Third, Jesus's epistemic position, his awareness of and progression into his vocation as messiah, is facilitated via his endowment with the Spirit. This extends even to his awareness of his communion and intimacy with the Father, his "Abba consciousness."[32] And the fourth dimension of

---

27. Moltmann, *Spirit of Life*, 58; see also Moltmann, *Way of Jesus Christ*, 73.

28. Mark 1:9–11; Matt 3:16; Luke 3:22; John 1:32.

29. Moltmann, *Way of Jesus Christ*, 73; see also 89–90.

30. Moltmann, *Spirit of Life*, 61–63.

31. Moltmann, *Way of Jesus Christ*, 91. See also Althouse, "Implications of the Kenosis," 155.

32. See Moltmann, *Trinity and the Kingdom*, 74. Also Habets, *Anointed Son*, has protracted discussion on this, with consistent reliance on and reference to Moltmann

pneumatological agency in Christ's kenosis emerges at the cross, and here it is inversely evident in his lack of agency, his lack of power, his helplessness. On the cross, Jesus is truly vulnerable, seemingly abandoned. Power had flooded forth from him at a touch to heal broken bodies,[33] but on the cross, his own broken body receives no such salve. The Spirit's work on the cross is to withhold and possibly even to co-suffer,[34] and thereafter to upsurge as the agent of Christ's resurrection from the dead.[35] As truly kenotic and truly human, Christ is truly dependent on the Spirit throughout the course of his life, death, and resurrection (and even beyond, though this anticipates the work of later chapters).

Moltmann's Relational Kenosis (III): Others

The self-emptying of Christ in relation to his human community—we could call this the "Christic communal kenosis"—consists most overtly in Christ's loving *solidarity* with others. It is fundamentally a kenosis, a self-limiting or self-exposure, in regard to Christ's lived *security*. Those whom Christ associates with, heals, and empowers are the *ochlos*, the crowds, the nobodies, the marginalized.[36] They are the people whom the powerbrokers and religious authorities fear and thus oppress.[37] To draw close to them, Jesus enters into danger, real danger, of the kind felt the world over by oppressed peoples. My reading of Moltmann again supplies four distinct facets which we can briefly highlight.[38]

First, Jesus lacks financial security. He is poor in the economic sense, "without any income or provision for the future."[39] Second, Jesus separates himself from the standard cultural bulwark of his family system, arousing the suspicion of his mother and brothers and disassociating from them (see

---

(136–38).

33. The woman with the hemmorhage (Mark 5:25–34; Matt 9:20–22; Luke 8:43–48) is the most cited. We will return to this gospel motif in subsequent chapters.

34. See my comments on the kenosis of the Spirit, *Way of the Kenotic Christ*, 113–15.

35. Or at least, it functions as such in Paul's *kainos* theology, Rom 6:10–11.

36. The "people" of Jesus are the "hungry, the unemployed, the sick, the discouraged . . . the sad . . . the suffering . . . the subjected, oppressed, and humiliated people . . . [the] crippled, homeless . . . . The poor are 'non-persons,' 'sub-human,' 'dehumanized,' 'human fodder'" (Moltmann, *Way of Jesus Christ*, 99).

37. See Matt 24:16.

38. For more detail on what follows, see Youngs, *Way of the Kenotic Christ*, 120–25.

39. Moltmann, *Way of Jesus Christ*, 100.

Mark 3:21–34).[40] This places Jesus in deep proximity to many in ancient Palestine who had been rejected by, or simply lost the blessing and comfort of, family. Third, and most obviously, Jesus foregoes political security by not relinquishing his compassionate mission even when it consistently drives him into frictional contact with legal authorities.[41] Fourth, and most dangerously, for it is the dimensionality most associated with his execution, Jesus contested his own socioreligious security. "Not only did he repeatedly render himself ritually impure through his association with the sickly, immoral, and unclean, but his theological claims also constituted the depth of social self-emptying of identity, for it they are what led to the most repeated charge against him: *blasphemer*."[42] Most radically, this included Jesus consciously jettisoning or resisting the presumed "messianic" categories of his broader society, leading to conflict, violence, and misunderstanding with everyone from his nearest followers (e.g., Peter, see Matt 16:16–27) to those who mocked him as he hung dying on the cross (Matt 27:39–44).

Moltmann's Relational Kenosis (IV): Body

The self-emptying of Christ in relation to his body—we could call this the "Christic sarxiological kenosis"—consists most overtly in Christ's loving vulnerability in the midst of suffering flesh. It is fundamentally a kenosis, a self-limiting or self-exposure, in regard to Christ's *bodily dignity and health*.[43] Moltmann is anti-dualist across all dimensions of his work, resisting both the ancient metaphysical dualisms derived from ontology and the modern dualisms derived from secular science.[44] This anti-dualism causes Moltmann to anticipate many later developments in the contemporary christological school known as "deep incarnation," which emphasizes that, via the bodily life of Jesus, the incarnation fundamentally knits all natural cosmology and its interrelationships into God's life.[45]

---

40. See Moltmann, *Way of Jesus Christ*, 142–44.

41. Moltmann describes Jesus and his ministry as "politically dangerous" (*Way of Jesus Christ*, 163, see further 160–64).

42. Youngs, *Way of the Kenotic Christ*, 123.

43. For more detail on what follows, see Youngs, *Way of the Kenotic Christ*, 125–31.

44. See Youngs, *Way of the Kenotic Christ*, 125, also 16–18.

45. See Gregersen, "Cur Deus Caro," and the surrounding articles published alongside it in *Theology and Science* (2013); see also the recent (2019) major statement from Edwards, *Deep Incarnation*; some effective overview is provided also in Niekerk and Niemandt, "Radical Embodiment of God."

This radicality (literally "rootedness") of the incarnation as a body in the midst of nature emphasizes Christ's *creatureliness*.[46] This means that the representative "death" suffered by Christ is not simply a human death, but it is rather, more expansively, a *cosmic* death, the death of a conscious piece of cosmic nature, a human piece:

> Jesus died the death of all living things. That is, he did not only die 'the death of the sinner' or merely his own 'natural death'. He died in solidarity with the whole sighing creation, human and non-human—the creation that 'sighs' because it is subject to transience [*Vergänglichkeit unterworfenen*]. He died the death of everything that lives. . . . The sufferings of Christ are therefore also 'the sufferings of this present time' (Romans 8.18), which are endured by everything that lives.[47]

The kenosis of Christ takes him into an *embrace of a cosmic vulnerability*, of dying material existence; he suffers material suffering; he suffers the pangs of hunger, exhaustion, as well as pierced and shredded flesh.[48] The one who in his divine form took on "the form of a slave" (Phil 2:7) was emptied to the point of being "enslaved" to a "body of death," like the one Paul rails against in Rom 7:24. "This enslavement, this self-emptying, fetters Christ's flesh to the powers of the old and broken creation—namely, the powers of dissolution, entropy, and death; indeed he was 'subjected to futility' (Rom 8:20)."[49]

Conclusion—Toward a Transformational Kenotic Christology

I have deliberately kept my exposition of Moltmann's unique kenotic Christology concise in this chapter for two reasons. One, as I have demarcated in footnotes and otherwise, my full treatment of Moltmann's Christology can be found elsewhere. But two, the actual circumscription of Moltmann's doctrinal stance is penultimate to this book. It serves us here as an example of a robustly kenotic Christology that has developed within the same stretch of recent theological history as "third-wave

---

46. See Gunton, *Christ and Creation*, ch. 2.

47. Moltmann, *Way of Jesus Christ*, 169–70 (German: 191).

48. See Moltmann, *Way of Jesus Christ*, 154–59, 193–97, 253, 255, 258; also Schmiechen, *Saving Power*, 138–39; Neal, *Theology as Hope*, 157–59; Bauckham, *Theology*, 210.

49. Youngs, *Way of the Kenotic Christ*, 128.

kenotic Christology" and yet differs from that movement in numerous obvious ways. Moltmann's christological attentiveness is differently placed. His kenosis is not an ontological formula employed to solve conceptual difficulties, respond to critics, or to "render the incarnation intelligible." While he shares the commitments to *humanity* and *history*, Moltmann is able to speak to these commitments in more meaningful ways because his christological work is *keyed to reality*. His Christology is hemmed by the empirical world of the past (as presented by cultural-historical study and the biblical witness itself) and the present (the concerns and tools of churchly reflection in the here-and-now), employing the future's eschatological pressure as a lever to unseat traditional affirmations when they no longer adequately address those realities.

In short, I contend that Moltmann's kenotic Christology is uniquely poised as a *transformational kenotic Christology*, one that furthers ecclesial praxis and reflection on that praxis. But to see if it truly does so, we must rigorously apply our three transformational questions that were developed in chapter 6. Can Moltmann's Christology be used to bear the intensely empirical weight that these questions apply, and thereby indicate a Christology that can be robustly meaningful in the midst of the real concerns of the living church?

8

Transforming Kenosis (I)

What Does the Kenotic Christ Accomplish?

THIS CHAPTER BRINGS THE two movements of the book together by focusing our account of Moltmann's kenotic Christology through the heuristic christological questions that we developed through our earlier examination of transformation theology. By way of reminder, those "transformational questions" for Christology were arrayed as follows:

> What has Jesus Christ accomplished? (I shorten the question from its earlier iteration to allow for Jesus's both past and ongoing accomplishments.)
>
> Where is Jesus Christ?
>
> What has Jesus Christ made possible in the world?

We recall, in light of these questions, that many forms of properly kenotic Christology, since their inception in the work of Thomasius, have tended toward an overtly *concept-focused* mode of Christology. They have been characterized by a christological attentiveness toward abstract ideas, and this has facilitated a lack of emphasis on Christ's historical accomplishment, his current presence in the world, and the living praxis of Christ's church. These problematic lacunae have become even more pitched in third-wave kenotic Christology, since the major proponents of that movement have explicitly annunciated a desire to defend and explicate Christ's *full humanity* and apply the significance of it to *the life of the church*. These goals are admirable, but the speculative, abstract focus of the enterprise has hampered christological contributions along these lines. In contrast to this, the venture of transformation theology advocates for a world-focused christological attentiveness where history, presence, and praxis are highly directive.

The remaining and necessary step of the book thus emerges: utilizing our transformational heuristic questions to strategically interrogate the *christological attentiveness* of Moltmann's approach. The goal of these chapters is, therefore, to show how Moltmann's unique articulation of Christ's fourfold relational kenosis can relate to the questions of Christ's historical achievement, his current presence, and his ongoing significance for Christian praxis, thereby generating specifically rehabilitative points for kenotic christological thinking.

Transformation of World

Because it is in the world of space and time, and nowhere else, that God made "the pioneer of [our] salvation perfect through suffering" (Heb 2:10), transformation theology argues that christological attentiveness must look to the world (in history and in current life) in its discussions of Jesus and in its applications of christological doctrine. This is why transformational questioning deliberately summons more concrete emphases which point toward the world rather than away from it. According to transformation theology this sort of attentiveness promotes the resistance of

> any easy circumvention of the difficult demands of space and time by the infinitely varied and sophisticated strategies of the human mind, which—for all their richness—have often become oriented almost entirely to structures of meaning and conception to the exclusion of what must remain the more primary *reception* of causally embodied reality . . . . [Transformational thinking] remains properly responsive and attentive to the sensible embodiment within which human reason has its origin and ground.[1]

When we allow such an orientation to drive us back into the Gospel accounts, we are empowered to do so with focus that inquires after the manner in which the actual world was changed by the life—the *enacted decisions*—of Christ. Phrased as a question, we could put it thusly: *What new realities were inaugurated in the enacted decisions of Jesus of Nazareth*? When we employ questions like this one "[we] are searching for an explanatory account of a real embodied event in which God himself enters into human history and fundamentally transforms this history through the historical redemption of it."[2]

In responding to this question via Moltmann's kenotic Christology, it is my contention that Moltmann's fourfold christological kenosis directly

1. "Prologue," 5.
2. Janz, *Command*, 139.

corresponds to a fourfold "fundamental transformation of history," in which new (or changed) realities in space and time are produced. In short, Moltmann's Christology suggests that the manner in which Christ historically enacts his redemptive achievements ("changes the world") *is kenotic*; kenosis is *the way of transformation*. Said another way, kenosis stands as the primary means of redemptive transformation throughout the past and continuing human career of Jesus Christ.

Moving forward in this chapter and those that follow, I will utilize the joint term *kenotic-transformation*, and by this I mean a change in reality that is facilitated directly by one of the four dimensions of Christ's relational self-emptying.[3] But before going on to fuller argumentation for and illustration of this, more definitional content must be given to the weighted terms "transformation" and "world."

Of our major transformational interlocutors, the notion of "world" has received its most forceful and detailed explication at the hands of Oliver Davies. Historically and theologically, Davies emphasizes that we are today living in the midst of a "second scientific revolution"[4] wherein neuroscience and quantum theory (among other fields) are disturbing the entrenched fortresses of modernity. No longer is anthropology forced to view the "mind" as something that stands "above" or "outside" the causal nexus of materiality, or something that operates apart from our embodiment in a disconnected way: "In the self of the 'second scientific revolution' . . . the opposition between materiality and mind has substantially broken down."[5] Our human mind and our human matter are now known to form a fundamental and irreducible unity.[6] Our human identity cannot be understood dualistically as located in an abstract "mind" or immaterial "soul," for we are matter; but neither can we be understood as "mere matter"—this is a non-reductive materialism. The unity goes beyond mere

---

3. One of the major points at issue in such a principle is *the key nature of both kenosis and transformation and their intrinsic christological relation*. By way of contrast, see the piece by Jeremy Treat, "Exaltation In and Through Humiliation," 96–114, where a conceptually similar thematic is presented but lacks in terms of historical ground or resulting praxis, owing to its focus on the (abstraction of) the two natures rather than on the lived, kenotic career of Christ and the transformations of world wrought by it.

4. Davies, *Theology of Transformation*, 43–44.

5. Davies, *Theology of Transformation*, 47.

6. Davies, *Theology of Transformation*, 46–48. "Mind is still a free domain that is other than materiality but this freedom is now one that is exercised within materiality and not from a point beyond it" (47–48).

psychosomatic unity, for the revolution has also prompted the realization that our materiality shares in the materiality of all the physical world; our embodiment cannot be divorced from "the world" (nature, cosmos, universe, etc.) at large, for our "embodiment is continuous with world."[7] Of particular significance for our discussion of "transformation," Davies claims that this "new self-understanding prompts us to think of ourselves as being not only *in* the world, as subject, but simultaneously to think of ourselves being also *of* the world and indeed, more correctly still, as ourselves *being* world."[8] If this language and way of thinking stands, then this means that a change in a person—in their feelings, thoughts, and actions, no less than in their appearance and health—constitutes a *change of world*. That is, when *we are changed* (transformed), it can be said, quite literally, that the *world has changed* (transformed).[9]

This equips us for our discussion of "transformation." On a straightforward rendering of "change/transformation," Davies's extension of *world* to human materiality, thought, and feeling would seem to imply that any time a human being engages in any action or thought, it could legitimately be said that "the world has changed." Transformational thinking embraces this conclusion to an extent, but leaves room for a more radical understanding of transformation as a change of worldly *possibility*. In short, the most fundamental transformations are the wholly "new;" they are those happenings which make possible that which was not possible before the transformational newness. In short, we are talking here about divine initiative that, when it enters into our historical space-time, can alter the dimensions of what is possible within that space-time. The Trinity is the agent of the world's change, and the incarnate (and ongoing) life of Christ is the centermost pivot of such worldly change.

Paul Janz is instructive in his discussion of "the new." Since true transformation does not come about under human initiative (since humans in

---

7. Davies, *Theology of Transformation*, 46–48. And further: "For contemporary science, we are indistinguishable from the universe in which we find ourselves in the basic constitution of our material. . . . . Where we are distinct is in the richness and depth of the subjectivity which that materiality of unparalleled complexity supports" (Davies, *Theology of Transformation*, 48). Moltmann aligns with this when he says that a human being "is nature and has a nature" (*Ethics of Hope*, 72).

8. Davies, *Theology of Transformation*, 48.

9. Significantly for our project, this blending of world and self via a cosmic anthropology has also been iterated by Moltmann: "We human beings are aligned toward the cosmos and dependent on it. . . . The elements of the cosmos are present in our physical constitution. We are a part of the cosmos" (*Ethics of Hope*, 69).

their own strength can only do what is *already* possible), it must simply be "'the new' of the new creation, as the *wholly* new of the coming righteousness, or as the *wholly* new of the coming kingdom of God."[10] Janz maintains that the new, as divine initiative, is not an apprehendable alternative to the *status quo* of the world nor is it disjunctive with the world, but that "it is rather *wholly generative ex nihilo* from *within* all life and present real existence."[11] This "divine causality in creation *ex nihilo*" echoes almost exactly Moltmann's famous category of *novum*.[12] For Moltmann, this is the "eschatologically new" which can only be brought to the present by God, and thus cannot be described as any natural development out of what had gone before.[13] The *novum* is nowhere more clearly revealed than in Christ's resurrection from the dead:

> For the raising of Christ involves not the category of the accidentally new, but the expectational category of the eschatologically new. The eschatologically new event of the resurrection of Christ, however, proves to be a *novum ultimum* both as against the similarity in ever-recurring reality and also as against the comparative dissimilarity of new possibilities emerging in history.[14]

Foundational transformations of this kind are thus transformations wrought in the life, death, and resurrection of Christ, and it is these transformations which make possible new acting/being/thinking for the church in the world, or, to adopt a deliberately more radical phrasing, *the church as world* (in the sense of being a part of the world, an anticipation of the new creation in the midst of the old). Drawing on some similarly concerned work from Rowan Williams,[15] Janz states that the messianic events enacted by Jesus are "authenticated most fundamentally in the way that, *as* foundational events, they are *still generative* as a present reality

---

10. Janz, "Coming Righteousness," 99.

11. Janz, "Coming Righteousness," 102.

12. The category is key for Moltmann's presence-focused eschatological reasoning. For an early statement, see Moltmann, "Die Kategorie Novum in Der Christlichen Theologie," 243–63.

13. Moltmann: "The absolute is not, *via eminentiae* or *via negationis*, extrapolated from the presently available reality, but is thought in the category of the coming totality of new being" ("Theology as Eschatology," 11; see further 14–15).

14. Moltmann, *Theology of Hope*, 179; see also 180; Moltmann, *Way of Jesus Christ*, 214.

15. See Williams, "Finality of Christ," and "Trinity and Revelation," 93–106 and 131–47, respectively.

within the embodied life of particular persons and communities in space and time today."[16]

When we speak, then, of *transformation*, we are operating with the following implicit gloss: *transformations are the Christic inauguration of novum which are generative in the continued living and being of those who follow in the way of Jesus.* It is these generative possibilities which constitute the Christian's living freedom and contrast it from the old order of sin and death; as Moltmann says, "We shall now be free from the damning power of our past, because the generative power for a new future will be embedded in our present."[17] Our earlier stated nomenclature of "kenotic-transformation" thus emerges with more clarity. What we aim to delineate in response to our three heuristic questions is a constructive development of Moltmann's kenotic Christology as it emphasizes and applies the ongoing generative force of Christ's kenotically facilitated transformations.

Christ's Accomplishment: Kenotic-Transformation of Worldly Realities

Each of the following sub-sections returns to a respective kenotic relationship in the Christic life (Christ's relation to the Father, to the Spirit, to human sociality, and to cosmic materiality), recapitulating some of the structure of chapter 6. But whereas that chapter focused on explicating the content of Moltmann's kenotic Christology, these sub-sections are focused on illustrating how, in each of those distinct kenotic relations, Christ sacrificially enabled a true transformation of worldly realities. We are here then specifically concerned with enumerating the accomplishments of the kenotic Christ, demonstrating what kenosis means for how Christ specifically altered the world itself.

Christ's Kenotic Submission of Human Will

Following our earlier ordering, I first examine Christ's kenotic obedience to the Father's will. I want to briefly but clearly delineate what sort

---

16. Janz, "Coming Righteousness," 104.

17. Moltmann, "Justification and New Creation," 164. Also: "God [is] the ground of the freedom from past and transiency and of the possibilities of the new, and, through both, the ground of the transformation of the world" (Moltmann, "Theology as Eschatology," 11).

of kenotic-transformation is effected by this kenotic relation on the part of Christ. In this kenotic obedience to the Father, Jesus is, in the words of Janz, "the one man, the only man—the one to whom alone 'God gives the Spirit without limit'—who lives his entire life in the *perfect unity* and obedience of a *fully human will* with the *perfect will of God*."[18] This constitutes a transformation of world, because humans and their human will are continuous with world; if human will is changed, is conformed in this way, then "world" has therefore been transformed. This "better righteousness" of Christ which is "accomplished"[19] as he overcomes temptation and walks the hard road of obedience, had never been instantiated in the world (that is, in human willing) before.[20] As Moltmann emphasizes that Jesus possessed a "fallen" human nature,[21] Janz says that Christ was "inhabiting even the law of covetous desire and covetous freedom, or the law of sin and death, yet without sin."[22] Christ was thus really tempted and truly susceptible to temptation, and yet conquered them through his unwavering obedience.[23] His own desiring faculty, as a fully human faculty, is transformed, *perfected*, by this enacted kenotic obeying.

There is no gospel event more illustrative of the transformational force of Christ's kenotic obedience than the dark scene in Gethsemane, where Christ distinguishes his human will from that of the Father while simultaneously submitting that will to the Father's. As Davies emphasizes, it is in the willing embrace of his own self-contradiction that we find the final perfecting (transforming) of Christ's human freedom:

> In choosing freely to undergo crucifixion, in conformity with the divine law of a total, self-giving love, Jesus thus also chose freely to lose this defining human freedom of the power of acting.... The renunciation of that capacity allowed him to offer himself in the fullness of his embodied life, to the divine imperative to love, in what was nevertheless a free and deliberate act. The stretching of his human freedom upon the Cross, was paradoxically the most total, free conforming of Jesus' humanity to the divine sovereignty

---

18. Janz, *Command*, 148.
19. Janz, *Command*, 150–51.
20. Janz, "Coming Righteousness," 92.
21. E.g., Moltmann, *Way of Jesus Christ*, 51–52.
22. Janz, *Command*, 144–45.
23. So also Habets, *Anointed Son*, 265–67.

in him. . . . His passion was the fundamental transformation of his embodied intentionality as a human being.[24]

This true progression into the "better righteousness" of God through the dramatic journey of the loving obedience of the human Son, resonates deeply with passages such as Heb 5:8–9: "Although he was a Son, he learned obedience [*emathen . . . hypkoēn*] through what he suffered; and having been made perfect [*teleiōtheis*], he became the source of eternal salvation for all who obey him."[25] On these words, we find hearty agreement with the exegesis of Stephen Long (himself a kenotic thinker in regards to Christology): "[Christ's] obedience, learned through suffering, makes him perfect. In other words, he brings his perfection as the 'exact imprint' of God into creation, into its space and time, and achieves it there."[26]

So when we read that "[Jesus] threw himself on the ground and prayed, 'My Father, if it is possible, let this cup pass from me; yet not what I want but what you want'" (Matt 26:39), we stumble to the threshold of perhaps the chief kenotic moment of the Gospel accounts. The completion of the transformation of human will, which Christ took on as something broken and unconformed to God's will, emerges in the pain of Golgotha, in Christ's freely chosen renunciation of freedom and life. By Christ's kenotic obedience, human willing and freedom is transformed in his very self.

Christ's Kenotic Healing of Human Brokenness

We now explore what aspect of kenotic-transformation Moltmann articulates in regard to Christ's dependence on the Spirit. According to Moltmann's Christology, as we saw in our previous chapter, Moltmann sees Christ's human acting, his carrying out of his (obedient) will by acting upon his environment through embodied intention, to be animated by the Spirit. As the obedient Son who has been given the Spirit "without measure" (John 3:34; cf. Luke 4:1) Jesus is "impelled" by the Spirit (*ekballei*, Mark 1:12) and undertakes his ministry "in the Spirit's power" (Luke 4:14) for the "Spirit is upon him" (Luke 4:18). This suggests that in Jesus, the divine Son does not

---

24. Davies, *Theology of Transformation*, 115.

25. The passage has a vexed exegetical history, owing largely to the confusion it presents for traditional christological paradigms. Allen's commentary speaks approvingly, with Cullman, of a "functional perfecting" of Jesus's will through suffering obedience, see Allen, *Hebrews*, 214–15, also 326, 329.

26. Long, *Hebrews*, 100.

manifest his own divine power when he performs his acts. As truly man, he is wholly dependent upon God's Spirit.[27] In this kenotic dependence, he *facilitates the Spirit's efficacy in the world* in an unprecedented way—the coming of the Spirit through the ministry of Jesus is thus another transformation of world that is enabled by the kenosis.

Moltmann well emphasizes the strange near-passivity (kenotic dependence) of Jesus at the key point of many miraculous healings in the Gospels:

> [In] nine stories about individual healings, the faith of the people concerned is said to have been responsible. Jesus either sees the faith which comes to meet him, as in the healing of 'the man sick of the palsy' (Mark 2:5), or actually says: 'your faith has made you well', as in the case of the woman with the issue of blood (Mark 5:34). In these stories Jesus always talks about faith in this way, absolutely and without any object. *Where there is faith, the power which goes out of Jesus 'works wonders'*. Where faith is lacking—as in his home town, Nazareth—he cannot do anything. 'He marvelled because of their unbelief' (Mark 6:6).[28]

As implied by Moltmann here and elsewhere,[29] the Spirit's mending of worldly afflictions is given passage via the humble ministry of Jesus; it could be said that *the Spirit goes "through" or "across" Jesus, or that he serves as a kenotic "bridge" or "doorway" for the Spirit*—for the "power goes out from him;" it does not say that "*he* put forth *his* own power."[30] This power (*dynamis*) is often synonymous with the Spirit in the Gospel accounts, for the *dynamis* is to be understood as *tē dunamei tou pneumatos* ("the power of the Spirit"), as Gerald Hawthorne, Gordon Fee, and other exegetes have compellingly argued.[31]

Jesus ministers in the manner of a vessel who is "filled" with the Spirit and from whom the Spirit is then "poured out," to the point where "all in the crowd were trying to touch him, for power was coming out from him

---

27. Stephen Davis and C. Stephen Evans make this point as well in their kenotic reflections (see "Conclusion," 320), as do many third-wave kenoticists. The issue with their points, and their difference from Moltmann, consists in their handling of the divine attributes and their lack of transformational import, as discussed in ch. 2.

28. Moltmann, *Way of Jesus Christ*, 111. Emphasis added.

29. See Moltmann, *Spirit of Life*, 190–91.

30. A point made in many contemporary Spirit Christologies—e.g., Hawthorne, *Presence and the Power*, 155; Pinnock, *Flame of Love*, 85–88.

31. Hawthorne, *Presence and Power*, 154–55; Fee, *God's Empowering Presence*, 35–36, 120, 643–44; Pinnock, *Flame of Love*, 25; See also Moltmann, *Source of Life*, 68–69.

and healing all of them" (Luke 6:19). This remarkable statement from Luke's Gospel is salient on two fronts: the mass, contagious, spontaneous healing which seems to be taking place and Jesus's kenotic passivity at the center of it (see also Mark 3:10, 6:56; Matt 14:36). The world is transformed (in the healings) but these transformations only come through Christ's kenotic reliance upon and openness to the Spirit. As the obedient Son, Jesus is granted the Spirit at his baptism in untold abundance of presence and power. The obedience and the dependence are thus mutually constitutive. The Spirit's transforming efficacy is brought into the world via Christ's kenosis. We see then that Moltmann's kenotic Christology provides another answer to the heuristic question concerning Christ's historical accomplishments: Christ not only accomplished the conforming of human will to the Father's through his obedience; he also accomplished the healing of worldly affliction by the Spirit's power through his reliance on that Spirit.

Christ's Kenotic Solidarity in Social Affliction

We now turn to the next level of the Christic kenosis in Moltmann's thought: the solidarity of Christ, the kenotic identification with oppressive social and relational affliction in the human situation. As the transformational healings are an extension of Christ's transformational obedience, so does his transformational healing extend into his transformational solidarity with the oppressed and his transformational participation with them in the midst of life. "Jesus takes as his family 'the damned of the earth,'"[32] claims Moltmann, for "he is the brother of the poor, the comrade of the people, the friend of the forsaken, the sympathizer with the sick. He heals through solidarity, and *communicates his liberty and his healing power through his fellowship.*"[33] This societal and interpersonal action of Jesus, his kenosis of stature and identity which aligns him with the *ochlos*, is another route of kenotic-transformation. Because of his obedience to the Father and dependence on the Spirit, Christ is no mere sympathizer. His solidarity is transformative; he enters into the situatedness of the poor and alters their self-understanding and their public perception through

---

32. Moltmann, *Way of Jesus Christ*, 149.
33. Moltmann, *Way of Jesus Christ*, 149, emphasis added.

his enacted decisions.[34] It could be said that Jesus *creates new world* for the poor, the "sinners," and the outcasts.[35]

The social kenosis should not be underestimated. Christ constantly endures social humiliation, despisement, religious umbrage, and suspicion. As a mighty prophet of God, he still willingly "pollutes" himself by eating with "sinners and tax collectors" (Mark 2:15-16; Luke 15:2). Even while seeking his own prayer and respite, the hunger of the poor compels him to "have compassion" (*splanchizomai*) and to feed them (Mark 6:30-44; Matt 14:13-21). When a "sinful woman," likely a prostitute, intimately washes his feet with her hair in a public place and in the midst of religious leaders (Luke 7:36-50),[36] he accepts and cherishes her. Christ is derided because of these extreme examples of solidarity (see Luke 7:34 // Matt 11:19; Luke 7:39) and his disciples are questioned scornfully on his account (Matt 9:11). But such derision does not override Christ's kenotic call, and he transformatively confers hope, dignity, and wisdom in each of his interactions with the poor and outcast. Moltmann refers to this collectively as "the life" brought to the afflicted through the solidarity of Jesus:

> Where the sick are healed, lepers are accepted, and sins are not punished but forgiven, there *life* is present. Freed life, redeemed life, divine life is there, in this world, in our times, in the midst of us. Where Jesus is, there is life. The basic characteristic of the life of Jesus is not the consolation of the beyond, not even the hope in the future, but his becoming human, becoming flesh, his healing of life, accepting of the oppressed, and making alive the frozen relationships between human beings. For that reason we find in the company of Jesus all the woe of humanity—the demon possessed, the incurably diseased, the lame, the blind, the dumb, the dead.... [Jesus's] passion yearns for life and hates death; it desires freedom and hates slavery; it is love and knows no apathy.[37]

---

34. *In the End, the Beginning*, 68; Moltmann, *Spirit of Life*, 125.

35. Moltmann, *Passion for Life*, 55-56.

36. Identifying the woman as a prostitute is acceptable among exegetes, though it is not definite, since the text only identifies her as a *hamartolos*, a sinner. I. H. Marshall says that the woman is "probably" a prostitute (*Gospel of Luke*, 304); Darrell Bock suggests the same (*Luke*, 218). John T. Carroll does not speculate (*Luke*, 177), and Robert Stein emphasizes simply that the nature of her sin must have involved "moral not ceremonial matters" (*Luke*, 236).

37. Moltmann, *Passion for Life*, 24.

Clemens Sedmak, a proponent of transformation theology and an ethicist, comments also on this compassion of Jesus, saying that "Compassion is a dynamic where the boundaries of the self are continually renegotiated."[38] This aligns with Moltmann's understanding of the "friendship" or "compassion" or "solidarity" of Jesus: it is identification that challenges the self's boundaries and securities and impels an emptying into the world, a sympathetic co-affliction in order to bring about healing.[39]

Instructively, Sedmak also draws a clear connection between this sort of kenotic movement and the possibility of transformation: "Jesus teaches us that love is disruptive . . . striving for *extending the boundaries of the self in a kenotic move*, since divine causality can enter the individual person in a situation of self-emptying."[40] In short, Christ's kenotic posture of self is what facilitates the inbreaking of divine presence and divine power and thereby constitutes radical transformations in other selves (and thus the world), within the nexus of often oppressive and distortionary human relations. Again Moltmann: "By forgiving their sins he restores to them their respect as men and women; by accepting lepers he makes them well. . . . [Jesus] reveals God's friendship to the unlikable, to those who have been treated in such unfriendly fashion. As the Son of man, he sets their oppressed humanity free."[41]

In his recent work on a theology of vulnerable hospitality, which draws substantially on Moltmann's thought, Thomas Reynolds effectively sums this kenotic-transformational trajectory:

> [Jesus] directs his ministry toward human vulnerability, embracing it completely in the life-giving shape of welcoming persons who are in a variety of ways especially vulnerable and without welcome. The marginalized and oppressed thus find liberation through Jesus's presence. . . . They find liberation not by sheer

---

38. Sedmak, "Wound of Knowledge," 152.

39. "These 'sufferings of Christ' are also the sufferings of the poor and vulnerable, the people (*ochlos*) and all the weaker creatures. People who suffer violence discover what happens to them in what happened to Jesus. . . . He himself becomes a victim among other victims. In this sense 'the sufferings of Christ' are not just Jesus' sufferings; they are the sufferings of the poor and weak, which Jesus shares in his own body and his own soul, in solidarity with them (Heb. 2:16–18; 11:26; 13:13)" (Moltmann, *Spirit of Life*, 130–31).

40. Sedmak, "Wound of Knowledge," 153, emphasis added.

41. Moltmann, *Passion for Life*, 56.

power and might, which Jesus intentionally avoids, but by love's vulnerable solidarity.⁴²

This vulnerability on the part of Jesus reaches its deepest point on the cross, where he dies the death of a rebellious Jew and a slave,⁴³ and the transformation is therefore itself radicalized when he is raised into the new life promised to all with whom he is identified and who identify with him. On this front, Moltmann is especially compelled by Jesus's comparison of his impending death to the "fruitful dying" of a grain of wheat (John 12:24): "But if it falls into the earth, it becomes alive, even if it then dies. It does not remain as it was, but *brings forth fruit through its transformation*. . . . Herein I find the secret of the passionate dying of Jesus, and the secret of passion in our own life."⁴⁴ By kenotic identification, the ashamed self-perception of the oppressed and broken structures of human relating are transformed. This is thus a third answer, corresponding to the third dimension of Christ's kenosis in Moltmann's thought, to the question of Christ's historical accomplishment.

Christ's Kenotic Transfiguring of Cosmic Materiality

The obedience, dependence, and solidarity of Jesus have all been discussed in the foregoing paragraphs primarily in terms of enacted decisions on the part of Jesus. In his human freedom, he embraces the rigors of his kenotic call—it is in freedom that he binds himself to his messianic role even as it gradually dawns upon him. But what we have yet to emphasize adequately is his *embodiment* itself, and this leads us back to the fourth and final dimension of the Christic kenosis in Moltmann's thought: Christ's kenotic embrace of the travails of vulnerable, material flesh. What is the kenotic-transformation in this case? How may it be named?

As with all of us, every act, every dependent decision, every feeling of identification, is instantiated most fundamentally in Jesus's *body*, his actual flesh and bone, space-time existence. We must reemphasize, with Oliver Davies, that the body is the seat of our most truly human expressions of freedom and limit.⁴⁵ Our bodies are the extension of our human willing into the world;

---

42. Reynolds, *Vulnerable Communion*, 229.
43. Moltmann, *Way of Jesus Christ*, 167–69; Moltmann, *Spirit of Life*, 130–31.
44. Moltmann, *Passion for Life*, 25. Emphasis added.
45. See Davies: "[We must recognize] that our freedom must be within materiality, if it is to be a real freedom. A freedom that is 'outside' materiality can only be the idea of

they are the means by which humans do anything at all, and they are what limit us in myriad ways. A transformational outlook on Christology cannot neglect focused discussion on the body of Jesus, and the Gospel accounts reward this scrutiny. Such attentiveness pervades Moltmann's discourse on Christ's kenotic, fleshly vulnerability, as we will see below.

I've noted the transformational focus on the body in the work of Oliver Davies,[46] and it is to these reflections we return here, but now with Moltmann's kenotic Christology arrayed. Recall that Davies sees a "cosmic drama" at work in the embodiment of Jesus, whereby the divinity is gradually less and less concealed over the course of Jesus's life.[47] These progressive and revelatory life stages are identified by Davies as the "mortal," "Easter," and "exalted" life of Jesus, corresponding to birth-ministry-death, then the resurrection appearances, and then post-ascension.[48] Helpful as they are, in the discussion below, we will only partially follow these categorizations, for the following reasons. Davies is surely right to emphasize the remarkable alterations in Jesus's embodiment following the resurrection and ascension, as well as their progressive and gradual revelation of Jesus's divine status.[49] However, Moltmann's thought allows us to expand these stages, and also to place even more emphasis on *Jesus as world* (as embodied human in continuity with nature). This is due mainly to Moltmann's explicit kenosis of body, whereby he sees Christ as deeply and intimately identified with the whole created order, its transitoriness, and its travail. Moltmann does not emphasize the incarnational kenosis as a divestiture of divine attributes but rather as a radical identification with the creation: Christ becomes a creature.[50] As creature, then, Christ is part of the "old creation;" he is born with mortal human flesh under the dominion of death (Rom 6:17; 8:3). What this kenotically "deep" reading

---

freedom. The theological reorientation which we are calling for here must be one which takes as its ground not so much our freedom of thought, but rather the freedom of our intelligence and will to come to judgment about ourselves which is only really operative in and through the freedom of our acts" (*Theology of Transformation*, 52).

46. The bulk of which is to be found in "Lost Heaven" and "Interrupted Body," in Davies et al., *Transformation Theology*, 11–59 and Davies, *Theology of Transformation*, throughout but esp. 103–18.

47. Davies, "Interrupted Body," 46–48.

48. Davies, *Theology of Transformation*, 112–18.

49. Davies, *Theology of Transformation*, 60, 111.

50. There is strong parallel here with Gunton's thinking in *Christ and Creation*, esp. Lecture 2: "Christ the Creature."

of the incarnation allows us to see is how, in the transformations of his own real embodiment, Christ is a true microcosm—a *mikrou kosmon*—of the changed materiality of the new creation.[51]

To illustrate this, we will in each of the following sub-sections discuss different "stages" in the embodiment of Jesus, drawing on Moltmann's thought to show how in each of these stages, Christ's embodiment—his very flesh—undergoes a transformative process.

The Anointed Body of Jesus.

Notoriously, the Gospels tell us little about Jesus before his baptism. But in the accounts we do have, laying aside for the moment the vexed historical and hermeneutical questions, everything concerning his embodiment is seemingly typical. He is born as humans are born[52] and grows up as children typically do, maturing in both body and mind, although possessed of a perhaps preternatural wisdom or precociousness, as we see in the single childhood story of Luke 2:41–52. Though, even in this passage it should be emphasized that the reaction of his parents seems to indicate that this was not a usual sort of occurrence in the life of the young Jesus.[53]

But things change at his baptism and anointing; the Spirit and its power are thereafter abundantly and immediately present in Jesus's physical form, extending even to his clothing (e.g., Mark 5:27–30). Moltmann notes that at the baptism "Jesus is uniquely endowed with the Spirit, his anointing is 'without measure' (John 3:34), and the Spirit 'rested' on him . . . This energy is . . . the worker of all his works."[54] Jesus's physical self, we could say, becomes *enspirited*, not in any vague internalized or inspirational sense, but in a tangible and proximate sense. Key moments in the Gospel narratives convey the uniqueness of his anointed embodiment—e.g., the account of Jesus walking on the water (Mark 6:48–50) and the accounts of Jesus mysteriously eluding capture by a large crowd (Luke

---

51. See Bauckham: "[Jesus is] the one human being whose story will finally prove to be identical with the story of the whole world" ("Future of Jesus Christ," 101).

52. Moltmann, *Way of Jesus Christ*, 85.

53. Moreover the boy Jesus is *learning from the teachers* while in the temple: ἀκούοντα αὐτῶν καὶ ἐπερωτῶντα αὐτούς ("listening to them and asking questions of them," Luke 2:46).

54. Moltmann, *Way of Jesus Christ*, 90, 91; see also Moltmann, *Trinity and the Kingdom*: "[Jesus] preaches and acts in the power of the Spirit" (122). See also Welker, *God the Revealed*, 284.

4:30; John 8:59). Certainly these things are taking place by the power of the Spirit, but that does not change the fact that they are occurrences in space and time, and involve a real body, a body whose material existence, in these moments, exhibits remarkable qualities due to its pervasive and unprecedented endowment with that Spirit. As Moltmann puts it: "The indwelling of the Spirit brings the divine energies of life in Jesus to rapturous and overflowing fullness."[55] Davies expresses a similar outlook in his account of the "mortal life" of Jesus, saying that his body "seems to be the site of a natural and immediate healing power" and that it can "manifest unique physical properties."[56] (But Davies's articulation of the stages does not mention the fact that these unique facets of Jesus's embodiment only seem to emerge after his baptismal anointing.[57]) We now turn to a stage of the embodiment that is not recognized as a distinct stage by Davies, but that is suggestively handled in Moltmann's writing: the passion of Christ and his dying body within it.

The Dying Body of Jesus

Christ's torture, crucifixion, and death is not treated as a stage within the developing Christic embodiment by Davies, but some of Moltmann's commentary allows us to suggest tentatively that it could be seen as such. In Davies's estimation, the major drama at Gethsemane and Golgotha involves the alignment and perfection of Jesus's human will,[58] and we have seen that Moltmann both supports and furthers such a conclusion via his articulation of Christ's kenotic obedience. But does Jesus's *embodiment* change? Of course Christ's body undergoes the trials of the crucifixion, but this would seemingly not constitute a changed embodiment, only an affliction of the already established anointed embodiment. (After all, if we are going to speak of a genuine change in embodiment it would seem to

---

55. Moltmann, *Spirit of Life*, 61.

56. Davies, "Interrupted Body," 46; Davies, *Theology of Transformation*, 112–13.

57. Davies does vaguely refer to some continuity between the pre- and post-baptismal life, saying that Jesus exhibits "unusual authority" even as a boy (*Theology of Transformation*, 112). The citation given by Davies here, however, is to Luke 3:16, which does not support the point. It seems that Davies must be intending to refer to the story of the boy Jesus at the temple at the end of Luke 2.

58. Davies, *Theology of Transformation*, 114–15; also Davies, "Interrupted Body," 46–47.

require some clear alteration in the bodily properties of Jesus, akin to the shift which occurred at his anointing.)

But here we will recall that Moltmann's kenosis of body means that, in his identification with the world, Christ suffers the sufferings of the whole created order in his crucifixion: "In 'the sufferings of Christ' the end-time sufferings of the whole world are anticipated and vicariously experienced."[59] Admittedly, Moltmann can be a bit unclear on this, sometimes seeming to say only that Christ dies as all living things in a transient created order must die.[60] But especially when he brings more cosmological themes to bear, Moltmann makes it sound like something more radical is taking place in the body of Jesus:

> Jesus . . . dies the death of everything that lives in solidarity with the whole sighing creation. The sufferings of Christ are therefore also 'the sufferings of this present time' (Rom. 8:18), which are endured by everything that lives. But we can also say, conversely, that created beings in their yearning for life suffer 'the sufferings of Christ'. The Wisdom of the whole creation, which is here subject to transience, suffers in Christ the death of everything that lives (1 Cor. 1:24).[61]

In short, Moltmann could be seen to be saying that Jesus, in his Passion, mysteriously takes on a co-suffering solidarity with all living things: "He himself bears the world's suffering."[62] This would seemingly be an alteration of physical properties in a significant way, and would definitively constitute a transformation of Christ's embodiment facilitated by the kenosis of body. If we pair this with Moltmann's staurological denunciation of divine impassibility, then he appears to suggest that, at the cross, via the mediating embodiment of Jesus, all of creation's sufferings enter into the divine experience. This point is further supported by Ryan Neal's interpretation of Moltmann: "[While] *CG* [*Crucified* God] relied heavily upon the cross as the site of divine suffering and its meaning for God, in

---

59. Moltmann, *Way of Jesus Christ*, 155.
60. Moltmann, *Way of Jesus Christ*, 169.
61. Moltmann, *Way of Jesus Christ*, 170.
62. Moltmann, *Spirit of Life*, 130. See also H. P. Santmire, "So That He Might Fill All Things," 264. Santmire interprets this as a continuing identification of creation's sufferings with Christ even post-exaltation, which some of Moltmann's passages, especially in *God in Creation*, could be seen to support.

WJC [*Way of Jesus Christ*] divine suffering is more capacious, knowing no spatial or temporal limit."[63]

Such an implied position on Moltmann's part, though undeniably speculative in some regards, may find scattered support in the strong cosmic christological passages of Colossians, where Christ is said to have "reconciled by his blood *all things*" whether "in heaven or on earth or under the earth" (Col 1:18–19) and where "the gospel" is said to have been "proclaimed to *every creature under heaven*" (Col 1:23).[64] We add to these considerations the radical cosmic effects that immediately surround Christ's death in the Matthean narrative (the sky darkened, the ground shaken, the dead raised—see Matt 27:45, 51–53), as well as the suggestive passages that discuss the church's "sharing" (*koinōnia*) in the "sufferings" (*pathēma*) of Christ, implying that the sufferings of the church, which certainly extend temporally and materially beyond the crucifixion, are somehow possessed by Christ himself, grounding the church's sharing of them (Phil 3:10; 1 Pet 4:13). If these points are taken, then Christ's extended staurological sufferings would seem to indicate some change in his embodiment during the height of his Passion, though any strict description of this certainly remains elusive.[65]

The next stage of the embodiment, however, inspires much clear thinking and agreement, and forms the most protracted discussions in both transformation theology and Moltmann: the resurrected body.

The Easter Body of Jesus

There has been lively and wide-ranging debate over the nature of Christ's post-resurrection body, much of it catalyzed in recent times by the welter of scholarship leveled by N. T. Wright's *The Resurrection of the Son of God*.[66] Over and against interpretations of Jesus's risen existence as an intangible "presence with God"[67] or an internalized visionary experience on the part of

---

63. See Neal, *Theology as Hope*, 158, see further 158–59. See also Moltmann, *Spirit of Life*, 130–31.

64. Note the agreement of Gregersen on the implication of these passages, "Deep Incarnation and Kenosis," 260.

65. Graham Ward makes several points about the body of Christ and its extended, displaced existence in its suffering which are consonant with our Moltmannian points here: "Bodies," 168–73.

66. Wright, *Resurrection of the Son of God*.

67. A recent example can be found in Schmisek, "Body of His Glory," 23–28.

early Christians,[68] Wright vigorously contends that Christ was "alive again," fully "physical," though with altered physical attributes,[69] grounding his position in Paul's longest discourse on the resurrected body (1 Cor 15:20–56).[70] Such an understanding of the resurrected body is also championed by Anthony Thiselton's important work on First Corinthians.[71] Oliver Davies is in agreement with the general lines of both these thinkers, saying that "the resurrection body is not a 'new' body: it is the same body of his birth, but now with radically new physical properties."[72] These new properties—unbound by walls, covering vast distances instantaneously; initially not identifiable as Jesus[73]—when appreciated in tandem with the distinctly corporeal properties (consumes food, can be touched, etc.),[74] are rightly said by Davies to exhibit an "outrightly ambiguous ontology."[75]

Moltmann has also long emphasized the bodily nature of the resurrected Jesus, over and against other interpretive schemas: "Christ's resurrection is bodily resurrection or it is not a resurrection at all. . . . It is not merely spirit which continues to be efficacious or his cause which goes on."[76] He has also been adamant that in the resurrection of Jesus the new creation of all things has begun.[77] If Jesus dies as an extension of

---

68. Rarely defended outright, but Pieter F. Craffert comes close: "'Seeing' a Body into Being," 89–107, esp 98–101.

69. See Wright, *Resurrection of the Son of God*, 8, 477–78.

70. Wright, *Resurrection of the Son of God*, 348–61. For some incisive and nuanced interacton with Wright's points, see Welker, *God the Revealed*, 127–35.

71. Thiselton, *First Epistle to the Corinthians*, 1276–81.

72. Davies, "Interrupted Body," 47.

73. Spatially unbound: see John 20:19, 20:26; Luke 24:31, 24:36; not immediately recognizable: John 20:14, 21:4; Luke 24:16–17.

74. See Luke 24:37–43; John 20:27; 21:12–13.

75. Davies, *Theology of Transformation*, 116. This does more justice to the strangeness of the body than Wright's bland descriptors of "unusual" and "somewhat different" (*Resurrection*, 605, 611).

76. Moltmann, *Way of Jesus Christ*, 256–57.

77. In his earlier work, Moltmann predictably emphasizes the eschatological and temporal nature of the resurrection, thus downplaying its corporeal nature somewhat (though never denying it), e.g., *Theology of Hope*, 204–5, 223; *Crucified God*, 170–71; *Trinity and the Kingdom*, 84–85 (more ambiguous here). Following his ecological turn, the emphasis becomes much more cosmological and thus bodily: *God in Creation*, 8, 225; *Way of Jesus Christ*, ch. 5; *Jesus Christ for Today's World*, 81–85; *Source of Life*, 122; *Sun of Righteousness*, ch. 5—this last work contains Moltmann's most detailed articulation of a bodily resurrection.

the old creation in his staurological embodiment, then he is raised as the inaugurator of the new creation in his Easter embodiment. The kenotic incarnational basis of the former is manifestly key to the realization of the latter.[78] Moltmann well understands the "interstice" nature of the risen embodiment, seeing it as a key stage in the life of Jesus:

> What is the relation between the transfigured Easter body of the risen Christ and the pre-Easter mortal body of Jesus? . . . What did Mary see when she saw Jesus? Was it his pre-Easter body or his transfigured body? Did she see her Rabboni or her Lord? Evidently both, for she encountered Jesus while he was on the way and in transition from his earthly flesh and blood to his transfigured body. He is *no longer* a dead body, but he has *not yet* ascended to the Father. He is no longer part of mortality but he is not yet in glory either.[79]

Moltmann is firm about the continuous identity of Jesus's changing embodiment—this is a true body that is truly transformed: "It must be the same pre-Easter, crucified, dead and buried body of Jesus which has been raised, has ascended to God and is transfigured in the glory of God. Without the identity with Jesus' bodily existence, his resurrection cannot be conceived."[80]

The world is changed by this as well, for Jesus as creature is part of the world, and he has been remade. Thus, in him, the world's cosmic remaking is initiated. Moltmann combines the themes of raising, resurrection, transfiguration, and transformation under the heading of "*Christ's transition to the new creation.*"[81] In a compelling statement, Moltmann avers: "[With] the raising of Christ, the vulnerable and mortal human nature we experience here is raised and transformed into the eternally living, immortal human nature of the new creation; and with vulnerable human nature the

---

78. Stephen Williams, though more aware than most commentators about the importance of kenosis for some aspects of Moltmann's Christology ("Moltmann on Jesus Christ," 109–11), wholly neglects this "binding" of the created order to Jesus via his kenotic embodiment; this oversight may be at the root of Williams's frustration with Moltmann's thinking on these more cosmological issues (117–19).

79. Moltmann, *Sun of Righteousness*, 49. Cf. Davies: "Both mortal and post-resurrection life have a forward momentum and appear in the scriptural record as transitional forms of embodiment in the progression from mortal to exalted Lord" (*Theology of Transformation*, 117).

80. Moltmann, *Sun of Righteousness*, 51.

81. Moltmann, *Way of Jesus Christ*, 257. Cf. the comments in Darrell Cosden, *Theology of Work*, 148–49.

non-human nature of the earth is transformed as well."[82] The resurrection embodiment is thus the true *novum*, a transformation brought about by divine causality (Rom 8:11; Eph 1:20; Acts 2:24) which has fundamentally reshaped the world *in the body of Jesus*; it is a radically new possibility emerging in history; it is the wellspring of Christian hope, "the beginning of the new creation of all things,"[83] and "a new reality, a new arrangement in which the dead are raised and all creation is transformed."[84] This is thus the maximal expression of kenotic-transformation. Christ's deepest moment of kenosis is the death upon the cross, and this is the necessary step which carries his embodiment into its glorious transformation.

Conclusion: From Body to Location

The resolute attentiveness of transformation theology, combined with a constructive reading of Moltmann, has produced in this chapter a radically embodied statement on kenotic Christology. Christ's very body—the site of a "cosmic drama"—undergoes in its living motion and activity the transformation that beckons the whole created order. The transformation of the Christic body is effectuated by the kenosis, and it is itself the nexus of further transformations, which ripple outward from the lived accomplishments of Jesus Christ—transformations from covetous to obedient, from broken to healed, from isolation to companionship, and from distance to co-suffering. But to be truly embodied, the body of the kenotic Christ must be located, not only in the past, but also in the present. And so our next heuristic question emerges: *Where* is the kenotic Christ?

---

82. Moltmann, *Way of Jesus Christ*, 258. Likewise, "[Christ] has been raised inclusively, as the head of the new humanity and as the first-born of the whole creation" (Moltmann, *In the End*, 75).

83. Moltmann, *In the End*, 55. Cf. Devin Singh's summation: "Christ embodies the promise of what will be, not only for humankind but for all of creation" ("Resurrection as Surplus and Possibility," 254).

84. This statement emerges in Singh's explication of Moltmann's views in "Resurrection as Surplus and Possibility," 257.

9

Transforming Kenosis (II)

Where Is the Kenotic Christ?

I HAVE DISCUSSED HOW all four dimensions which Moltmann perceives within Christ's kenosis (Father, Spirit, sociality, materiality) result in tangible transformations of world. Thereby, I used our first transformational question to examine and apply Moltmann's Christology. This brings us to recapitulate our notion of kenotic-transformation: kenosis is the "way" of transformation; it is the "foolishness of God" that Paul extols as the "power and wisdom of God" (1 Cor 1:18–25). Christ's emptying unto death—in obedience, dependence, solidarity, and travail—is that *skandalon,* that "stumbling block," which changes the world and moreover anticipates the change of world which results from the living acts of those who are "in Christ."

We recall that Moltmann's Christology emphasizes concrete and continuous development in Jesus. Amidst all of our discussed kenotic-transformations, the world is changed in its encounters with Jesus and in his own self. His obedient will brings into being new righteousness and new relation with God; his dependence on the Spirit brings about radical healing and untold power; his solidarity with the oppressed shatters societal, interpersonal, and relational barriers; and his vulnerable identification with the transient created order allowed it to be borne into his death and raised (proleptically) to life with his resurrection. Along the way, Christ is not only the subject of these kenotic-transformations, but also the object—Moltmann describes this as "Christ-in-his-becoming, the Christ on the way, the Christ in the movement of God's eschatological history."[1] Having become incarnate as a creature of the old creation (in a "body of death"), he instantiates that creation's transformation in his own body, relations, will, and actions. Jesus Christ is not simply new-creation-in-person, but *old-creation-made-new-creation in person.* God the Son becomes Jesus

---

1. Moltmann, *Way of Jesus Christ,* 33.

of Nazareth by incarnation, but he is transformed into the Lord of God's oncoming kingdom via his kenotic-transformations.[2]

These kenotically inaugurated, Christic transformations of world have great implications for the praxis of the church, and this will be broached more fully when we engage with our third heuristic question in chapter 10. But ahead of that, we must turn to the question of the *exalted, current, ascended life of Christ*. What does Moltmann do with the ascension? We saw clearly that this was a vexed issue in third-wave kenotic Christology in our earlier chapters. So we now must explore what understanding of the ascension is present in Moltmann and inquire whether he is able to hurdle the lack of clarity which attends so many other kenotic approaches. We will have to press the question about whether Moltmann is able to present any meaningful way of linking the *kenosis* of Christ to his *exalted state*—that is, does the Son's kenosis continue even post-ascension, or is it merely an exceptional episode in the eternal life of the Son?

The Summons of the Ascension

This heuristic question is perhaps the most simple: *Where is Jesus Christ?* And yet it is one of the most effective queries for the focusing of christological attentiveness, for it concerns not only the nature of Christic location but concerns it in the *present tense*, in the here and now. It is well-recognized that the course of Christ's transformed embodiment reached a threshold of sorts at his ascension. Due to the clear scriptural portrayal of Christ's withdrawn visible presence (Luke 24:51; Acts 1:9, 1:22, 1 Tim 3:16) and yet equally clear conviction of his continuing and efficacious presence,[3] the state of the ascended Jesus summons critical reflection about its relationship to his mortal life. This scriptural difficulty, compounded by the cosmological and historical theses of the Enlightenment,[4] has given

---

2. This rendering of kenotic-transformation as the path to the redeemed cosmos via the lived body of Christ has certain ancient resonances in Irenaeus, and possibly points toward ecumenical engagment with Catholic and Eastern Orthodox reflections on salvation, e.g., regarding the links between kenosis and theosis, or deification. See Lefsrud, *Kenosis in Theosis*.

3. See Davies, "Interrupted Body," 50. This is especially evident scripturally in statements of Christ being "with" individuals and the church (e.g., Matt 18:20; 28:20; Acts 18:10) and statements of Christ being "in" individuals and the church (e.g., Col 1:27) or individuals or the church described as "in" Christ (e.g., Eph 2:10).

4. In addition to Davies's description of these factors (e.g., *Theology of Transformation,*

rise to a situation in which "by and large, contemporary theology... has ignored the topic of the ascension."[5] In contrast to this trend, transformation theology founds itself on a strong articulation of the presence of Christ in the world today, calling for a fresh expression of ascension thinking in light of the scientific revolutions of the late-modern world.[6] The foundational importance of the ascension is well-summed by Christoph Schönborn: "[The exaltation] is in a sense the christological article that has the most ecclesiological relevance.... That is not surprising, since it has to do precisely with the *present* relationship of Christ to his Church."[7] In short, an underdeveloped Christology (by way of neglecting the exaltation) results in an impoverished ecclesiology, thereby vitiating our perspective on Christian life and action in the world.[8]

The ancient church, compelled by the scriptural witness, answered the question by saying that "Christ is in heaven" or "he is seated at the right hand of God."[9] Tranformation theology pushes us to discover if new language cannot be used to articulate this theological point in our present-day context. Davies makes the case that "[in] the early Christian world, to say that Jesus Christ was in heaven, was to affirm his universal Lordship and so was to say that he could also be present on earth.... [It was also] to affirm that he is still in this same world but now in a radically different form."[10] This belief in Christ's hidden but very real presence within the mundane is what has "shaped human life as Christian life"[11] in the ecclesial reality of the past and should still do so today.

35–43), see Farrow, *Ascension and Ecclessia*, esp. 165–71; *Ascension Theology*. esp. 25–31. Farrow's emphasis is more philosophical and anthropological while Davies's is more cosmological, but both assessments are largely consonant.

5. Kärkkäinnen, *Christ and Reconciliation*, 357; Kärkkäinen makes the statement more radical further on, claiming that "Western theology has ignored the ascension with its focus on the cross" (363). Kelly Kapic and W. V. Lugt are more measured, saying that the ascension is "given relatively little attention in comparison with the cross and resurrection," ("Ascension of Jesus," 23).

6. See especially Davies, *Theology of Transformation*, ch. 1.

7. Schönborn, *God Sent His Son*, 344.

8. This point is perhaps best made in Farrow, *Ascension and Ecclesia*, esp chs. 5–6; also *Ascension Theology*, esp. chs. 4–5.

9. E.g., Melito of Sardis, *Peri Pascha* 104; Irenaeus of Lyons, *Adversus haereses* 3.16.9; Leo the Great, *Tractatus* 73.4; John Damascene, *De fide orthodoxa*, 4.2.

10. Davies, *Theology of Transformation*, 5, 119.

11. Davies, *Theology of Transformation*, 5.

We have already seen, in chapter 6, the basic outline of a transformational theology of the exalted Christ. Just as his human body took on new properties in his Easter life, so too, for Davies, does the body of the exalted Christ possess *a new kind of materiality*; Jesus is fundamentally and permanently in relation to space and time, but he is now related to them in new ways.[12] This is where the Spirit's relation to the exalted Christ is most highlighted, for it is the Spirit that "[makes] real to us the body of Christ" and "makes the power of God actual in the world."[13] According to this line of thinking, the Spirit *does not substitute* for the historically incarnate Christ, for the incarnation never ends; rather, the Spirit *mediates* the exalted embodiment of the incarnate (and now glorified) Christ to the world.[14] Similarly expressed by Farrow, the Holy Spirit "does not in fact present himself but the absent Jesus."[15] Recall that Davies helpfully argues that this pneumatic mediation serves as the facilitation of Christ's glorified self into our own not-yet-glorified reality. What is brought to us is Christ; the Spirit is what brings him and enables our interaction and union with him.

At this juncture, we must bring this line of discussion to bear on Moltmann and his christological views. Secondary engagement with Moltmann's perspective on the ascension/exaltation of Christ is quite sparse in current literature. Stephen Williams, for his part, has commented critically, saying that "the exaltation of Jesus Christ is something which Moltmann is wary of, to put it mildly."[16] In support of this assessment, Williams cites two passages in Moltmann, one from *Theology of Hope* and the other from *The Crucified God*. However, an examination of those two passages reveals that it is not actually the exaltation that Moltmann is wary of, but rather the manner in which the doctrine has been applied in defense of certain ideas in doctrinal history. Specifically, Moltmann expresses concern that the established church can lose its focus on the cross and on the future-oriented movement of the kingdom once the exaltation becomes ensconced as a static and abstract reality only accessible via formalized, institutional ritual:

> With this change from the apocalyptic of the promised and still outstanding lordship of Christ to the cultic presence of his eternal,

---

12. Davies, "Interrupted Body," 50.
13. Davies, *Theology of Transformation*, 50, 51.
14. Davies, *Theology of Transformation*, 89–90; Davies, "Interrupted Body," 39.
15. Farrow, *Ascension and Ecclesia*, 257.
16. Williams, "Moltmann on Jesus Christ," 114.

> heavenly lordship there goes at the same time also a waning of theological interest in the cross.[17]

> [Christ's] humiliation on the cross faded into the background behind the present experience of his exaltation to be Kyrios, to be the Lord who ushers in the end-time. . . . There was no longer any need to think of the earthly way of this Lord to the cross.[18]

Moltmann's thoughts here thematically dovetail with his censure of the non-prophetic, compromised, and imperialistic church,[19] as opposed to his vision for a distinctly kenotic *Kirche unter dem Kreuz* ("church under the cross"), a point we shall visit in more detail shortly.[20]

So, Williams's censure somewhat misconstrues what Moltmann finds bothersome about the exaltation. However, Williams's point is effective insofar as it highlights the fact that Moltmann does not provide any major positive statement on the exalted Christ in either *Theology of Hope* or *The Crucified God*.

A related issue has attended recent engagement with Moltmann's understanding of the present Christ (*Christus Praesens*). Idar Kjøsvik's work has engaged the theme at length in Moltmann, but it has mainly focused on its eschatological dimension and its articulation in *The Church in the Power of the Spirit*.[21] Because Kjøsvik takes that particular work as his "*wichtigste materielle Gegenstand*,"[22] and since that work precedes Moltmann's "cosmological" turn in the mid-1980s, Kjøsvik's analysis misses out on the more presential and world-focused dimensions that the doctrine accrues in Moltmann's later work.

Kjøsvik remains focused on the "temporal" aspect of Christ's current state (Christ is raised "into the future" and comes to us from the future in his Parousia) but not on the "spatial" or "cosmological" aspect of Christ's current state.[23] Functionally, this means that Kjøsvik's examination

---

17. Moltmann, *Theology of Hope*, 158.

18. Moltmann, *Crucified God*, 179

19. His most trenchant critique of these tendencies comes in his historical analysis of eschatology in Moltmann, *Coming of God*, 159–84.

20. Moltmann first refers to "the church under the cross" in *Crucified God* (202), but develops the notion at greatest length in *Church in the Power of the Spirit* (e.g., 65, 85–97, 357–61).

21. Kjøsvik, *Christus Praesens*.

22. Kjøsvik, *Christus Praesens*, 260.

23. E.g., "Here is where Moltmann's answer to the question 'Where is Christ present?'

of Moltmann comes quite close to detecting a program of substitution of Christ by the Spirit: "[The] future is emphasized, in the present it is anticipated by the Spirit; this would better be called the doctrine of 'the present Spirit' and 'the future Christ.'"[24] This is one of the reasons why Kjøsvik ultimately argues that Moltmann does not do enough justice to the *current* presence of Christ in his church.

To this, again, we would note that the temporal and eschatological language for Christ's presence is more prominent in Moltmann before the publication of *God and Creation*, to the neglect of cosmology and a real sense of Christ's current presence in the world (as Kjøsvik notes). But, as with many aspects of Moltmann's theology, subsequent developments and writings bring formerly neglected themes into broader and deeper expression. Once these developments are viewed holistically (again, acknowledging that we are rendering Moltmann's perspective more systematically than he himself sometimes does), it emerges that Moltmann's view on the exalted Christ is fairly directive for his theological outlook on the themes of ecclesial participation in new creation, *Christus praesens*, the nature of Christian hoping, and transformed Christian acts. We now briefly analyze each of these.

The Power of the New Creation

The first theme is specifically aligned toward new creation, as embodied in Christ. Though Moltmann does not always use the same strong "embodiment" language as transformation theology in discussing the exalted Christ, he makes it clear that the exaltation has eschatological significance for the church and for human becoming in fellowship with Christ:[25] "His followers will be drawn into his humiliation here and his exaltation

---

can be found. His first answer is 'Jesus is raised into the coming kingdom of God.' Moltmann's question is spatial, but his answer is temporal" (Kjøsvik, *Christus Praesens*, 277, my translation).

24. Kjøsvik, *Christus Praesens*, 277, my translation. Original: "[Die] Zukunft betont, gegenwärtig werden sie im Geist antizipiert und sie gehören wohl eher zu Lehre vom 'Spiritus Praesens' und 'Christus Futurus.'"

25. Cf. Habets, *Anointed Son*: "So as *arche* (or *protokos* of Col. 1:15), original human, and now as *telos*, ultimate human, Jesus Christ is our model, our exemplar, even our template. And what we shall become is already inherently related to what we are becoming. . . . This is achieved or actualized through the power of the Holy Spirit. It is through the Holy Spirit that believers participate in the one incarnation (but they do not replicate the incarnation)" (271).

there."[26] The drawing of believers into the new creation develops in Moltmann not only as a result of Christ's sending of the Spirit,[27] but also the Spirit's mediation of Christ: "regeneration or rebirth as new creation is christologically based, pneumatologically accomplished, and eschatologically orientated."[28] Davies pursues a largely consonant line of thinking in his transformational discourse: "The Spirit, which is 'poured out on all flesh', facilitates the conforming of creation to the transformation effected in the body of Christ, who is 'raised up' above all things."[29] Furthermore, Moltmann suggestively argues that a "transfiguring efficacy emanates from" the exalted body of Jesus,[30] recalling quite directly the powers of the Spirit which emanated from him during his earthly life:

> The raised body of Christ therefore acts as an embodied promise [*verkörperte Verheißung*] for the whole creation. It is the prototype of the glorified body. . . . It is the perfected body, so it provides the hope for 'the resurrection of the body'. It partakes of God's omnipresence, so its bodily presence is therefore spatially unbound [*ist darum räumlich ergrenzt*]. It partakes of God's eternity, so its presence is no longer temporally restricted [*nicht mehr zeitlich bedingt*]. It lives in the heaven of God's creative potencies and reigns with them, and is no longer tied to the limited potentialities of earthly reality. So in this body and through it the powers of the new creation act upon and penetrate the world.[31]

Here Moltmann verges on two key affirmations: the transformed body of Christ as the source of the world's continual transformation and the Spirit ("power of the new creation") being identified as that transfiguring efficacy that proceeds from the body of Christ. Just as Christ's humanity was transfigured by the Spirit in his raising (Rom 8:11), so does Christ give the Spirit, which is his "gift" for the "building up [*oikodomēn*]" of his body (Eph 4:7,11). Importantly, this means that Moltmann strongly implies that *Christ's kenotic reliance on the Spirit continues, even now, in his exaltation*, and it continues

---

26. Moltmann, *Spirit of Life*, 145, emphasis added.

27. E.g., Moltmann, *Trinity and the Kingdom*, 122–24.

28. Moltmann, *Trinity and the Kingdom*, 147. Moltmann consistently highlights this dual-mediation (the Spirit comes through Christ, Christ is made present by the Spirit). See also Davies, *Theology of Transformation*, 69–70.

29. Davies, *Theology of Transformation*, 141.

30. Moltmann, *Way of Jesus Christ*, 258; see also Cosden, *Theology of Work*, 148.

31. Moltmann, *Way of Jesus Christ*, 258 (German: 281). I have slightly altered Kohl's English translation here.

to effectuate transformation of the world insofar as the Spirit's energies are thereby enabled to break into the created order. The Spirit thus mediates the worldly extension of the kenotic, transformational, Christic body. We see this unfolded further as we turn our attention to Moltmann's notion of the pneumatological mediation of the exalted Christ.

The Mediation(s) of the Present Christ

Substitution of Jesus by the Spirit, rightly bemoaned by Davies, is impossible for Moltmann due to his view of the perichoretic relations and roles in the course of trinitarian history.[32] We can see this explicitly illustrated in his references to the exalted Christ and the outpoured Spirit: "The experience of the Spirit makes Christ—the *risen* Christ—present, and with him makes the eschatological future present too."[33] As with transformation theology, Moltmann finds Christ's presence to be pneumatologically mediated, and, though boundless (that is, unbound by spatial limitation), Christ is also uniquely present in certain dimensions of ecclesial and worldly array.

So, where is Christ's presence to be found in this unique sense? As answered by Oliver Davies, the exalted Christ is "with us on earth, in the poor and vulnerable, the sacraments, the Church, and in the Bible."[34] The transformational emphasis here is toward Christ and toward the world *simultaneously*; so, again, none of these things "substitute" for Christ but rather they mediate "his presence in the world in power, in and through the Spirit of Pentecost."[35]

Moltmann's most protracted and ecclesiologically specific discourse on the presence of Christ comes in *The Church in the Power of the Spirit*.[36] Drawing on his revelation-as-promise paradigm, as well as his promissory-messianic hermeneutic,[37] Moltmann is able to articulate the presence of

---

32. Most programmatically in Moltmann, *Trinity and the Kingdom*; see also analysis and summary in Youngs, *Way of the Kenotic Christ*, 83–88.

33. Moltmann, *Spirit of Life*, 147; see also Moltmann, *Way of Jesus Christ*, 238–39.

34. Davies, *Theology of Transformation*, 58, emphasis added.

35. Davies, *Theology of Transformation*, 89; see 88–93 for the discourse against trinitarian, eucharistic, or biblical "substitution" for the exalted Christ.

36. This discourse commences, in fact, with Moltmann's own version of our second transformational heuristic question: "[If] the church finds the place of its truth and its true constitution in the presence of Christ, the difficult question arises: where, then, is Christ present?" (122). See also Kjøsvik, *Christus Praesens*, 259–60.

37. On both these methodological emphases in Moltmann, see Youngs, *Way of the*

Christ in multiple dimensions, basing each one on the promises given by (or in) the Messiah himself:

> Christ is . . . present where he has expressly given the assurance of his presence. And here we must distinguish between the promises of his presence in something other than himself, and the promise of his presence through himself. . . . If we enquire about the promises of his presence in this way, we find three different groups of assurances in the New Testament: (*a*) By virtue of his identifying assurance, Christ is present in the apostolate, in the sacraments, and in the fellowship of the brethren. (*b*) By virtue of his identifying assurance, Christ is present in 'the least of the brethren'. (*c*) By virtue of his assurance, Christ is present as his own self in his parousia.[38]

Owing to the limitations of our study, we cannot examine Moltmann's thinking on the Parousia in any depth.[39] However, from the other elements in the above listing, it becomes clear that Moltmann envisions a program of mediation, wherein Christ is made present "by virtue of" the church, the sacraments, and the poor.[40] This leads to a thickly circumscribed ecclesiology where Christ, via the Spirit, is truly present: "This is a Real Presence in the Spirit through identification [*Realpräsenz im Geist kraft Identifikation*] . . . [W]here the apostolate, baptism, the Lord's supper and brotherly fellowship occur in Christ's name [*Christi Namen geschehen*], there is the church."[41]

Later in the same work, Moltmann produces a sweeping understanding of the Eucharist, combining the emphases of Zwinglian memorial, Lutheran real presence, and Moltmann's own eschatological outlook into a missional and empowering understanding of the sacrament which brings Christ as crucified, risen, exalted, and still-to-come Lord into a real encounter with the community of faith.[42] This is mediated, once again, by the Spirit's power: "It is the Spirit who allows Christ to be truly present in the meal and gives us fellowship with him. . . It is the Spirit who, as the power of the kingdom,

---

Kenotic Christ, ch. 1.

38. Moltmann, *Church in the Power of the Spirit*, 122–23.

39. Moltmann's most important discourse on Christ's Parousia is found in *Way of Jesus Christ*, ch. 7. See further the discussion by Bauckham, "Future of Jesus Christ," 97–110.

40. For an impassioned accounting of Christ's presence in "the hungry, the thirsty, the alien, the naked, the sick, and the imprisoned," see Moltmann, *Passion for Life*, 103–4.

41. Moltmann, *Church in the Power of the Spirit*, 125 (German: 144); I have altered Kohl's translation slightly (her English edition reads "presence" for *Namen*).

42. Moltmann, *Church in the Power of the Spirit*, 252–58.

gives a foretaste [*Vorgeschmack*] of the new creation in the feast."[43] Moltmann orients the entire existence of the church toward the future which God will bring, but in his mature understanding of the Spirit he declares that this "can only be understood pneumatologically" because the church "is the eschatological creation of Spirit."[44]

The eschatological dimension noted here, and which scholars like Kjøsvik are right to emphasize, should not be treated as though Christ's real presence in the here-and-now is disallowed or unexpressed by Moltmann.[45] But this is perhaps to beg the question: how exactly can the eschatological reading and presential reading be held together in Moltmann's understanding of the *Christus Praesens*? It hinges on Christ's simultaneous identity as the one who is with us (presentially, by his Spirit) and the one who is "ahead" of us—that is, further along the eschatological path that God has charted for all of creation. Kjøsvik's analysis overlooks these dual elements,[46] and so finds Moltmann's understanding of Christ's presence deficient for the current church (moreover, he overestimates the influence of Ernst Bloch on Moltmann's thinking for this doctrinal issue).[47] On the contrary, Moltmann holds tightly together the present Christ and that presence's pneumatological mediation, over and against Kjøsvik's critique; as Moltmann himself says in response: "What Kjøsvik calls 'real-presence' cannot in my opinion be against 'spiritual-presence', [which is] the present Christ in the power of the Holy Spirit . . . because what could be more real than the creative and life-quickening powers of God's spirit?"[48]

---

43. Moltmann, *Church in the Power of the Spirit*, 257 (German: 283).

44. Moltmann, *Church in the Power of the Spirit*, 33; see further 197–99.

45. Cf. Moltmann, "Nachwort," in Kjøsvik, *Christus Praesens*: "Die alte Unterscheidung zwischen a 'präsentischen Eschatologie' und einer 'futurischen Eschatologie' ist hinfällig" (331).

46. Again, Kjøsvik, while to be commended for a sustained engagement with this topic in Moltmann's thought, is too one-sided in his focus on the temporal-future-eschatological side aspect of Christ's presence in Moltmann's thinking. E.g., "The past-perspective on Moltmann's historical outlook provides an answer for who the *coming Christ* is, but not for who the *present Christ* is. Through the identification of the person of Jesus Christ with the coming Christ, we can [only] indirectly answer who the present Christ is" (*Christus Praesens*, 300, my translation).

47. Moltmann, "Nachwort," in Kjøsvik, *Christus Praesens*: "Der Verfasser [Kjøsvik] überschätzt den Einfluss von Blochs Zukunftphilosophie auf die Entwicklung meiner Theologie" (331).

48. Moltmann, "Nachwort," in Kjøsvik, *Christus Praesens*, 331; my translation.

The Animation of Christian Hope

Moltmann asserts that the actual conversion to a living Christian hope, though based on the resurrection of Jesus, is only made effective in the world by Christ's continuing life as exalted Lord. It is Christ's current and future Lordship alongside belief in his resurrection that dialectically serve to sustain Christian hoping and acting in the world:

> [F]aith in the resurrection is only alive in acknowledgment [Bekenntis] of the present lordship of Christ (Rom. 10:9f.). Without new life, without the ability to love and the courage of hope in the lordship of Christ, faith in the resurrection would decay into belief in particular facts, without any consequences. Without faith in the resurrection, new life in the lordship of Christ would cease to be a radical alternative to human forms of sovereignty and—adapting itself religiously, morally or politically—would lose its power to overcome the world [*seine weltüberwindende Kraft einbüßen*].[49]

For Moltmann, life under Christ's continuing lordship is what prevents the resurrection from becoming a mere matter of mental assent to the occurrence of a past event. His christological pneumatology emerges here with surprising force as he emphasizes that the exalted Christ "pours out" the Spirit and that this outpouring is the source of believer's "regeneration" (Titus 3:5–7) into a transformative partaking of the resurrected existence of Christ. The "Spirit is mediated through Christ," says Moltmann," [and] it must at this point be called 'the Spirit of Christ'. . . . [It] has to be understood as the quickening power of the resurrection (Rom 8:11)."[50] The Spirit is the mediator of *regeneration*, which stands not as an internalized, pietistic conversion experience for the believer (Moltmann explicitly wants to go beyond this understanding[51]) but as an assuredly *transformative* category; it is the inauguration of Christian life, love, and hope as *newly instantiated realities* in the world.[52] Regeneration is nothing other than the mediation of Christ's own current and continuing

---

49. Moltmann, *Church in the Power of the Spirit*, 98 (German: 117).

50. Moltmann, *Spirit of Life*, 146.

51. "Neither the Reformation nor the Pietistic and revivalist theologians took this cosmic, apocalyptic character of 'rebirth' into account, however. They always viewed regeneration from the very outset as something that happens in human beings themselves. They saw rebirth only as an inward personal experience in the soul, not as an expectation for the whole suffering and dying world" (Moltmann, *Spirit of Life*, 145). Calvin's thinking on the redemption of the body is overlooked by Moltmann in this analysis, however.

52. Recall that "in the world" means "in a person," for we are continuous with "world."

life to the Christian in their lived reality. Thus, the resurrection, as the beginning of the new creation which now irrupts into the world by the movement of the Spirit, remains generative as a real source of transformative power: "In the activity of the Spirit, consequently, the renewal of life, the new obedience and the new fellowship of men and women is experienced. The marks of the eschatological experience of the Spirit [*eschatologische Geisterfahrung*] are boundless freedom, exuberant joy and inexhaustible love."[53] The source of these new realities is fundamentally *the body of Jesus*, which Moltmann argues now "lives in the heaven of God's creative potencies" and "is no longer tied to the limited possibilities of earthly reality."[54] The new creation is thus contained in the possibilities which Christ offers to his church through his Spirit to actualize—that is, to *enact*, to *make real*—in the world. Christ's own body, his glorified human self, is brought into the world, made available in the midst of our space and time, by the Spirit. What is most unique about Moltmann's articulation of these points is what separates him from other theologies of the ascension, including transformation theology: the Christic life which is mediated by the Spirit is, and remains, a *kenotic* life. *Christ's fourfold kenotic relations endure even now as the necessary way in which the kingdom comes*, and so participation in Christ, as his church, as an extension of his Christic and kenotic life, is also necessarily participation in this kenotic way, these kenotic-transformations of world. This pivotal and highly original outlook—connecting *kenosis*, *ascension*, and *ecclesia*—generates significantly renewed and deepened contexts for Christian *praxis*.

The Embodiment of the Exaltation in Christic Praxis

Moltmann redoubles the transformational emphasis in his later work by declaring that the risen, exalted Jesus *continues to act through the Spirit even now*. Moltmann writes: "Jesus goes on acting in the Spirit," and this includes the healing "of those who are sick;" "Jesus continues to minister in the Spirit," and this includes "forgiv[ing] sins and lift[ing] the oppressive burden of guilt;" "Jesus continues to act in the Spirit" and this includes "gather[ing] the 'foolish,' 'weak,' 'low and despised' and those who are of no account."[55] Healing, forgiving, and gathering-in-solidarity, as ministries of the Christian church, are thus revealed to be further mediations "in act"—or

---

53. Moltmann, *Trinity and the Kingdom*, 124 (German: 139–40).
54. Moltmann, *Way of Jesus Christ*, 258.
55. Moltmann, *Experiences in Theology*, 147.

we could say *enacted mediations*—of the pneumatic presence of the glorified Jesus in the world. His newness of life is communicated through the lived decisions and actions of his church, mirroring or, more radically, *extending* Jesus's own continuing kenotic reliance on the Spirit's efficacy.[56] This framework, wherein the ascended Christ's own life is mediated to the church through the Paraclete, we can refer to heuristically as the "Christic" dimension of ecclesiology. In this sense, the kenotic dependence of Jesus on the Spirit is perpetuated even in his exalted life. Jesus depends on the Spirit's power in the extension of his Christic life into the world, and the church depends on the Spirit's mediation of that Christic life.

However, as mentioned above, Moltmann's thought implies that Christ's fourfold kenotic relations have *all* continued in the midst of his exalted life, not solely his kenotic reliance on the Spirit. Moltmann routinely emphasizes that Christ is obedient to the Father still and ultimately, as indicated by the eschatological moment in which Christ "returns the kingdom" to the Father (1 Cor 15:24,28).[57] Christ also continues his solidarity with the lowly, for the Spirit mediates his presence in their midst, and Christ explicitly identifies himself with their hunger, thirst, nakedness, sickness, and imprisonment (see Matt 25:35–36).[58] And finally, Christ continues to suffer with his church, present in their suffering and persecution (Acts 9:4),[59] and by co-suffering with them, he co-suffers with the world, continuing his kenotic relationship to fleshly transience. This is a necessarily radical extension of the Christic kenosis; as Moltmann says, quoting Pascal, "Christ will be in agony until the end of the world."[60] The world's

---

56. See the points made by Liston, *Anointed Church*, 128–29; see also Twelftree, *People of the Spirit*, esp. 31–34.

57. "Then comes the end, when *he hands over the kingdom* to God the Father, after he has destroyed every ruler and every authority and power ... then *the Son himself will also be subjected* to the one who put all things in subjection under him, so that God may be all in all" (emphasis added). See Moltmann, *Crucified God*, 255–56; Moltmann, *Coming of God*, 104–5; Moltmann, *Spirit of Life*, 102; Moltmann, *Way of Jesus Christ*, 101, 104.

58. "*I was hungry* and you gave me food, *I was thirsty* and you gave me something to drink, *I was a stranger* and you welcomed me, *I was naked* and you gave me clothing, *I was sick* and you took care of me, *I was in prison* and you visited me" (emphases added). See Moltmann, *Church in the Power of the Spirit*, 126–30; Moltmann, *In the End*, 70–71, 85; Moltmann, *Passion for Life*, 103–4.

59. Now as [Saul] was going along and approaching Damascus, suddenly a light from heaven flashed around him. He fell to the ground and heard a voice saying to him, "Saul, Saul, why do you *persecute me*?" (emphasis added).

60. Moltmann, *Way of Jesus Christ*, 157, see also 211.

transformation was begun in Christ's mortal life, radicalized at the cross,[61] and is now perpetuated via his resurrected-exalted self's pneumatic and enacted mediations in the world.

Paul himself eagerly writes of the process of Christ "being formed" in the Christian (*morphōthei Christos en humin*, Gal 4:19)—a striking biblical statement that conveys the church's effective and transforming relation to the ascended Jesus. Just as in Christ's earthly sojourn the glory of God became gradually more revealed in him, so too is the glory of God gradually more revealed in the world, for the "the creation waits with eager longing for the revealing of the children of God" (Rom 8:19).

Conclusion—From Location to Action

This chapter contributes substantially to the applications of transformational attentiveness, while also revealing the deeply attenuated relationship between Christ's self-emptying and his ascension that lies latent in Moltmann's thought. Most significantly, and worthy of further exploration, Moltmann indicates that the ascended Christ is *still kenotic*, and his kenosis, as his incarnate status, perpetuates as a feature of the divine life (since it is true of a divine person); moreover, by the mediation of the Spirit, the enacted life of the church is the *extension* of Christ's own ongoing, kenotic life into the world, thus transforming world.

At this point, however, our discourse has organically shifted to the threshold of our final heuristic question, which concerns the *specific praxiological possibilities* that are made available by Christ for his church. We turn in our final chapter to that discussion. We have seen how Moltmann clearly goes beyond many manifestations of third-wave kenotic Christology, which typically lack any sustained or specific attention for Christ's current presence and very little connection of that presence to Christ's historical kenotic life. We have also seen how this lack among kenoticists impoverishes their oft-stated commitment to the "practical life of Christians and the Church."[62] Moltmann's kenotic Christology helps to renovate this deficiency as well, for his views on Christ's mediated, ecclesial presence open up trajectories that specifically point toward praxis.

---

61. Gal 6:14: "May I never boast of anything except the cross of our Lord Jesus Christ, by which the world has been crucified to me, and I to the world."

62. Evans, "Introduction," 3.

10

Transforming Kenosis (III)

What Does the Kenotic Christ Make Possible?

WHAT IS THE PRAXIOLOGICAL horizon engendered by a Moltmannian view of the exalted, kenotic Christ? In seeking to answer this question our driving idea of *kenotic-transformation* reaches its farthest constructive extension. To anticipate the perspective to be argued for in this chapter—and building fundamentally on what has preceded—I posit the following: *the kenotic-transformational life of the incarnate, exalted Christ is pneumatologically mediated to the church, thereby effecting through it further kenotic-transformations of the world.*

Such a formulation is deeply consonant with the fundamental concerns of transformation theology, as seen when Davies states that

> it is the Spirit who communicates the new order of life which floods from the transformed body of Jesus. . . . It is the Pentecostal giving of the Spirit which extends the irreversible transformation of the body of Jesus into the world and so makes it present too for us in the 'crowded spaces' of our own situational reality. We receive the Spirit in Christ, and Christ in the Spirit. And the reception of this life is that we become at the moment of acting in the name of Christ the mode of his presence in hiddenness in the world, and so also the mode of his power and display.[1]

I am here most interested in the notion of Christian acts instantiating the "mode of Christ's presence" in the world, and thus being themselves

---

1. Davies, *Theology of Transformation*, 70; and further, "Christ is not just an exemplar with whose life we are familiar: we feel that he is present to us and *in* us through the Holy Spirit. . . . Through the Spirit then, we already know implicitly what it is to be transformed *in him*. . . . The Christian experience is that the meaning of our life as a unity of Christian beliefs, practices, and acts becomes ever more expressive of, and participatory in, the meaning of Christ's own life, as made present to us through the Spirit, at the centre of our own historical living" (98).

the Christic transformations-in-act of the world. The key addition that Moltmann has brought to this paradigm is, of course, the manifold and relational christological *kenosis*, arguing that Christ's life, whether in his first-century ministry or presently in his mediated, exalted state, is kenotic (in, at least, the four relational dimensions we have detailed). The kenosis of Christ *has not ended*; in fact, we have argued to the contrary, with Moltmann, that the Christic kenosis extends now into Christ's body, the church, and that it is by specifically kenotic, Christic acts that the world is transformed, that old creation is made new. Some of Moltmann's most suggestive material to this end comes in his ecclesiological discourse, when he discusses the church as a *cruciform* community. Our first section below will explore this theme in Moltmann. Thereafter, however, a critical issue must be confronted: the *risks* of emphasizing kenotically-themed praxis, which have been ably highlighted by feminist thinkers in particular. After addressing some of those concerns as they pertain to Moltmann's outlook, we will explore his distinctly kenotic view of the Christian self and finally on the presence of all four of the Christic kenotic dimensions in the life of the faithful believer.

The Kenotic Church "Under the Cross"

Christ's kenotic, constitutive relations with the Father, the Spirit, the poor, and the world do not end at his exaltation; they are transformed. They remain a part of the Christic life, and as such are contained in that life that is mediated by the Spirit to the body of Christ, the church. For Moltmann, this means that *Christ's kenosis is gifted to the church as its true power and way in the world*; the church is to be a kenotic community: "Because of [Christ's sacrificial life] their life is also destined for self-giving [*Hingabe*]."[2] Grounding his thought in Mark 10:42–44,[3] Moltmann describes the self-giving church in the following way: "True dominion does not consist of enslaving others but in becoming a servant of others; not in the exercise of power, but in the

---

2. Moltmann, *Church in the Power*, 96 (German: 115). Strong support for an understanding of the church as radically kenotic can be found in the thought of both Donald MacKinnon and Michael Gorman. For MacKinnon, see Hopkins, *Exposed Life*, and Connor, *Kenotic Trajectory of the Church*. Gorman's most illustrative works on this score are his *Cruciformity* and *Inhabiting*.

3. "Whoever wishes to become great among you must be your servant, and whoever wishes to be first among you must be slave of all" (NRSV).

exercise of love; not in being served but in freely serving; not in sacrificing the subjugated but in self-sacrifice [*Selbsthingabe*]."[4]

Since Moltmann finds the most profound realization of Christ's kenosis to be manifested in his death on the cross,[5] a position that Phil 2:6–11 enforces and that our four-dimensioned framing of Moltmann's kenosis heavily supports,[6] he can refer to the church's kenotic shape and mode as the "church under the cross."[7] "Wherever men take up their cross and in their self-giving *are made like the one who was crucified*," says Moltmann, "there is the church."[8] Echoing this emphasis is the strong current of scholarship supporting an ethical, imitative dimension to the kenotic passage of Philippians 2.[9] The kenotic church is such because it is called to follow the way of its kenotic Lord. As David Horrell puts it, "[Christians] are to conform their character and practice [to] cultivate the virtues embodied in [Jesus]—humility, other-regard, confidence and joy in suffering."[10]

If Jesus Christ's willing kenosis of will, efficacy, status, and even body constitute the "way" in which he enacted his ministry, death, and resurrection,[11] then this kenotic trajectory can be brought into tight constructive unity

---

4. Moltmann, *Church in the Power*, 103 (German: 122).

5. Moltmann, *Trinity and the Kingdom*, 119; Moltmann, *God in Creation*, 89–90.

6. Phillippians 2 presents the kenosis and humility of Christ as culminating with his death, "even death on a cross." Each of the four dimensions designated within Moltmann's christological kenosis reaches its climactic expression at Golgotha: Christ's obedience to the Father's will is most deeply expressed in his willingess to suffer the cross; Christ's reliance on the Spirit is what sustains him on the cross and is through which he offers himself (Heb 9:14); Christ's identification with the poor carries all the way through to the very mode of his execution on the cross; Christ's unity with the transient created order is most fully expressed in the agony of his bodily dying.

7. Moltmann, *Church in the Power*, see 65, 85–97, 357–61.

8. Moltmann, *Church in the Power*, 65; Moltmann will also state that Christians "live from [Christ's] self-giving" (89).

9. We have noted several exegetes who support such a reading, though with differing nuances (R. Martin, M. Gorman, and N. T. Wright). Another supporting voice is found in Horrell, *Solidarity and Difference*, 225–36. Horrell rightly claims that the kenosis hymn in Phil. 2 is a "*crux interpretum*" for seeing a pervasive *imitatio Christi* in Paul's ethics and ecclesiology (225).

10. Horrell, *Solidarity and Difference*, 235.

11. It may seem strange to say that Christ "enacts" his resurrection, since both logically and biblically the Father and the Spirit appear to be the necessary agents of that event. However, on the basis of Moltmann's firmly established notion of "active kenosis" (*passio activa*), Christ can be truly said to enact ("bring about") his resurrection insofar as he enacts his kenotic roles, which are the necessary presuppositions of that resurrection.

with transformation theology's insistence that, as church, Christians enact the transformative life of Christ in the world by becoming, in the power of the Spirit, "human material cause for the sake of the other."[12] From this dual emphasis, arising at the juncture of Moltmann and transformation theology, we see light thrown upon the idea that, if the way of Jesus Christ is kenotic and transformational, Christ's church now serves as the *material cause of kenotic-transformations in the world*.

Under the strong aegis of both Luther and Bonhoeffer, Moltmann's vision of Christian calling allows for "no fundamental division between the general priesthood of all believers and the particular priestly ministry."[13] This focus on the "priesthood of all believers" clearly aligns Moltmann with the radical wing of the Reformation in terms of polity,[14] but it is also significant for his understanding of a kenotic church. In Moltmann, the church under the cross is kenotic, and thus must be made up of Christians whose individual lives and enacted decisions are kenotic in both foundation and expression. As T. D. Herbert writes, "[Moltmann] wishes to describe priesthood by reference to *theologia crucis* as the identifying mark of the Christian. Priesthood is a sacrificial event of kenotic identification."[15]

But such a view of the church's kenotic priesthood in the world needs to be duly aware of the "risks" that have been identified when a self-sacrificial ethical mode has been adopted. Feminist theologies in particular have highlighted these dangers and must be engaged. It will serve us well to now address these concerns and examine Moltmann's proposals in light of them.

The Risks of Kenotic Praxis

What should kenotic ecclesial action look like? How should it be understood, portrayed, and taught? These are important questions, for kenotic praxis framed as self-denial or self-effacement alone runs the risk of implying a docile passivity or resigned victimhood. Feminist theologians

12. Davies, *Theology of Transformation*, 238.
13. Moltmann, *Church in the Power*, 97, cf. also 301.
14. See McDougall, *Pilgrimage*, 140. For Moltmann's most programmatic statements, see his ecclesiological commentary in *Church in the Power*, 301–14; his social and historical commentary in *Passion for Life*, 113–26; and his political and more polemical commentary in *Trinity and the Kingdom*, 200–202. His most balanced discussion, summing and ameliorating some of these foregoing statements, appears in *Sun of Righteousness*, 22–28.
15. Herbert, *Kenosis and Priesthood*, 123.

have led the charge in denouncing the ways in which a merely "self-abnegating" model of enacted kenosis can lead (and has led) to the acceptance of denigrating treatment and status by those who have been oppressed throughout church history.[16] Aristotle Papanikolaou, summarizing many of these concerns, writes that the "oppressed state" of women and others in the history of Western theology has caused them to view "notions of self-sacrifice, self-abnegation, and service to others" as something which undermines the "struggle for full humanity and further justif[ies] oppressive structures."[17] Daphne Hampson famously denounced kenosis as often underwriting patriarchal power relations, wherein "sheer vulnerability ... is likely to lead to the exploitation of others."[18] In her view "self-emptying and self-abnegation are far from helpful" in protecting and furthering the concerns of women.[19] In the course of detailing Moltmann's advocacy for a form of kenotic Christology, a kenotic view of the church, and a kenotic understanding of Christian praxis, as we are doing here, such reservations should be addressed.

Though some critics search vigorously for an "abusive theology" in Moltmann's work (especially in *The Crucified God*[20]), Moltmann himself has always demonstrated a keen awareness that the church "has much abused the theology of the cross and the mysticism of the passion in the interest of those who cause the suffering."[21] Given his career-long attention to the issues of oppression and subjugation (not least as they concern the history of women), it is not surprising that Moltmann's Christ is not presented as a self-deprecating person or a simple passive victim. We find Moltmann favoring no self-annihilaton or self-denigration, such as that found in the radical "kenotic" devotion of Simone Weil, for example.[22] In

---

16. As Sarah Coakley puts it, "[The] rhetoric of kenosis [can constitute] the all-too-familiar exhortation to women to submit to lives of self-destructive subordination" ("*Kenosis* and Subversion," 4).

17. "Person, *Kenosis* and Abuse," 43. See also Mercedes, *Power For*: "The long legacy of female subjugation that has relied on women's sacrifice as the fundamental currency of patriarchal economies implicates self-emptying doctrine as a tool of hierarchical enforcement" (2).

18. Hampson, "Response," 124.

19. Hampson, *Theology and Feminism*, 155.

20. E.g., Feske, "Christ and Suffering in Moltmann's Thought," 92–101.

21. Moltmann, *Crucified God*, 49, also 48; see also Crysdale, *Embracing Travail*, 105–8.

22. See, e.g., Weil, *Gravity and Grace*, esp. 88–89. For a critical evaluation of Weil's

Moltmann's rendering, Christ is secure in his identity as the Son, out of which he calls God *Abba* with unprecedented intimacy. We recall further that it is a distinctive element of Moltmann's pneumatological Christology that the Spirit aids and preserves Jesus in this relational assurance even through the travails of death.[23] Christ is thus not presented by Moltmann as any victim *of* his kenotic relations, although *through* his kenotic acting he allows himself to be afflicted by sinful powers in his humiliating execution. The suffering—the weakness, the vulnerability, the giving up of one's securities—is the way in which transformation takes places; it is never suffering for suffering's sake alone. Moltmann makes this distinction clear:

> It is obvious that 'the first'—the powerful people of this world—were bound to react to [Jesus'] radical revaluation of their values with persecution, humiliation and execution.... But in taking his way to the cross, *Jesus was also making his own decision: his active love for sufferers becomes his suffering love with sufferers.* We understand his suffering obedience to God ... as his unreserved self-giving to the uttermost for the God-forsaken.[24]

It is only in the exercise of deep human freedom, founded in his identity as God's Son, that Christ willingly gives up his freedom to the suffering of the cross.[25] We have seen Davies emphasize this from a transformational perspective,[26] but it is Moltmann who, in his earliest work on these issues, openly framed the free self-surrender of Jesus in terms of an *active passion*: "It is no unwilling, fortuitous suffering [*unfreiwilliges, zufälliges Leiden*]; it is a *passio activa*."[27]

Hampson is right; pure vulnerability or silent passivity can make nothing but victims. But feminist thinker Ruth Groehout offers a resonant

---

extreme form of self-abnegation from a feminist thinker who favors kenotic language, see Groenhout, "Kenosis and Feminist Theory," 301–2. See also Katrina Duttenhaver's discussion of Weil's "self-annihilation" in *Love's Labor*, 161–64.

23. Moltmann, *Spirit of Life*, 64.

24. Moltmann, *In the End*, 69.

25. This reading of Christ's assured and willing self-sacrifice is echoed strongly in Crysdale, *Embracing Travail*, 53–55, esp. 54.

26. Davies, *Theology of Transformation*, 114–15.

27. Moltmann, *Trinity and the Kingdom*, 75 (German: 91); see also 81; Moltmann, *Crucified God*, 229–30. The fullest expression of his Christology links this theme clearly with the self-surrender, the kenosis: "In the event of the surrender, Jesus is not merely the object; he is the subject too. His suffering and dying was a *passio activa*, a path of suffering deliberately chosen" (Moltmann, *Way of Jesus Christ*, 173).

counterbalance in her own writing on kenosis: "Self-sacrifice is something we [Christians] are called to. . . . Self-sacrifice should not be understood as a matter of spineless submission to whatever anyone else requests or demands. . . . [When] oriented toward service in the Kingdom rather than purposeless self-abnegation, self-sacrifice is important for those who call themselves followers of Christ."[28] Sarah Coakley and Anna Mercedes further stand as strong examples of feminist thought that re-expresses, rather than abandons, the motif of kenosis.[29] Coakley has supported Rosemary Radford Ruether's famous reading of Jesus's kenosis as an "emptying of patriarchal values" evidenced in his historical actions and sayings,[30] an assessment that accords in many respects with Moltmann's view of Christ's kenosis of social and cultural securities and norms.[31] Moreover Coakley suggests an understanding of kenosis as "choosing *never to have* 'worldly' forms of power" as the most effective application of Phil 2:6 to the person of Christ.[32] Alongside her focus on a constructive doctrinal statement for Christology as such,[33] she is also concerned with kenotic devotion in the Christian's present life, which, to her thinking, is best exemplified in the practice of contemplative prayer, a "regular and willed practice of ceding and responding to the divine."[34]

The recent work of Anna Mercedes articulates a more active sense of kenotic praxis, emphasizing that kenosis should be seen as "power for"—power *for* goals, *for* others, *for* self. As kenotic power, it consists in expressions of vulnerability in the name of changing negative situations or empowering others, involving the willing sacrifices that such activity may entail. Though she does not use the precise language, Mercedes's themes resonate with Moltmann's sense of a *passio activa*:

---

28. Groenhout, "Kenosis and Feminist Theory," 310–11.

29. See Coakley, "*Kenosis* and Subversion"; Mercedes, *Power For*, esp. 132–53; Groenhout, "Kenosis and Feminist Theory," esp. 305–12.

30. See Coakley, "*Kenosis* and Subversion," 25.

31. Moltmann specifically describes Jesus's overthrowing cultural patriarchal norms in *Way of Jesus Christ*, 142–45.

32. Coakley, "*Kenosis* and Subversion," 31. Coakley wishes to limit this solely to the human nature. For Coakley, kenosis mainly applies to the humble bearing of Jesus in his earthly life.

33. More fully explored in Coakley's essay, "Does Kenosis Rest on a Mistake?," 246–64.

34. Coakley, "*Kenosis* and Subversion," 34.

> Power for leans toward another or others; its focus and its desire remain for the thriving of this particular other or others. In this sense it is very much a self-giving, a self-emptying.... Though self-giving may appear as the *loss* of power, kenotic outpouring may also... bear a mighty current, opening a revelation of oneself, beckoning the becoming of another, resisting oppression, and redefining subjection.[35]

In the kenotic embrace of goals beyond oneself, one's self is reduced in the amount of focus it receives; selfish perpetuation of personal goals and self-absorbed construction of private idols is confuted by this active kind of kenosis. As Mercedes puts it, "Our self-emptying, when christic, is neither self-righteousness nor diffuse charity but rather always necessarily for another."[36]

Though Groenhout, Coakley, and Mercedes do not parrot one another—in fact, Mercedes stages much of her own interaction with Coakley as a dialogical critique[37]—we can still render their basic stances on kenotic praxis in a complementary statement: *the kenotic Christian life refuses to take up worldly forms of power and instead submits radically to God in its practices* (Coakley), *sustaining self-sacrifice in the service of justice, resistance, and solidarity on behalf of others* (Groenhout and Mercedes). These points align with the themes I have unearthed in Moltmann's thought, and thus they provide a safeguard against Moltmann's discourse on "the church under the cross" being read as a masochistic valorization of suffering for its own sake.

Taken together, Moltmann's kenotic church and the sort of kenotic praxis etched by feminist theologians seems to fundamentally illustrate the New Testament's emphasis on willingly, freely, even joyfully, ceding oneself to others in love and humility: "For you were called to freedom, brothers and sisters; only do not use your freedom as an opportunity for self-indulgence, but *through love become slaves to one another*" (Gal 5:13;

---

35. Mercedes, *Power For*, 135. See also the similar lines of thinking taken up by Groenhout, "Kenosis and Feminist Theory," 291–312. Groenhout claims that "self-sacrifice is something we [as Christians] are called to" (306), and claims further that "feminism has always accepted the presence of values that require the sacrifice of self-interest for the sake of justice" (308). Her valuation of self-sacrifice is thus not in terms of its oppressive history but instead its liberative potential; it is not the sacrifice of power or freedom for its own sake but the sacrifice or safety or security when challenging the "status quo" through being a "prophetic voice" (312). Kenosis is goal-oriented in this case, a power for change and transformation.

36. Mercedes, *Power For*, 150.

37. Mercedes, *Power For*, 30–38.

cf. also 1 Cor 5:14; 1 John 4:9–11). Christians are freed to love, and in that love ought to willingly bind themselves to others and to God.[38] Such is the shape of kenotic action that does not lend itself readily to exploitation and self-denigration.[39]

Moltmann, when discussing the ethical responsibility of Christian praxis, takes pains to emphasize that limitations should be recognized and that "no one is required to abrogate himself completely.... The person who despises himself will not be able to love his neighbor either."[40] This qualification is hugely important, as commentary on "kenotic selfhood" can often run toward self-dissolution. In recent work, Rowan Williams has suggested a way of approaching the kenotic self that verges on this: "[There] is nothing that is *possessed*, no solid self that owns, accumulates, gives or holds back according to will."[41] It is difficult to see enduring agency here, though, on balance, Williams seems to be aiming at the undoing of an illusory notion of *inflated* agency. Mark McInroy expounds on Williams's account in the midst of a broader discussion on deification, saying that "deification is the process of becoming a hypostasis, a person, not as a finite individual who relates to God and world as an individual, but instead as one whose *illusory self is undone* so that God's life might pour through."[42] Such reflections stand in a generative tension with the outlook of Catherine Keller, who in her own writing on kenosis has advocated for a vision of selfhood and agency that "strengthens both the sense of attachment and the sense of self, seeking not to overcome self but to experience and to articulate an *extensively relational* self."[43] These words hit very closely to Moltmann's specific and capacious understanding of transformational-kenotic praxis rooted in other-centered agency.

---

38. Thus, self-sacrifice need not be self-*abnegation*, but can rather serve as self-*realization* within one's Christic identity as part of the kenotic Lord's kenotic church.

39. But given the doctrine's potentiality for oppressive use, we strongly concur with Mercedes's observation that "Theological care around questions of *kenosis* continues to be necessary because abuse continues.... Thus, *kenosis* merits theological reconsideration, *through and with* honesty about the hazards of kenotic doctrine" (*Power For*, 152–53).

40. Moltmann, *Ethics of Hope*, 74.

41. Williams, "Deification, Hypostatisation, and Kenosis," 38.

42. McInroy, "To Become Like God," 8, emphasis added.

43. Keller, "Scoop Up the Water," 107. Emphasis added.

The Open Self: Embracing "Entrance" and "Limitation"

The emphasis on self-giving relationship as the proper way to understand kenosis is deeply seated in Moltmann's thought, often articulated in the language of "openness." Openness to others is what facilitates relationship; it is the initial and vulnerable step of kenosis. Kenotic praxis is thus fundamentally originated in relational openness, and both serve as facilitation of Christic transformation. Moltmann's first major work on ecclesiology was given the telling English title *The Open Church*.[44] In his introduction to that book, Douglas Meeks emphasized Moltmann's clear connection between the kenotic themes of relationship, passion, and suffering:

> The words "passion" and "suffering" will be found in this book. . . . [But they do] not mean passivity. . . . "Passion" and "suffering" mean not simply to be acted upon but also to be affected, changed, transformed, and matured by the lives of others. To be open, accessible, vulnerable is not the sign of passive impotence but the precondition of active historical life. Suffering also means the power to go outside of oneself and affect the other.[45]

This characteristic Moltmannian emphasis on alterity ("otherness" or "difference") enunciates the fact that there is no relationship without difference, thus differences—even challenging differences—must be borne—even suffered—for the sake of true relationship. In Papanikolaou's words: "'Otherness' is constituted in and through 'distance,' which is the precondition for real communion."[46] Within an irreducibly relational understanding of kenosis, we agree with Graham Ward's declaration that "there cannot be true *kenosis*. . . without true difference."[47]

Moltmann's theological epistemology itself comes to hinge on a phenomenology of difference, which is also a phenomenology of relational suffering, or passion. On Moltmann's reading, the "other" calls us to suffer

---

44. Later reprinted as *Passion for Life*.

45. Meeks, "Introduction," 16.

46. Papanikolaou, "Person, *Kenosis* and Abuse," 51. He is drawing here on Balthasar's articulation of *diastasis*, or the necessary "distance/difference" between the Trinitarian persons in order for them to truly commune with one another (rather than simply being modes of one single divine monad, without any *diastasis*).

47. Ward, "Kenosis," 44. See the analytic points about the nature of individuated identity in Strawson, *Individuals*, 99–102.

not out of malice, but simply out of its difference, calling for change and acknowledgment from us in the thick of the encountering moment:

> If [we] encounter something strange, something different or new, we feel pain. We sense the resistance of what is alien, the contradiction of the other, the claim of the new. The pain shows us that we must change ourselves if we want to understand the alien, perceive the other, and comprehend the new. *The pain shows that we must open ourselves if we want to take in the other*, the alien or the new, and that we cannot adapt it to ourselves or make it like ourselves without destroying it.[48]

If we follow the discourse closely here, we find Moltmann making an explicit and progressive connection between the themes of otherness, suffering, relationship, and *self-opening*. Self-opening often stands as a Moltmannian gloss for his active, relational sense of kenosis;[49] rather than self-emptying in the sense of self-abnegation, we have here self-emptying in the sense of self-extension and ceding of self-concern. Instead of kenosis as passive abnegation, we have kenosis as active vulnerability. This is, in fact, the Phil 2:6–8 picture once again; the Son's *extension* into human life (rather than a cessation of his divine life) carries along with it the whole warp and weft of relational differences encountered via his incarnate human self.[50] Kenosis is thus *com-passionate* by definition, and, in the words of Oliver

---

48. Moltmann, *Experiences in Theology*, 170, emphasis added; see also Moltmann, *God for a Secular Society*, 143–49. This phenomenological, epistemic stance was initially situated thickly within Moltmann's dialectical method (during his most anti-analogical phase) and is drawn principally from Ernst Bloch and the Greek philosopher Anaxagoras, see also Moltmann, *Crucified God*, 25–28; Moltmann, "Antwort auf die kritik an 'Der gekreuzigte Gott,'" 188–89. There is, of course, also a detectable alignment here with the thought of someone like Emmanuel Levinas, e.g., *Totality and Infinity*, 35–48 (see further, Janz, *Command*, 61–63). Moltmann, however, does not reference Levinas often (though he is aware of him: *God for Secular Society*, 19, 135n1) and exhibits no direct line of dependence on his thought.

49. This applies in both anthropological and theological contexts for Moltmann. He often speaks of God "opening himself" for the world's history, thus enabling relationship with the world and the possibility of suffering for God. See Moltmann, *Church in the Power*, 59–64. Moltmann's discourse on what he calls "the open Trinity" or "self-opening Trinity" should, then, be read as an expression of his outlook on kenosis as relationship, vulnerability, and pathos (see Moltmann, *Trinity and the Kingdom*, 89–95; Moltmann, *Spirit of Life*, 291, 294–95; Moltmann, *God in Creation*, 242; Moltmann, *Experiences in Theology*, 323; Moltmann, *Sun of Righteousness*, 156–57; "Trinitarian History of God," esp. 82–86).

50. Gorman makes a similar point; see *Becoming the Gospel*, 39–40.

Davies, forms "the site of intensified or enriched existence" rather than any negation of existence.[51] For Moltmann, this is key not only for the practice of the Christian life, but also for the understanding of Christian identity: "Our knowledge of ourselves develops in *our understanding emptying of ourselves* in confrontation with the other."[52]

Moltmann utilizes both "entering" and "openness" language to very similar discursive ends in his kenotic discussions, e.g., "In my perception of others I subject myself to the pains and joys of my own alteration, not in order to adapt myself to the other, but in order to *enter into* it. There is no true understanding of the other without this empathy. Together with the other I *enter into* a process of reciprocal change."[53] If kenosis is, at its most basal level, understood as self-emptying and self-limitation, then Moltmann's articulation of the open self, the entering self, which relates to world and God and is thereby limited and suffers, is also his articulation of the kenotic self.[54] We can also call this the vulnerable self or even the "exposed self,"[55] and it is in this mode of exposure, of kenosis, that the self is rendered vulnerable, transformable, and truly capable of love; as Moltmann says, "Only a loving life *exposes itself* to the wounds of disappointment, contradiction, sickness and death."[56] Williams and McInroy, though they present some open questions about the precise nature of the *self* in the midst of kenotic relating, suggest some parallel thinking in this regard. Williams notes that interpersonal and lived kenosis leads to "an intensified vulnerability . . . precisely in our *opening* to the otherness of God and our neighbour."[57] And McInroy (who, again, is concerned to relate kenosis to theosis) writes, "The deified person is one whose protective, self-isolating walls have been torn down, one who is exposed to—and

---

51. Davies, *Theology of Compassion*, xix.

52. Moltmann, *Way of Jesus Christ*, 244, emphasis added.

53. Moltmann, *God for a Secular Society*, 145. Emphasis added.

54. See Moltmann, *Passion for Life*, 30–31, which explicitly ties our "suffering of others" to Christ's "suffering for us."

55. "If we expose ourselves . . . we discover the new in the reality we encounter" (Moltmann, *Science and Wisdom*, 145). Moltmann considers "apathy" to be the result of the "closed-off," that is, non-kenotic, person (see Moltmann, *Passion for Life*, 21–22; Moltmann, *Ethics of Hope*, 62). MacKinnon's articulation of the "exposed life" of a Christian who foregoes the easy security of dogma and institutional history is *apropros* on this front as well (see "Kenosis and Establishment," 33–34).

56. Moltmann, *God in Creation*, 268, emphasis added.

57. Williams, "Deification, Hypostatisation, and Kenosis," 43–44. Emphasis mine.

defenseless against—the need of the world, and one who carries out into the world the self-giving of the Father, Son, and Spirit."[58]

This opening-entering movement, moreover, is always depicted by Moltmann as both a Christic and transformational occurrence: "The suffering of [Christ's] love has changed everything," he writes, "and the more we go outside of ourselves, the more we will discover and experience this change ourselves. If God wants so much to suffer us that he so deeply suffers for us, because of us, and with us, then *we also become free to be transformed*."[59] The initial movement of kenosis is opening-entering; it is a call to act, a call to a particular posture; a manifesto for aligning oneself with Christic transformation by turning to Christ and to the world simultaneously. Once this "turning" has taken place, the kenotic relations of Christ can be extended through the Christian's own obedience to the Father, empowerment by the Spirit, identification with the lowly, and willingness to suffer bodily. The varied kenosis of Christ's life becomes that of the church.

The Fourfold Christic Kenosis in the Christian Life

The dimensions of these kenotic exposures in the Christian's life thus reflect and extend those of Jesus Christ. In the power of the Spirit, the Christian both anticipates the new creation and participates in transformational realities in the here and now.[60] This is the furthest praxiological extension which emerges from our multi-layered analysis of Moltmann's kenotic Christology. Mediation by the Spirit serves as the connection between Christ's humanity and ours; as Liston writes: "[The] Spirit is sent through the incarnate Christ specifically to unite the church with Christ's humanity. Our humanity is joined with Christ's humanity by the Spirit."[61]

As Christ obeys, the church obeys, in kenotic submission. This is not servile obedience to a divine, imperial taskmaster,[62] but the kenotic extension of self in openness to one's heavenly Father. Christian obedience, for

58. McInroy, "To Be Like God," 9.

59. Moltmann, *Passion for Life*, 32, emphasis added.

60. See also Gorman, *Becoming the Gospel*, 16–20.

61. Liston, *Anointed Church*, 127. And further: "The church then, should be understood precisely as the pneumatologically enabled relational union between believers' humanity and that of the incarnate Son" (128).

62. Moltmann sees the image of God as "ruler" and the Aristotelian divine attributes as mutually formative in the tradition; see Moltmann, *Sun of Righteousness*, 87–89; also Moltmann, *Crucified God*, 249–51; Moltmann, "New Paradigm of Transcendence," 3.

Moltmann, does not take the form of subservience, but co-working on the *missio Dei*, partaking of the same status of "sonship" that Jesus possesses—hence the church's cry of *Abba*, mirroring the immediate and filial consciousness of the kenotic Son (Rom 8:15; Gal 4:6). As Moltmann puts it, Jesus "recognizes a new community among the people who do the will 'of my Father in heaven' (Matt 12:50)."[63] Moreover, the will of the Father and kenotic obedience to that will are strongly emphasized by Paul Janz as the expressed form of the "perfect obedience" and "embodied will" of Jesus's incarnate life.[64] Admittedly, Moltmann's aversion to hierarchy occasionally renders his discussions of human obedience to God somewhat unclear, but this is less of an issue in the passages where he explicitly grounds his discourse in Jesus's depiction (and embodiment) of God's rule.[65]

But, just as in the past and ongoing ministry of Jesus, the Christian's kenosis of will (obedience) must be paralleled and sustained by the kenosis of efficacy, for it is the Spirit that *enables* obedience and the transformation of personal life and conduct, while also distributing the "powers of the age to come" (healings, prophecy, etc.—see 1 Cor 12:1–11). When Christians expose themselves in open vulnerability, even weakness, they must rely upon the Holy Spirit: "In praying for the coming of the Spirit, men and women *open themselves* for his coming."[66] In their lack, the Spirit gives: "The Spirit of God makes the impossible possible [*macht Unmögliches möglich*]; he creates faith where there is nothing else to believe in; he creates love where there is nothing lovable; he creates hope where there is nothing to hope for."[67] The church cannot be the church in its own (human) powers; the only church is "the church in the power of the Spirit."[68] Moltmann talks about the power of the Spirit in an expansive sense, highlighting pneumatological sustenance for the whole of the Christian life. For in the Spirit "the hitherto unexplored creative powers of God are thrown open"[69] and "new chances and possibilities for the gospel" are manifested.[70] The power

---

63. Moltmann, *Way of Jesus Christ*, 144.
64. Janz, *Command*, 148–51.
65. See esp. Moltmann, "God the Father," 11–16; also Moltmann, *Spirit of Life*, 115–16.
66. Moltmann, *Spirit of Life*, 74, emphasis added.
67. Moltmann, *Church in the Power*, 191 (German: 216).
68. Moltmann, *Church in the Power*, throughout, but esp. 33–37.
69. Moltmann, *Spirit of Life*, 115; see also 111, 190.
70. Moltmann, *Spirit of Life*, 103.

of the Spirit is not only present in filial identity, obedience, and new possibilities for Christian acting, but also in the strength to sustain Christian acts when they are difficult or painful.[71]

It is these kenotic relationships with the Father and the Spirit which provide the transformational resources which compel the embrace of the other two kenotic relations: with the lowly and with bodily transience itself. Often this means suffering. Moltmann sees a consistently borne *theologia crucis* (which is the pinnacle of kenosis) to be the "mark of the Christian."[72] Moltmann explicitly links his self-sacrificial vision for the "community of the crucified" (the church) with Christ's kenosis, saying that Christians should become like "the one who became man, the God who humbled himself [*sich erniedrigenden*] and whose love reached to the point of suffering death,"[73] clearly echoing the kenosis hymn.

As regards the poor—that is, victims and perpetrators who are either poor materially or poor in righteousness—Moltmann advocates a program of solidarity and co-suffering love, which would entail both identification and acts of charity. Michael Welker has articulated a similar stance for this aspect of the church's kenotic life, calling it an *ethos of free, creative self-withdrawal*.[74] Such a thickly relational understanding allows us to see how, in the words of Herbert, kenosis should not be understood as "surrender of self and loss of identity, but rather [as] the very opposite,"[75] for the priestly role of the Christian emerges as an expressed and enacted testimony to "Christ's self-giving [*Hingabe*] and in self-giving for the reconciliation of the world."[76]

Moltmann follows the Christian's lived kenosis all the way into the fourth Christic dimension as well: the kenosis of body. In relation to the transience and decay of the world, Moltmann highlights the fact that Christians are often called to suffer in their mortal flesh, most clearly in the case of martyrs.[77] There is a stark specificity here that is often lacking in academic

---

71. Moltmann, *Spirit of Life*, 73–74.
72. Moltmann, *Spirit of Life*, 123.
73. Moltmann, *Church in the Power*, 85 (German: 103–4).
74. See Welker, *God the Revealed*, 223–34. He stages this as a radicalizing of the "ethos of free self-limitation" promoted by W. Huber (*Konflikt und Konsens*, 205–6).
75. Herbert, *Kenosis and Priesthood*, 123, drawing on Moltmann, *Crucified God*, 214.
76. Moltmann, *Church in the Power*, 97.
77. For Moltmann's reflections on martyrdom, see *Way of Jesus Christ*, 153–54; 196–204; *Crucified God*, 55–60; "Cross as Military Symbol of Sacrifice," 259–61.

theology. Moltmann is speaking of physical pain and the clear suffering and humiliation that this visits upon the sufferer. There is no ecclesial example of this more striking than martyrdom. "The martyr," says Moltmann, "is united to Christ in a special way. [The] martyrs *anticipate in their own bodies the sufferings* . . . which come upon the whole creation; and dying, they witness to the creation that is new."[78] Michael Gorman too speaks of the suffering, weakness, and even death of the Christian's material body as an extension of apostolic cruciformity, or kenosis: "The metaphor of dying with Christ is not merely meant to refer to self-giving love or the termination of selfish desires. It includes . . . a variety of concrete, physical pains suffered for the sake of the gospel of the crucified Christ."[79] Indeed, in Paul's discourse to the Galatians he can speak of his own wounds thusly, in radical Christic identification: "I carry *the scars of Jesus* on my own body."[80]

This sort of physical martyrdom need not be understood as only the dramatic torture or execution of the Christian in the name of their faith (though this is certainly included) but should be radically extended into all aspects of worldly life, mirroring what Rowan Williams has referred to as the "quotidian" character of Christian martyrdom.[81] In all enacted decisions, Christian bodies are "laid on the line"—they are vulnerable, as embodied beings, to undergo even the most quotidian sufferings, no matter how undramatic their form.[82] Again as Paul writes, the death of Jesus is to be always "carried" (*peripherō*) in the very body of the Christian, as something to which they are being "given up" (*paradidōmi*) (2 Cor 4:10–11).[83]

As we can see, the foundation for specific kenotic-transformations of the world is the fourfold kenotic relationality of Christ's continuing life as mediated through his church (his "body") in living acts. This kenotic life is no curse on the church but its very gift and life, a graced participation in the radical extension of Christic humanity into the world by the Spirit; in Moltmann's words: "[The Spirit] leads us into the 'fellowship of the sufferings of Christ', into conformity to his death, into the love which exposes

---

78. Moltmann, *Way of Jesus Christ*, 203–4.

79. Gorman, *Inhabiting the Cruciform God*, 288, see further, 283–89. See also Kar Yong Lim, *Sufferings of Christ Are Abundant in Us*, 160–92.

80. My translation, Gal 6:17.

81. See Medley, "'Always Carrying in the Body the Death of Jesus,'" 475–93.

82. Richard Beck renders a similar point, saying that "martyrdom is a discipline of daily living" consisting in "routine acts of daily self-expenditure" (*Slavery of Death*, 79).

83. Note that this is the same technical verb employed by Paul to speak of the "giving up" of Christ to the bodily suffering of the cross (see Rom 8:32; Gal 2:20; Eph 5:2).

itself to death because it is upheld by hope."[84] These kenotic dimensions of Christian life constitute the church's identity fundamentally.[85] Moltmann's capacious kenotic vision for ecclesiology and praxis is powerfully summed by Richard Bauckham:

> The Church which finds its identity in identification with the crucified Christ can be involved in the world only be identification with those with whom Christ identified. The principle of its life cannot be the love of like for like, but openness to those who are different[.] The Church's critical openness to the world in hope gains new dimensions when combined with the openness of suffering love.[86]

In a turn of phrase from Donald MacKinnon, Christian kenotic identity consists in both the "peril and the promise of the Incarnation."[87] The Word, that is, the Word-made-flesh, makes his authority known in the proclamation of his kingdom, and that kingdom is proclaimed in the specific activity of his church, his body, which enacts "new possibilities in reality" which have been "authored" by the Word.[88]

This brings to crescendo the program of this book. I have intended, through the employment of the critical lens offered by transformation theology and our strategic deployment of Moltmann's doctrine of Christ to offer a "rehabilitative" course for future kenotic christological reflection. In the three areas of christological discourse where we saw third-wave kenotic Christology struggle most characteristically—history, presence, and praxis—we have seen Moltmann's kenotic Christology proffer manifold insights and correctives.

Conclusion—The Kenotic Christ and the Transformed World

Once Moltmann's unique form of kenotic Christology was summarized in chapter 7, it remained the task of these final three chapters to apply our

---

84. Moltmann, *Theology of Hope*, 212.

85. Further recent argumentation for an intensely kenotic view of ecclesiology can be found in Gorman's trilogy: *Cruciformity* (2001); *Inhabiting the Cruciform God* (2009); *Becoming the Gospel* (2015).

86. Bauckham, *Moltmann: Messianic Theology in the Making*, 115–16.

87. MacKinnon, "Kenosis and Establishment," 33.

88. Moltmann and Lapide, "Dialogue," 158.

transformational heuristic questions to it. In so doing, I have argued that, while Moltmann occasionally suffers from a lack of clarity and rigor in his theological pronouncements, his overall vision of worldly transformation, the mediation of the ascended (and still kenotic) Christ, and the Christic role of the church in the continued enactment of kenotic-transformations, provides a broadly rehabilitative resource for ongoing work in kenotic Christology. Perhaps most importantly, we see how Moltmann's kenosis links together the bodily ministry of Jesus, the ongoing kenotic life of the ascended Christ, and the continuing enactment of kenotic relations via churchly praxis, in a way that informs, expands, and radicalizes elements of even transformation theology's christological reflections.

The following quotations from Oliver Davies and Moltmann have been reserved for this final concluding section, because in tandem they serve to exemplify the rehabilitative vision for churchly life and action that can empower further reflection on the (ongoing) transformational kenosis of Jesus Christ. Davies distills the themes thusly:

> In his exaltation then, the true life of Christ becomes also participatively the true en-Spirited and so also embodied life of the Church. This is not a new reality that is imposed upon us, but it comes rather through the perfecting of our human freedom, which is at the core of our own intentionality, through Christ's own freedom in act as communicated through the Holy Spirit. If we come to live by the power of his intentionality, we live also according to our own free distinctiveness and integrity, or what makes us truly ourselves.[89]

In this study we have seen, through textual evidence and logical connection, Moltmann's agreement with these ideas. But what Moltmann's Christology adds to them is of monumental importance: *their inalienably kenotic character*, in both a christological and Christic sense, understood in a robust fourfold relationally, and calling the human self to open, transformative vulnerability as the extension of Christ's will and life. As Moltmann says:

> It is true that in a world of high consumption, where anything and everything is possible, nothing is so humanizing as love, and a conscious interest in the life of others, particularly in the life of the oppressed. *For love leaves us open to wounding and disappointment. It makes us ready to suffer.* It leads us out of isolation into a fellowship with others, with people different from ourselves, and

---

89. Davies, *Theology of Transformation*, 134.

> this fellowship is always associated with suffering. *It changes the world*, in so far as it puts life into a static situation and overcomes the death urge which turns everything into a possession or an instrument of power.[90]

Such a quotation is striking in its resonance with the themes we have explored, even more so because it occurs in Moltmann's earliest major christological work: *The Crucified God*. It affirms, in a foundational way, the trajectory of this study: *Christ, theology, and the life of the church cannot be sundered*. For theology to retreat from the world into conceptual abstraction and apologetic stratagems is to leave behind its very ground, its holy ground, its incarnate God. Theology must resolve, with the apostle Paul, "to know nothing but Jesus Christ and him crucified" so that faith "may not rest on human wisdom, but on God's power" (1 Cor 2:2,5).

---

90. Moltmann, *Crucified God*, 62–63, emphasis added. See also Bingaman, *All Things New*, 88–89.

Bibliography

Allen, David. *Hebrews*. New American Commentary 35. Nashville: B&H, 2010.
Allison, Dale C., Jr. "The Embodiment of God's Will: Jesus in Matthew." In *Seeking the Identity of Jesus: A Pilgrimage*, edited by Beverly Roberts Gaventa and Richard B. Hays, 131–46. Grands Rapids: Eerdmans, 2008.
Althouse, Peter. "Implications of the Kenosis of the Spirit for a Creational Eschatology: A Pentecostal Engagement with Jürgen Moltmann." In *The Spirit Renews the Face of the Earth,* edited by A. Yong, 155–73. Eugene, OR: Pickwick, 2009.
———. *Spirit of the Last Days: Pentecostal Eschatology in Dialogue with Jürgen Moltmann.* London/New York, T. & T. Clark, 2003.
Anderson, James. *Paradox in Christian Theology: An Analysis of Its Presence, Character, and Epistemic Status.* Exeter: Paternoster, 2007.
Athanasius. *Orationes I.* In *The Orations of St. Athanasius: Against the Arians*, translated by W. Bright, 1–67. Oxford: Clarendon, 1873.
Baillie, D. M. *God Was in Christ.* New York: Scribners, 1948.
Balthasar, Hans urs Von. *Mysterium Paschale.* Translated by Aidan Nichols. Edinburgh: T. & T. Clark, 1990.
Barth, Karl. *Church Dogmatics*, Vol. I/2. Translated by G. W. Bromiley. Edinburgh: T. & T. Clark, 2009.
Barth, Karl. *Church Dogmatics*, Vol. II/1. Translated by G. W. Bromiley. Edinburgh: T. & T. Clark, 2000.
———. *Church Dogmatics*, Vol. IV/1. Translated by G. W. Bromiley. Edinburgh: T. & T. Clark, 2010.
———. *The Epistle to the Philippians.* Translated by J. W. Leith. Richmond, VA: John Knox, 1962.
———. *The Word of God and the Word of Man.* Translated by Douglas Horton. London: Hodder and Stoughton, 1928.
Bauckham, Richard. *God Crucified: Monotheism and Christology in the New Testament.* Grand Rapids: Eerdmans, 1999.
———. "The Future of Jesus Christ." *Scottish Bulletin of Evangelical Theology* 16 (1997) 97–110.
———. *Jesus and the God of Israel: God Crucified and Other Studies on the New Testament's Christology of Divine Identity.* Grand Rapids: Eerdmans, 2009.
———. "Moltmann's Messianic Christology." *Scottish Journal of Theology* 44 (1991) 319–31.
———. *Moltmann: Messianic Theology in the Making.* London: Marshall Pickering, 1987.
———. *Theology of Jürgen Moltmann.* Edinburgh: T. & T. Clark, 1995.
Beck, Richard. *The Slavery of Death.* Eugene, OR: Cascade, 2014.

Beck, T. David. *The Holy Spirit and the Renewal of All Things: Pneumatology in Paul and Jürgen Moltmann.* Eugene, OR: Pickwick, 2007.

Berkhof, Louis. *Systematic Theology, Volume 2.* Grand Rapids: Eerdmans, 1938.

Bingaman, Brock. *All Things New: The Trinitarian Nature of the Human Calling in Maximus the Confessor and Jürgen Moltmann.* Edinburgh: James Clarke and Co., 2015.

Bock, Darrell. *The NIV Application Commentary: Luke.* Grand Rapids: Zondervan, 1996.

Bonhoeffer, Dietrich. *Christ the Center.* Translated by E. H. Robertson. San Francisco: Harper, 1978.

———. *Discipleship.* Minneapolis: Fortress, 2015.

———. *Ethics.* Minneapolis: Fortress, 2005.

———. *Letters and Papers from Prison.* Minneapolis: Fortress, 2015.

Bonzo, J. Matthew. *Indwelling the Forsaken Other: The Trinitarian Ethics of Jürgen Moltmann.* Eugene, OR: Pickwick, 2009.

Brown, David. *Divine Humanity: Kenosis Explored and Defended.* London: SCM, 2010.

———. *The Divine Trinity.* London: Duckworth, 1985.

Bruce, A. B. *The Humiliation of Christ.* 4th ed. Edinburgh, T. & T. Clark, 1895.

Burge, Gary. *The Anointed Community: The Holy Spirit in the Johannine Tradition.* Grand Rapids: Eerdmans, 1987.

Bulgakov, Sergius. *The Lamb of God.* Translated by Boris Jakim. Grand Rapids: Eerdmans, 2008.

Buxton, Graham. "Moltmann on Creation." In *Jürgen Moltmann and Evangelical Theology: A Critical Engagement,* edited by S. W. Chung, 40–68. Eugene, OR: Pickwick, 2012.

Calvin, John. *Institutes of the Christian Religion.* Translated by H. Beveridge. Edinburgh: The Calvin Translation Society, 1845.

Carroll, John T. *Luke: A Commentary.* Louisville, KY: Westminster John Knox, 2012.

Cassirer, Ernst. *Philosophy of the Enlightenment.* 3rd ed. Princeton: Princeton University Press, 2009.

Coakley, Sarah. "Does Kenosis Rest on a Mistake? Three Kenotic Models in Patristic Exegesis." In *Exploring Kenotic Christology,* edited by C. Stephen Evans, 246–64. Oxford: Oxford University Press, 2006.

———. "The Identity of the Risen Jesus: Finding Jesus Christ in the Poor." In *Searching for the Identity of Jesus,* edited by B. R. Gaventa and R. Hays, 301–22. Grand Rapids: Eerdmans, 2008.

———. "*Kenosis* and Subversion." In *Powers and Submissions: Spirituality, Philosophy, and Gender,* 3–39. Oxford: Wiley-Blackwell, 2002.

———. "What Does Chalcedon Solve and What Does It Not? Some Reflections on the Status and Meaning of the Chalcedonian 'Definition.'" In *The Incarnation,* edited by S. T. Davis et al., 143–63. Oxford: Oxford University Press, 2002.

Congar, Yves. *I Believe in the Holy Spirit.* Translated by D. Smith. New York: Seabury, 1983.

Connor, Timothy G. *The Kenotic Trajectory of the Church in the Theology of Donald MacKinnon.* London: Continuum, 2011.

Cook, Michael. *The Jesus of Faith: A Study in Christology.* Mahwah, NJ: Paulist, 1981.

Cooper, Ian. "Reading Beyond Community: D.F. Strauss's *Das Leben Jesu* and Nietzsche's *Also sprach Zarathustra*." *The Modern Language Review* 103 (2008) 456–70.

Cooper, John W. *Panentheism: The Other God of the Philosophers.* Grand Rapids: Baker, 2006.

Cosden, Darrell. *A Theology of Work: Work and the New Creation.* Cumbria, UK: Paternoster, 2004.

Craffert, Pieter. "'Seeing' a Body into Being: Reflections on Scholarly Interpretations of the Nature and Reality of Jesus' Resurrected Body." *Religion and Theology,* 9 (2002) 89–107.

Crisp, Oliver. *Jonathan Edwards on God and Creation.* New York: Oxford University Press, 2012.

Crouter, Richard. *Friedrich Schleiermacher: Between Enlightenment and Romanticism.* Cambridge: Cambridge University Press, 2005.

Crysdale, Cynthia. *Embracing Travail, Retrieving the Cross Today.* New York/London: Continuum, 2000.

Cupitt, Don. "The Christ of Christendom." In *The Myth of God Incarnate,* edited by John Hick. London: SCM, 1977.

Dalimayr, Fred. "The Discourse of Modernity: Hegel and Habermas." *Journal of Philosophy.* 84 (1987) 682–92.

Davies, Oliver. "Evolution, Language and the Biblical Text: Towards a Theological Synthesis." In *Theologians on Scripture,* edited by Angus Paddison, 37–52. London/New York: Bloomsbury T. & T. Clark, 2016.

———. "The Interrupted Body." In *Transformation Theology,* edited by Oliver Davies et al., 37–61. New York/London: T. & T. Clark, 2007.

———. "Lost Heaven." In *Transformation Theology,* edited by Oliver Davies et al., 11–36. New York/London: T. & T. Clark, 2007.

———. *Theology of Compassion: Metaphysics of Difference and the Renewal of Tradition.* London: SCM, 2003.

———. *Theology of Transformation: Faith, Freedom, and the Christian Act.* Oxford: Oxford University Press, 2013.

Davies, Oliver, et al., eds. *Transformation Theology.* New York/London: T. & T. Clark, 2007.

Davis, Stephen. "John Hick on Incarnation and Trinity." In *The Trinity,* edited by S.T. Davis et al., 251–72. Oxford University Press, 1999.

———. "Is Kenosis Orthodox?" In *Exploring Kenotic Christology,* edited by C. Stephen Evans, 246–64. Oxford: Oxford University Press, 2006.

———. *Logic and the Nature of God.* Grand Rapids: Eerdmans, 1983.

———. "The Metaphysics of Kenosis." In *The Metaphysics of the Incarnation,* edited by Anna Marmodoro and Jonathan Hill, 114–33. Oxford: Oxford University Press, 2011.

———. "Jesus Christ: Savior or Guru?" In *Encountering Jesus: A Debate on Christology,* edited by S.T. Davis, 38–59. Atlanta: John Knox, 1988.

Davis, Stephen, and C. S. Evans. "Conclusion: The Promise of Kenosis." In *Exploring Kenotic Christology,* edited by C. Stephen Evans, 313–21. Oxford: Oxford University Press, 2006.

Dawe, Donald. *The Form of a Servant: An Historical Analysis of the Kenotic Motif.* Westminster, 1963.

Dawson, Gerrit Scott. *Jesus Ascended: The Meaning of Christ's Continuing Incarnation.* London/New York: T. & T. Clark, 2004.

DeHart, Paul J. "Ter mundus accipit infinitum: The Dogmatic Coordinates of Schleiermacher's Trinitarian Treatise." *Neue Zeitschrift für Theologie und Religionphilosophie* 52 (2010) 17–39.

De Nys, Martin J. *Hegel and Theology.* Bloomsbury: London, 2009.

Dembski, W. "Schleiermacher's Metaphysical Critique of Miracles." *Scottish Journal of Theology* 49 (1996) 443–65.

Duttenhaver, Katrina. *Love's Labor: The Relational Self in Simone Weil's Mystical-Political Theology*. PhD diss., University of Notre Dame, 2010.

Earman, John. *Hume's Abject Failure: The Argument Against Miracles*. New York: Oxford University Press, 2000.

Edwards, Denis. *Deep Incarnation: God's Suffering Love for Creatures* (Maryknoll, NY: Orbis Books, 2019).

Erdozain, Dominic. *The Soul of Doubt: The Religious Roots of Unbelief from Luther to Marx*. New York: Oxford University Press, 2016.

Evans, C. Stephen. *The Christ of History and the Jesus of Faith: The Incarnational Narrative as History*. New York: Oxford University Press, 1996.

———. *The Historical Christ and the Jesus of Faith: The Incarnational Narratives as History*. Oxford: Clarendon, 1996.

———. "Introduction: Understanding Jesus the Christ as Human and Divine." In *Exploring Kenotic Christology*, edited by C. Stephen Evans, 1–24. Oxford: Oxford University Press, 2006.

———. "Kenotic Christology and the Nature of God." In *Exploring Kenotic Christology*, edited by C. Stephen Evans, 190–217. Oxford: Oxford University Press, 2006.

———. "Methodological Naturalism in Historical Biblical Scholarship." In *Jesus and the Restoration of Israel: A Critical Assessment of N.T. Wright's Jesus and the Victory of God*, edited by Carey C. Newman, 180–205. Downers Grove, IL: InterVarsity, 1999.

———. "The Self-Emptying of Love: Some Thoughts on Kenotic Christology." In *The Incarnation: An Interdisciplinary Symposium on the Incarnation of the Son of God*, edited by Stephen T. Davis et al., 246–72. Oxford: Oxford University Press, 2002.

Farrow, Douglas. *Ascension and Ecclesia: On the Significance of the Doctrine of the Ascension for Ecclesiology and Christian Cosmology*. Edinburgh: T. & T. Clark, 1999.

———. *Ascension Theology*. New York: T. & T. Clark, 2011.

Fee, Gordon. *God's Empowering Presence: The Holy Spirit in the Letters of Paul*. Peabody, MA: Hendrickson, 1994.

———. "The New Testament and Kenosis Christology." In *Exploring Kenotic Christology*, edited by C. Stephen Evans, 25–44. Oxford: Oxford University Press, 2006.

———. *Paul's Letter to the Philippians*. New International Commentary on the New Testament. Grand Rapids: Eerdmans, 1995.

Feenstra, Ron. "A Kenotic Christological Model of Understanding the Divine Attributes." In *Exploring Kenotic Christology*, edited by C. Stephen Evans, 139–64. Oxford: Oxford University Press, 2006.

———. "Reconsidering Kenotic Christology." In *Trinity, Incarnation, and Atonement: Philosophical and Theological Essays*, edited by R. J. Feenstra and C. Plantinga, 128–52. Indiana: University of Notre Dame Press, 1989.

Feske, Millicent. "Christ and Suffering in Moltmann's Thought." *The Asbury Theological Journal* 55 (2000) 85–104.

Feuerbach, Ludwig. *The Essence of Christianity*. Tranlated by George Eliot. Cambridge: Cambridge University Press, 2011.

Fisk, Bruce. "The Odyssey of Christ: A Novel Context for Philippians 2:6–11." In *Exploring Kenotic Christology*, edited by C. Stephen Evans, 45–73. Oxford: Oxford University Press, 2006.

Forrest, Peter. *Developmental Theism: From Pure Will to Unbounded Love*. Oxford University Press, 2007.

———. "The Incarnation: A Philosophical Case for Kenosis." *Religious Studies* 36 (2000) 127–40.
Funk, Robert W. *The Five Gospels: What Did Jesus Really Say?* New York: Harper Collins, 1997.
Gibbs, John G. "The Relation Between Creation and Redemption According to Phil. II 5–11." *Novum Testamentum* 12 (1970) 270–83.
Gockel, Matthias. "Mediating Theology in Germany." In *The Blackwell Companion to Nineteenth Century Theology*, edited by David Ferguson, 301–18. Wiley-Blackwell, 2010.
Gore, Charles. *Dissertations on Subjects Connected with the Incarnation*. New York: Charles Scribner, 1895.
———. "Holy Spirit and Inspiration." In *Lux Mundi: A Series of Studies in the Religion of the Incarnation*, edited by Charles Gore, 315–64. London: John Murray, 1890.
Gorman, Michael J. *Becoming the Gospel: Paul, Participation, and Mission*. Grand Rapids: Eerdmans, 2015.
———. *Cruciformity: Paul's Narrative Spirituality of the Cross*. Grand Rapids: Eerdmans, 2001
———. *Inhabiting the Cruciform God: Kenosis, Justification, and Theosis in Paul's Narrative Spirituality*. Grand Rapids: Eerdmans, 2009.
Gorringe, Timothy. *Redeeming Time: Atonement Through Education*. London: Dartman, Longman & Todd, 1986.
Granados, Jose. "The First Fruits of the Flesh and the First Fruits of the Spirit: The Mystery of the Ascension." *Communio* 38 (2011) 6–38.
Gregersen, N. H. "Deep Incarnation and Kenosis: In, With, Under, and As: A Response to Ted Peters." *Dialog* 52 (2013) 251–62.
Gregory, Brad. *The Unintended Reformation: How a Religious Revolution Secularized Society*. Cambridge, MA: Harvard University Press, 2015.
Gregersen, N. H. "Cur Deus Caro: Jesus and the Cosmos Story." *Theology and Science* 11 (2013) 370–93.
Grenz, Stanley, and Roger Olson. *20th Century Theology: God and the World in a Transitional Age*. Downers Grove, IL: InterVarsity, 1992.
Griffin, D. R. *God, Power, and Evil: A Process Theodicy*. Louisville, KY: Westminster John Knox, 2004.
Grillmeier, Alloys. *Christ in Christian Tradition: Volume 2, Part 1: From the Council of Chalcedon to Gregory the Great*. Atlanta: John Knox, 1987.
Groenhout, Ruth. "Kenosis and Feminist Theory." In *Exploring Kenotic Christology*, edited by C. Stephen Evans, 291–312. Oxford: Oxford University Press, 2006.
Gunton, Colin. *Christ and Creation*. Eugene, OR: Wipf & Stock, 2005.
———. *Yesterday and Today: A Study of Continuities in Christology*. London: SPCK, 1997.
Gutierrez, Gustavo. *A Theology of Liberation*. Translated by Caridad Inda and John Eagleson. Maryknoll, NY: Orbis, 1973.
Habets, Myk. *The Anointed Son: A Trinitarian Spirit Christology*. Eugene, OR: Pickwick, 2010.
Hall, Francis J. *The Kenotic Theory*. New York/London & Bombay: Longmans, Green, and Co., 1898.
Hampson, Daphne. "Response." In *Swallowing a Fishbone? Feminist Theologians Debate Christianity*, edited by D. Hampson, 112–24. London: SPCK, 1996.
———. *Theology and Feminism*. Oxford: Wiley-Blackwell, 1991.

Harteshorne, Charles. *Omnipotence and Other Theological Mistakes*. New York: State University of New York, 1984.
Harvie, Timothy. *Jürgen Moltmann's Ethics of Hope*. Burlington, VT: Ashgate, 2009.
———. "Living the Future: The Kingdom of God in the Theologies of Jürgen Moltmann and Wolfhart Pannenberg." *International Journal of Systematic Theology* 10 (2008) 149–64.
Hawthorne, Gerald. "In the Form of God and Equal to God." In *Where Christology Began*, edited by R. P. Martin and B. J. Dodd, 96–110. Louisville, KY: Westminster John Knox, 1998.
———. *Philippians*. Word Biblical Commentary. Waco, TX: Word, 1983.
———. *The Presence and the Power: The Significance of the Holy Spirit in the Life and Ministry of Jesus*. Eugene, OR: Wipf & Stock, 1991.
Hebblethwaite, Brian. "Jesus, God Incarnate." In *The Incarnation: Collected Essays*, 21–26. Cambridge: Cambridge University Press, 1987.
Head, Jonathan. "Scripture and Moral Examples in Pietism and Kant's *Religion*." *Irish Theological Quarterly* 83 (2018) 217–34.
Hegel, G. W. F. *Lectures on the Philosophy of Religion*. Translated and edited by Peter Hodgson. Berkeley: University of California Press, 1988.
———. *Vorlesungen über die Philosophie der Weltgeschichte*. Edited by Georg Lasson. Leipzig: F. Meiner, 1920.
Heil, John Paul. *Philippians*. Atlanta: SBL, 2010.
Herbert, T. D. *Kenosis and Priesthood: Towards a Protestant Re-Evaluation of the Ordained Ministry*. Carlisle: Paternoster, 2009.
Hick, John. "Christology and the World Religions." In *The Myth of God Incarnate*, edited by John Hick, 167–85. Louisville, KY: Westminster, 1977.
———. "An Inspiration Christology for a Religiously Plural World." In *Encountering Jesus: A Debate on Christology*, edited by S. T. Davis, 5–21. Atlanta: John Knox, 1988.
———. "Literal and Metaphorical Christologies." In *Jesus Then and Now: Images of Jesus in History and Christology*, edited by M. Meyer and C. Hughes, 143–53. Harrisburg, PA: Trinity International, 2001.
Hitchens, Christopher. *God Is Not Great: How Religion Poisons Everything*. New York: Hachette, 2007.
Höhne, David. "Moltmann on Salvation." In *Jürgen Moltmann and Evangelical Theology: A Critical Engagement*, edited by S. W. Chung, 152–73. Eugene, OR: Wipf & Stock, 2012.
Hopkins, Luke. *The Exposed Life: The Kenotic Ecclesiology of Donald MacKinnon*, BTh Thesis, University of Newcastle, 2011.
Horrell, David G. *Solidarity and Difference: A Contemporary Reading of Paul's Ethics*. New York: T. & T. Clark, 2005.
Horrell, J. Scott. "The Eternal Son of God in the Social Trinity." In *Jesus in Trinitarian Perspective*, edited by Fred Sanders and Klaus Issler, 44–79. Nashville: B&H, 2007.
Huber, W. *Konflikt und Konsens: Studien zur Ethik der Verantwortung*. Münschen: Kaiser, 1990.
Hume, David. *Enquiry Concerning Human Understanding (1772)*. Cambridge: Cambridge University Press, 2007.
Hurtado, Larry. "Jesus as Lordly Example in Philippians 2:5–11." In *From Jesus to Paul*, edited by P. Richardson and J. C. Hurd, 113–26. Waterloo, ON: Wilfred Laurier University Press, 1984.

Issler, Klaus. "Jesus' Example: Prototype of the Dependent, Spirit-Filled Life." In *Jesus in Trinitarian Perspective*, edited by Fred Sanders and Klaus Issler, 189–225. Nashville: B&H, 2007.

Jacobs, Alan. *Original Sin: A Cultural History*. New York: HarperCollins, 2009.

Janz, Paul. "The Coming Righteousness." In *Transformation Theology*, edited by Oliver Davies et al., 89–113. New York: T. & T. Clark, 2007.

———. *The Command of Grace: A New Theological Apologetics*. London: T. & T. Clark, 2009.

———. *God, the Mind's Desire*. Cambridge: Cambridge University Press, 2004.

———. "Revelation as Divine Causality." In *Transformation Theology*, edited by Oliver Davies et al., 63–88. New York: T. & T. Clark, 2007.

———. "What is 'Transformation Theology'?" *American Theological Inquiry* 2 (2009) 9–28.

Jeroncic, A. *A Peaceable Logic of Self-Integration: Jürgen Moltmann's Theological Anthropology and the Postmodern Self*. PhD diss., University of Chicago, 2008.

Jowers, Dennis. "The Theology of the Cross as Theology of the Trinity: A Critique of Jürgen Moltmann's Staurocentric Trinitarianism." *Tyndale Bulletin* 52 (2001) 248–50.

Kant, Immanuel. *The Critique of Pure Reason*. Translated by W. S. Pluhar. Cambridge: Hackett, 1996.

Kapic, Kelly M., and Wesley Vander Lugt. "The Ascension of Jesus and the Descent of the Holy Spirit in Patristic Perspective: A Theological Reading." *Evangelical Quarterly* 79 (2007) 23–33.

Kärkkäinen, Veli-Matti. *Christ and Reconciliation*. Grand Rapids: Eerdmans, 2013.

———. *Christology: A Global Introduction*. Grand Rapids: Baker Academic, 2003.

Keller, Catherine. "Scoop Up the Water and the Moon is in Your Hands: Feminist Theology and Dynamic Self-Emptying." In *The Emptying God: A Buddhist-Jewish-Christian Conversation*, edited by J. B. Cobb and C. Ives, 102–15. Maryknoll, NY: Orbis, 1990.

Kelly, Anthony. *Upward: Faith, Church, and the Ascension of Christ*. Collegeville, MN: Liturgical, 2014.

Kelsey, Catherine. *Thinking About Christ with Schleiermacher*. Louisville, KY: Westminster John Knox, 2003.

Kim, Grace Ji-Sun. "Jürgen Moltmann." In *Beyond the Pale: Reading Theology from the Margins*, edited by M. A. De La Torre and S. M. Floyd-Thomas, 245–54. Louisville, KY: Westminster John Knox, 2004.

Kjøsvik, Idar. *Christus Praesens: Jürgen Moltmanns Geschichtverständnis und die Lehre vom gegenwärtigen Christus*. Neukirchener Verlag, 2008.

Kurz, W. "Kenotic Imitation of Paul and of Christ in Philippians 2 and 3." In *Discipleship in the New Testament*, edited by Fernando F. Segovia, 103–26. Philadelphia: Fortress, 1985.

Langford, Jerome. *Galileo, Science, and the Church*. Ann Arbor: University of Michigan Press, 1992.

Langmead, Ross. *The Word Made Flesh: Towards an Incarnational Missiology*. American Society of Missiology Dissertation Series. Lanham, MD: University Press of America, 2004.

Law, David. *Kierkegaard's Kenotic Christology*. Oxford: Oxford University Press, 2013.

———. "Luther's Legacy and the Origins of Kenotic Christology." *Bulletin of the John Rylands Library* 93 (2017) 41–68.

Lawson, John Stewart. *Conflict in Christology. A study of British and American. Christology from 1899-1914*. London, SPCK, 1947.
Lefsrud, Sigurd. *Kenosis in Theosis*. Eugene, OR: Pickwick, 2020.
Lessing, G. E. "On the Proof of the Spirit and the Power." In *Lessing: Philosophical and Theological Writings*, edited by H. B. Nisbet, 83–88. Cambridge: Cambridge University Press, 2005.
Levinas, Emmanuel. *Totality and Infinity*. Translated by A. Lingis. Pittsburgh: Duquesne University Press, 1969.
Lewis, Alan. *Between Cross and Resurrection: A Theology of Holy Saturday*. Grand Rapids: Eerdmans, 2001.
Lim, Kar Yong. *'The Sufferings of Christ Are Abundant in Us': A Narrative Dynamics Investigation of Paul's Sufferings in 2 Corinthians*. London: T. & T. Clark, 2009.
Linahan, Jane. *The Kenosis of God and Reverence for the Particular: A Conversation with Jürgen Moltmann*. PhD diss., Marquette University, 1999.
Liston, Gregory, J. *The Anointed Church: Toward a Third Article Ecclesiology*. Minneapolis: Fortress, 2015.
Livingston, James. *Modern Christian Thought: The Enlightenment and Nineteenth Century*. Minneapolis: Fortress, 2006.
Long, D. Stephen, *Hebrews*. Louisville, KY: Westminster John Knox, 2011.
Loomer, B. "Paul Tillich's Theology of Correlation." *The Journal of Religion* 36 (1956) 150–56.
Lösel, Steffen. *Kreuzwege: Ein ökumenisches Gespräch mit Hans Urs von Balthasar*. Zürich: Ferdinand Schöningh, 2001.
Luy, David. *Dominus Mortus: Martin Luther on the Incorruptibility of God in Christ*. Minneapolis: Augsburg Fortress, 2014.
MacKinnon, Donald. "Does Faith Create Its Own Objects?" In *Philosophy and the Burden of Theological Honesty*, edited by John McDowell, 209–22. London: T. & T. Clark, 2011.
———. "Kenosis and Establishment." In *The Stripping of the Altars*, 13–40. London: The Fontana Library, 1969.
———. "The Myth of God Incarnate." In *Themes in Theology: The Three-Fold Cord*, 137–44. Edinburgh, T. & T. Clark, 1987.
———. "Our Contemporary Christ." In *Borderlands of Theology and Other Essays*, edited by G. W. Roberts and D. E. Smucker, 82–89. Eugene, OR: Wipf & Stock, 2011.
———. "Some Notes on the Irreversibility of Time." In *Explorations in Theology*, 90–98. London: SCM, 1979.
———. "'Substance' in Christology: A Cross-Bench View." In *Philosophy and the Burden of Theological Honesty*, edited by John McDowell, 237–54. New York: T. & T. Clark, 2011.
———. "The Tomb Was Empty." In *Philosophy and the Burden of Theological Honesty*, edited by John McDowell, 255–60. New York: T. & T. Clark, 2011.
Mackintosh, Hugh Ross. *The Doctrine of the Person of Jesus Christ*. New York: Charles Scribner's Sons, 1912.
Mariña, Jacqueline. "Christology and Anthropology in Friedrich Schleiermacher." In *The Cambridge Companion to Friedrich Schleiermacher*, 151–70. Cambridge: Cambridge University Press, 2005.
Marshall, I. H. *The Gospel of Luke*. New International Greek Testament Commentary. Grand Rapids: Eerdmans/Paternoster, 1978.

Marx, Karl. *Critique of Hegel's 'Philosophy of Right.'* Translated by Annette Jolin and Joseph O'Malley. Cambridge: Cambridge University Press, 1970.
McCormack, Bruce. "The Person of Christ." In *Mapping Modern Theology*, edited by Kelly Kapic and Bruce McCormack, 149–74. Grand Rapids: Baker, 2012.
McCormack, Bruce, and Kimlyn Bender. *Theology as Conversation: The Significance of Dialogue for Contemporary Theology*. Grand Rapids: Eerdmans, 2009.
McDougall, Joy Ann. *Pilgrimage of Love: Moltmann on Trinity and the Christian Life*. New York: Oxford University Press, 2005.
McGrath, Alister. *Luther's Theology of the Cross*. Oxford: Blackwell, 1985.
———. *The Making of Modern German Christology, 1750–1990*. Downers Grove, IL: Intervarsity, 1994.
McInroy, Mark. "To Be Like God Is to 'Give Assistance Freely, Impartially, and Universally': A Patristic-Constructive Modle of *Theosis* as Hospitality to the Neighbor." Paper Presented at the 2021 Annual Meeting of the American Academy of Religion (San Antonio, Texas).
Medley, Mark. "'Always Carrying in the Body the Death of Jesus': Baptism, Martyrdom, and Quotidian Existence in Rowan Williams' Theology." *Anglican Theological Review* 94 (2012) 475–93.
Meeks, Douglas. "Introduction." In *The Passion for Life: A Messianic Lifestyle,* translated by Douglas Meeks, 13–18. Minneapolis: Fortress, 2007.
———. *Origins of the Theology of Hope*. Minneapolis: Fortress, 1974.
Mercedes, Anna. *Power For: Feminism and Christ's Self Giving*. Edinburgh: T. & T. Clark, 2011.
Moltmann, Jürgen. "Adventure of Theological Ideas." *Religious Studies Review* 22 (1996) 102–5.
———. "Antwort auf die kritik an 'Der gekreuzigte Gott.'" In *Diskussion über Jürgen Moltmanns Buch 'Der gekreuzigte Gott'*, edited by M. Welker, 165–90. Munich: Chr. Kaiser Verlag, 1979.
———. *A Broad Place: An Autobiography*. Translated by Margaret Kohl. Minneapolis: Fortress, 2008.
———. "Christian Theology and Its Problems Today." In *The Experiment Hope*, edited and translated by M. Douglas Meeks, 1–14. Philadelphia: Fortress, 1975.
———. *The Crucified God*. Translated by Margaret Kohl. Minneapolis: Fortress, 1993.
———. *The Coming of God*. Translated by Margaret Kohl. Minneapolis: Fortress, 2000.
———. "The Christian Hope—Messianic or Transcendent?" In *History and the Triune God*, translated by John Bowden, 91–109. London: SCM, 1991.
———. *The Church in the Power of the Spirit*. Translated by Margaret Kohl. Minneapolis: Fortress, 1993.
———. "Come Holy Spirit! Renew the Whole of Creation." In *History and the Triune God*, translated by John Bowden, 70–79. London: SCM, 1991.
———. "Creation as an Open System." In *Future of Creation: Collected Essays*, translated by Margaret Kohl, 115–30. Minneapolis: Fortress, 2007.
———. "Creation, Covenant, Glory." In *History and the Triune God*, translated by John Bowden, 125–42. London: SCM, 1991.
———. "The Cross as Military Symbol of Sacrifice." In *Cross Examinations,* edited by Marit Trelstad, 259–63. Minneapolis: Fortress, 2006.
———. "The Crucified God and Apathetic Man." In *The Experiment Hope*, edited and translated by M. Douglas Meeks, 69–84. Philadelphia: Fortress, 1975.

———. "Die Kategorie Novum in Der Christlichen Theologie." In *Ernst Bloch Zu Ehren*, edited by Siegfried Unseld, 243–63. Frankfurt: Suhrkamp, 1965.
———. *Experiences of God*. Translated by Margaret Kohl. Minneapolis: Fortress, 2007.
———. *Experiences in Theology*. Translated by Margaret Kohl. Minneapolis: Fortress, 2000.
———. *Ethics of Hope*. Translated by Margaret Kohl. Minneapolis: Fortress, 2012).
———. *God for a Secular Society: The Public Relevance of Theology*. Translated by Margaret Kohl. Minneapolis: Fortress, 1999.
———. *God in Creation*. Translated by Margaret Kohl. Minneapolis: Fortress, 1993.
———. "God is Unselfish Love." In *The Emptying God: A Buddhist-Jewish-Christian Conversation*, edited by J. B. Cobb and C. Ives, 116–24. Maryknoll, NY: Orbis, 1990.
———. "Gottesoffenbarung und Wahrheitsfrage." In *Parrhesia: Karl Barth zum actzigsten Geburstag*, edited by Eberhard Busch, 149–72. Zurich: Evz-Verlag, 1966.
———. "I Believe in Jesus Christ, the Only Son of God: Brotherly Talk of Christ." In *History and the Triune God*, translated by John Bowden, 31–43. London: SCM, 1991.
———. "I Believe in God the Father: Patriarchal or Non-Patriarchal Talk of God?" In *History and the Triune God*, translated by John Bowden, 1–18. London: SCM, 1991.
———. *In the End, the Beginning: The Life of Hope*. Translated Margaret Kohl. Minneapolis: Fortress, 2004.
———. "Is God Incarnate in All That Is?" In *Incarnation: On the Scope and Depth of Christology*, edited by N. H. Gregersen, 119–32. Minneapolis: Fortress, 2015.
———. *Jesus Christ for Today's World*, translated Margaret Kohl. Minneapolis: Fortress, 1994.
———. "Justice for Victims and Perpetrators." In *History and the Triune God*, translated by John Bowden, 44–56. London: SCM, 1991.
———. "Justification and the New Creation." In *Future of Creation: Collected Essays*, translated by Margaret Kohl, 149–71. Minneapolis: Fortress, 2007.
———. *On Human Dignity: Political Theology and Ethics*. Translated by M. D. Meeks. Minneapolis: Fortress, 2007.
———. *The Passion for Life: A Messianic Lifestyle*. Translated by Douglas Meeks. Minneapolis: Fortress, 2007.
———. *The Power of the Powerless*. Translated by Margaret Kohl. London: SCM, 1983.
———. *Science and Wisdom*. Translated by Margaret Kohl. Minneapolis: Fortress, 2003.
———. *The Source of Life: The Holy Spirit and the Theology of Life*. Translated by Margaret Kohl. Minneapolis: Fortress, 1997.
———. *The Spirit of Life*. Translated by Margaret Kohl. Minneapolis: Fortress, 2001.
———. *Sun of Righteousness, Arise! God's Future for Humanity and the Earth*. Translated by Margaret Kohl. Minneapolis: Fortress, 2010.
———. "Theologia Reformata et Semper Reformanda." In *Toward the Future of Reformed Theology*, edited by David Willis-Watkins, 120–35. Grand Rapids: Eerdmans, 1998.
———. "Theology as Eschatology." In *The Future of Hope*, edited F. Herzog, 1–24. New York: Herder & Herder, 1970.
———. *Theology of Hope*. Translated by James W. Leitch. Minneapolis: Fortress, 1993.
———. "The Theology of the Cross Today." In *Future of Creation: Collected Essays*, translated by Margaret Kohl, 59–79. Minneapolis: Fortress, 2007.
———. "The Trinitarian History of God." In *Future of Creation: Collected Essays*, translated by Margaret Kohl, 80–96. Minneapolis: Fortress, 2007.

———. "Trinitarian Personhood of the Spirit." In *Advents of the Spirit: An Introduction to the Current Study of Pneumatology*, edited by Lyle Dabney and B. E. Hinze, 302–14. Milwaukee: Marquette University Press, 2001.

———. "The Trinitarian Story of Jesus." In *History and the Triune God*, translated by John Bowden, 70–89. London: SCM, 1991.

———. *The Trinity and the Kingdom*. Translated by Margaret Kohl. Minneapolis: Fortress, 1993.

———. *The Way of Jesus Christ*. Translated by Margaret Kohl. Minneapolis: Fortress, 1993.

Moltmann, Jürgen, and Elisabeth Moltmann-Wendell. *Humanity in God*. New York: Pilgrim, 1983.

Moltmann, Jürgen, and Pinchas Lapide. "Dialogue." In *Jewish Monotheism and Christian Trinitarian Doctrine*, translated by Leonard Swindler, 59–81. Minneapolis: Fortress, 1981.

Moritz, J. M. "Deep Incarnation and the *Imago Dei*: The Cosmic Scope of the Incarnation in Light of the Messiah as the Renewed Adam." *Theology and Science* 11 (2013) 436–43.

Morris, Thomas. *The Logic of God Incarnate*. Cornell University Press, 1986.

———. "The Metaphysics of God Incarnate." In *Oxford Readings in Philosophical Theology*, edited by Michael Rea, 1:211–24. Oxford University Press, 2009.

Moule, C. F. D. "Further Reflexions on Philippians 2:5–11." In *Apostolic History and the Gospels*, edited by W. W. Gaque and R. P. Martin, 264–76. Grand Rapids: Eerdmans, 1970.

———. "The Manhood of Jesus in the New Testament." In *Christ, Faith, and History: Cambridge Studies in Christology*, edited by S. W. Sykes and J. P. Clayton, 95–110. Cambridge: Cambridge University Press, 1972.

Müller-Fahrenholz, Geiko. *The Kingdom and the Power: The Theology of Jürgen Moltmann* Minneapolis: Fortress, 2001.

Murphy, Nancey, and George F. R. Ellis. *On the Moral Nature of the Universe: Theology, Cosmology, and Ethics*. Minneapolis: Augsburg Fortress, 1996.

Neal, Ryan. "Jürgen Moltmann." In *Companion to the Theologians*, edited by Ian S. Markham, 461–71. West Sussex, UK: Wiley-Blackwell, 2009.

———. *Theology as Hope*. Princeton Theological Monograph Series 99. Eugene, OR: Pickwick, 2008.

van Niekerk, Pieter, and Nelus Niemandt. "The Radical Embodiment of God For a Christology of a New Era." *HTS Teologiese Studies/Theological Studies* 75 (2019).

Oakes, E. T. *Infinity Dwindled to Infancy: A Catholic and Evangelical Christology*. Grand Rapids: Eerdmans, 2011.

Olson, Roger. *The Journey of Modern Theology: From Reconstruction to Deconstruction*. Downers Grove, IL: InterVarsity, 2013.

O'Regan, Cyril. *The Heterodox Hegel*. Albany: State University of New York Press, 1994.

Page, Robert J. *Charles Gore, Anglican Apologist*. New York: Columbia University Press, 1955.

Pals, Daniel. *Ten Theories of Religion*. Oxford: Oxford University Press, 2021.

Pannenberg, Wolfhart. *Anthropology in Theological Perspective*. Translated by Matthew J. O'Connell. New York: T. & T. Clarke International, 1985.

———. "Die Aufnahme des philosophischen Gottesbegriffs als dogmatisches Problem der frühchristlichen Theologie." In *Grundfragen systematischer Theologie*, 1:296–346. Göttingen: Vandenhoeck & Ruprecht, 1967.

———. *Jesus—God and Man*, translated by L. L. Wilkins and D. A. Priebe. London: SCM, 1968.

Papanikolaou, Aristotle. "Person, *Kenosis* and Abuse: Hans Urs Von Balthasar and Feminist Theologies in Conversation." *Modern Theology* 19 (2003) 41–65.

Pinnock, Clark. *Flame of Love: A Theology of the Holy Spirit*. Downers Grove, IL: InterVarsity, 1999.

Polkinghorne, John, ed. *The Work of Love: Creation as Kenosis*. Grand Rapids: Eerdmans, 2001.

Prooijen, Ton van. *Limping but Blessed: Jürgen Moltmann's Search for a Liberating Anthropology*. Netherlands: Rodopi, 2004.

Purves, David R. "Relating Kenosis to Soteriology: Implications for Christian Ministry amongst Homeless People." *Horizons in Biblical Theology* 35 (2013) 70–90.

Quick, Oliver. "An Ethical Sermon." In *Doctrines of the Creed*, 80–85. London: Nisbet, 1938.

Ramsey, A. M. *An Era in Anglican Theology: From Gore to Temple*. London: Charles Scribner's Sons, 1960.

Reumann, John. *Philippians: A New Translation with Introduction and Commentary*. New Haven, CT: Yale University Press, 2008.

Reynolds, Thomas. *Vulnerable Communion: A Theology of Disability and Hospitality*. Grand Rapids: Brazos/Baker Academic, 2008.

Robinson, J. A. T. *The Body: A Study in Pauline Theology*. London: SCM, 1982.

Santmire, H. P. "So That He Might Fill All Things: Comprehending the Cosmic Love of Christ." *Dialog* 42 (2003) 257–78.

Schleiermacher, Friedrich. *The Christian Faith*. Edited by P. T. Nimmo. London/New York: T. & T. Clark, 2016.

———. *On Religion: Speeches to Its Culture Despisers*. Edited by Richard Crouter. Cambridge: Cambridge University Press, 1996.

Schmiechen, Peter. *Saving Power: Theories of Atonement and Forms of the Church*. Grand Rapids: Eerdmans, 2005.

Schmisek, Brian. "The Body of His Glory: Resurrection Imagery in Philippians 3:20–21." *Biblical Theology Bulletin* 43 (2013) 23–28.

Schönborn, Christoph. *God Sent His Son: A Contemporary Christology*. Translated by Henry Taylor San Fransisco: Ignatius, 2010.

Sedmak, Clemens. "The Disruptive Power of World Hunger." In *Transformation Theology*, edited by Oliver Davies et al., 115–41. New York: T. & T. Clark, 2007.

———. "The Wound of Knowledge: Epistemic Mercy and World Hunger." In *Transformation Theology*, edited by Oliver Davies et al., 142–66. New York: T. & T. Clark, 2007.

Senor, Thomas. "Drawing on Many Traditions: An Ecumenical Kenotic Christology." In *The Metaphysics of the Incarnation*, edited by Anna Marmodoro and Jonathan Hill, 88–113. Oxford: Oxford University Press, 2011.

Shults, F. LeRon. *Christology and Science*. Grand Rapids: Eerdmans, 2009.

———. *Reforming Theological Anthropology: After the Philosophical Turn to Relationality*. Grand Rapids: Eerdmans, 2003.

Shults, F. LeRon, and Jan-Olav Henriksen. *Saving Desire: The Seduction of Christian Theology*. Grand Rapids: Eerdmans, 2011.

Singh, Devin. "Resurrection as Surplus and Possibility: Moltmann and Ricoeur." *Scottish Journal of Theology* 61 (2008) 251–69.

Smith, James K. A. *Desiring the Kingdom: Worship, Worldview, and Cultural Formation*. Grand Rapids: Baker Academic, 2009.

Stein, Robert. *Luke*. New American Commentary Nashville: B&H Publishing, 1992.

Strawson, Peter. *Individuals: An Essay in Descriptive Metaphysics*. London: Methuen, 1977.

Strauss, D. F. *The Life of Jesus, Critically Examined*. Translated by George Eliot. Cambridge, MA: Harvard University Press, 1860.

Surin, Kenneth. "Some Aspects of the 'Grammar' of 'Incarnation' and 'Kenosis': Reflections Prompted by the Writings of Donald Mackinnon." In *Christ, Ethics, and Tragedy*, edited by K. Surin, 93–116. Cambridge: Cambridge University Press, 1989.

Swinburne, Richard. *The Christian God*. Oxford: Clarendon, 1994.

Sykes, S. W. "The Strange Persistence of Kenotic Christology." In *Being and Truth: Essays in Honor of John Macquarrie*, edited by Alistair Kee and Eugene T. Long, 349–75. London: SCM, 1986.

Tarnas, Richard. *The Passion of the Western Mind*. New York: Ballantine, 1991.

Taylor, Charles. *Sources of the Self: The Making of Modern Identity*. Cambridge: Cambridge University Press, 1989.

Taylor, Vincent. *The Person of Christ in New Testament Teaching*. London: Macmillan, 1958.

Thandeka. "Schleiermacher's Affekt Theology." *International Journal of Practical Theology*. 9 (2005) 197–216.

Thielicke, Helmut. *Modern Faith and Thought*. Grand Rapids: Eerdmans, 1990.

Thiselton, Anthony. *The First Epistle to the Corinthians: A Commentary on the Greek Text*. NIGTC. Grand Rapids: Eerdmans: 2000.

Thomasius, Gottfried. *Beiträge zur kirchlichen Christologie*. Erlangen: Theodor Bläsing, 1845.

Thompson, T. R. "Nineteenth Century Kenotic Christology." In *Exploring Kenotic Christology*, edited by C. Stephen Evans, 74–111. Oxford: Oxford University Press, 2006.

Tillich, Paul. *Systematic Theology*, Vol. 2. Chicago: University of Chicago Press, 2012.

Tindal, Matthew. *Christianity as Old as Creation: or, The Gospel, a Republication of the Religion of Nature*. Londo: S.N., 1730.

Torrance, T. F. *Space, Time, and Incarnation*. Edinburgh: T. & T. Clark, 1997.

Treat, Jeremy. "Exaltation In and Through Humiliation: Rethinking the States of Christ." In *Christology: Ancient and Modern*, edited by Oliver Crispand Fred Sanders, 96–114. Grand Rapids: Zondervan, 2013.

Tsui, Teresa Kuo-Yu. "Kenosis in the Letter of Paul to the Philippians." In *Godhead Here in Hiding*, edited by T. Merrigan and F. Glorieux, 242–52. Leuven: Uitgeverij Peeters, 2012.

Twelftree, Graham. *People of the Spirit: Exploring Luke's View of the Church*. Grand Rapids: Baker Academic, 2009.

Vial, Theodore. *Schleiermacher: A Guide for the Perplexed*. London: Bloomsbury, 2013.

Waddell, Peter. *Charles Gore: Radical Anglican*. London: Canterbury, 2014.

Wannenwetsch, Bernd. "The Whole of Christ and the Whole Human Being: Dietrich Bonhoeffer's Inspiration for the 'Christology and Ethics' Discourse." In *Christology and Ethics*, edited by F. LeRon Shults and Brent Waters, 75–98. Grand Rapids: Eerdmans, 2010.

Ward, Graham. "Bodies: The Displaced Body of Jesus Christ." In *Radical Orthodoxy*, edited by J. Milbank et al., 163–81. London: Routledge, 1999.

———. "Kenosis: Death, Discourse and Resurrection." In *Balthasar at the End of Modernity*, edited by L. Gardiner, 15–68. Edinburgh: T. & T. Clark, 1999.

Weil, Simone. *Gravity and Grace*. Translated by Arthur Wills. Lincoln: University of Nebraska Press, 1952.

Welch, Claude. *God and Incarnation in Mid-Nineteenth Century German Theology*. New York: Oxford University Press, 1965.

———. *Protestant Thought in the Nineteenth Century*. New Haven, CT: Yale University Press, 1972.

Welker, Michel. *God the Revealed: Christology*. Translated by Douglas Scott. Grand Rapids: Eerdmans, 2013.

Weston, Frank. *The One Christ*. London: Longmans, Green, 1914.

Williams, Rowan. "Deification, Hypostatisation, and Kenosis." In *Theosis/Deification: Christian Doctrines of Divinization East and West*, edited by John Arblaster and Rob Faesen, 35–48. Leuven: Peeters, 2018.

———. "The Finality of Christ." In *On Christian Theology*, 93–106. Oxford: Blackwell, 2000.

———. "Trinity and Revelation." In *On Christian Theology*, 131–47. Oxford: Blackwell, 2000.

Williams, Stephen. "Moltmann on Jesus Christ." In *Jürgen Moltmann and Evangelical Theology: A Critical Engagement*, edited by S. W. Chung, 104–25. Eugene, OR: Wipf & Stock, 2012.

Wright, N. T. *Climax of the Covenant*. London: T. & T. Clark, 1991.

———. "Jesus and the Identity of God." *Ex Auditu* 14 (1998) 42–56.

———. *Jesus and the Victory of God*. Minneapolis: Fortress, 1996.

———. *The Resurrection of the Son of God*. Minneapolis: Fortress, 2003.

———. *Surprised by Hope: Rethinking Heaven, the Resurrection, and the Mission of the Church*. New York: HarperOne, 2008.

Yerkes, James. *The Christology of Hegel*. Albany: State University of New York Press, 1983.

Youngs, Samuel, "Wounds of the Emptied God: The Role of Kenosis at the Cross in Christologies of Jürgen Moltmann and Sergius Bulgakov." *American Theological Inquiry* 4 (2011) 45–58.

———. *The Way of the Kenotic Christ: The Christology of Jürgen Moltmann*. Eugene, OR: Cascade, 2019.

Zachariades, Theodore. *The Omnipresence of Christ: A Neglected Aspect of Evangelical Christology*. Milton Keynes: Paternoster, 2015.

Index

Abba-consciousness (of Jesus), 6–10, 15, 82, 92
anhypostasia, 27
Anselm/Anselmian, 52
apatheia, 118
   apathy of humanity, 154n55
atonement, 9, 13, 84
ascension, 9–10, 19, 57–61, 81
Augustine, 73

Balthasar, Hans Urs von, 99, 152
baptism of Jesus, 103, 117, 122–23
Barth, Karl, viii
Bauckham, Richard, 99, 106, 122, 137, 159
Bonhoeffer, Dietrich, viii–ix, 65, 71, 77–78, 80, 83, 90, 95, 98, 146
boyhood of Jesus, 122–23

Calvin, John, 85–87, 139
Chalcedon, 1, 27, 36–38, 47, 82, 84, 90, 92
Christology
   cosmic, 84, 106, 111, 113, 120–28, 139,
   eschatological, 97, 107, 112–13, 126, 129, 133–41
   nineteenth-century (radical) kenotic, 1–3, 23, 26–30, 35, 40–41, 48, 58
   traditional forms of, x, 2, 8–10, 18–19, 23–26, 30, 35–37, 39–40, 43–44, 46–47, 51–53, 55–56, 67, 100, 107, 115
   trinitarian, 10, 26–29, 32, 53, 99–102, 136, 152
   two natures, 9, 14, 39, 82–84, 92–93, 100, 110
Christopraxis, 95
classical theism, 6–7, 100
Coakley, Sarah, 89, 92, 147–50
communicatio idiomata/communication of attributes,
cosmology/cosmic,
   see Christology
crucifixion, 114, 123–25
cruciform(ity), 144, 158–59

Davies, Oliver, 46, 63, 65–67, 70–78, 82–89, 92, 95, 100, 110–11, 114, 120–23, 126–27, 130–32, 135–36, 143, 146, 148, 154, 160
deep incarnation, 105, 125
doxology, 101

ecology/eco-theology, 126
ecumenical, 40, 97, 130
ecclesiology, viii, x, 10, 26, 34, 36, 51, 57–58, 61–63, 75, 76–77
embodiment, ix, 5, 33, 77, 81, 84–85, 88, 93, 120–28
enhypostasis, 9
eschatology, 97, 107, 112, 126, 129, 133–38, 140–41
exegesis, 99, 115
existentialism, 4–5, 19, 40–41

Fee, Gordon, 42, 54, 116
Feminism/feminist theology, 62, 144, 146, 148–50
Feuerbach, Ludwig, 16, 19–21, 23

INDEX

Gess, Wolfgang, 25, 35, 43, 48, 54
Gethsemane, 102, 114, 123
Gorman, Michael, 99, 144–45, 153, 155, 158–59
Gregersen, N.H., 105, 125
Gunton, Colin, 106, 121

Habets, Myk, 103, 114, 134
Hampson, Daphne, 147–48
Hawthorne, Gerald, 116
Hegelianism, 17, 46
hypostatic union, 1, 84

(im)mutability, 6, 21, 26–28, 43, 51, 56, 100
(im)passibility, 6, 26, 124
incarnation, viii, 8, 10, 12, 14–15, 25–27, 29, 31–45, 47–56

Janz, Paul, ix, 46–47, 65–83, 89, 91–93, 109, 111–14, 153, 156
Judaism, 38

Kenosis, xvi-xviii (*see also* self-emptying),
    Christ and Father (kenosis of will), 145, 156
    Christ and flesh (kenosis of body), 121, 124, 157
    Christ and others (kenosis of security), 104–5
    Christ and Spirit (kenosis of efficacy), 156
    immanent Trinity, 101
    in Moltmann's Christology, x, 1–2, 10, 64, 65, 79–80, 83, 90, 96–161
    in Philippians 2:6–11, 62, 145
    nineteenth-century (radical), 1–3, 23, 26–30, 35, 40–41, 48, 58
    relational (Moltmann), 101–6
kingdom of God/heaven, 58, 75, 85, 87, 95, 131

learning of Christ, 122
liberation theology, 76, 98, 100, 119
Luther, Martin, 2, 21, 73, 85, 146

Mackinnon, Donald, ix, 50, 65, 67–69, 78–80, 83, 93, 144, 154, 159
materiality, 15, 55, 84, 89, 94, 110–13, 120–22
McInroy, Mark, 151, 154–55
Mercedes, Anna, 147, 149, 150–51
messiah-in-becoming/messiah-in-process, 103, 129, 146, 151
Moltmann, Jürgen, 96–161

Neal, Ryan, 97, 124,
new creation, 87, 112, 122, 126–28, 134–35, 138, 140, 155

omnipotence, 2, 28,
omniscience, 28, 48–49, 51

Pannenberg, Wolfhart, 27, 35, 56
Pascal, Blaise, 141
perichoresis, 101
physicality, *see* cosmology/cosmic
pneumatologia crucis (pneumatology of the cross), 104, 148
political theology,
praxis, vii–viii, 28, 48–49, 57, 61–63, 65, 74, 76, 87, 89, 95, 107
prayers of Jesus, 102, 118
pre-existence (of Christ), 91

Rahner, Karl, 83, 101
reason (in theology), 2, 8, 47, 88, 101
resurrection, 9–10, 17, 19, 29, 58, 60, 75, 79, 84, 94–95, 104, 112, 121, 125–29, 131, 135, 139–40, 142, 145

sarx (and/or flesh), 105,
Schleiermacher, Friedrich, ix, 4–10, 14–16, 18–21, 23, 46, 82–83, 91–92
self-sacrifice/self-sacrificial, 145–51, 157
Shekinah, 101
soteriology, 62
sovereignty, 70, 114, 139
staurology, 124–25, 127
Strauss, D. F. W., 16–19, 23, 25, 33, 38

temple, 122–23
Tillich, Paul, 15

theology of the cross, 147, see also *staurology*,
Thomas Aquinas, 72,
Thomasius, Gottfried, ix, 24-35, 40-41, 48-49, 58, 60, 108
transformation theology, ix-x, 46, 59, 63-77, 80, 82-83, 85-88, 90-92, 94, 96, 98, 108-9, 119, 121, 125, 128, 131, 134, 136, 140, 143, 146, 159, 160
Trinity, 10, 28, 31, 59, 99, 111

virgin birth (of Christ), 2, 9
vulnerability, 100, 102-3, 105, 106, 119, 120, 121, 147, 148, 149, 153, 154, 156, 160

Welker, Michael, 122, 126, 157
Williams, Rowan, ix, 83, 112, 151, 154, 158
Wright, N. T., 3, 38-39, 79, 99, 125-26, 145

www.ingramcontent.com/pod-product-compliance
Lightning Source LLC
Chambersburg PA
CBHW062047220426
43662CB00010B/1685